WOMEN AND WORK

WOMEN AND WORK

Honest Answers to Real Questions

Carole Hyatt

M. EVANS AND COMPANY, INC.
NEW YORK

Library of Congress Cataloging in Publication Data

Hyatt, Carole.
  Women and work.

  Includes index.
  1. Women—Employment. I. Title.
HD6057.9.H9   650.1′4′088042   80-23984

ISBN 0-87131-324-3

M. Evans and Company, Inc.
216 East 49 Street
New York, New York 10017

DESIGN BY RFS GRAPHIC DESIGN INC.

Manufactured in the United States of America

9 8 7 6 5 4 3 2 1

*This book is for my husband Gordon and my daughter Ariel,
whose willingness to support me far exceeds
my 1950's expectations.*

Contents

Acknowledgments

I want to thank Patricia Linden for her extraordinary professionalism, organization, and communication. Without her assistance, total commitment, and wit, this book would not have been written.

My special thanks to my agent and friend, Julia Coopersmith. I totally appreciate her talent for making the most complicated situations look so easy.

A thank you to my business partner, June Esserman, whose fortitude and energy I deeply admire.

I am particularly indebted to the entire staff of Hyatt/Esserman Research Associates and The Center for Family Research for their intelligent input, keen eyes, backup, and out-and-out good humor.

Lastly, I wish to acknowledge and thank Barbara Toalson for her keen abilities to set priorities and organize a hectic work schedule.

How to Use This Book

To make material more accessible to the reader, the questions and answers have been grouped according to the general headings shown in the table of contents. Some of the questions could have been presented in a number of sections. If your concern, for example, is how to handle an office chauvinist, information in the section "The New Manners" may give you additional ideas or assistance that will supplement "What to Do about Chauvinism and Questions of Sex." Consult the index if you are interested in a particular topic or problem, or if you can't find exactly what you are looking for.

WOMEN AND WORK

Introduction

I'd been on the road for about three months, on a multi-city personal appearance tour for my book, *The Woman's Selling Game*, when I began to feel the way you do when a mosquito keeps buzzing and you can't shoo it away. Everywhere I went—bookstores, women's workshops, television talk shows—women kept buzzing the same question at me: "What should I wear?" The question seemed so trivial, and there were so many important subjects I'd been hoping to cover. I confess, I was becoming pretty annoyed.

Then, one night in St. Louis, the phone in my hotel room rang. My husband, Gordon, was calling, very pleased and excited. He wanted to know if I could get back to New York by the twentieth. "Listen to this," he said. "I just got the go-ahead to produce a documentary film in the Middle East, and you and I are invited to meet the Egyptian ambassador at a private dinner party on the twentieth. It's at the ambassador's official residence and half the UN delegation will be there. Can you make it?"

"Oh, Gordon," I exclaimed. "That's wonderful. I'm so pleased for you. Of course I'll make it, but what should I wear?"

And then I burst into laughter; Gordon must have thought I'd gone mad. What happened was, the instant I heard my own spontaneous reaction, I knew what all those women had really been asking. That pesky "What should I wear?" wasn't the buzzing of a mosquito; it was shorthand for the problems all of us have when we're faced with something new and strange. Women were saying, just as I had, "I'm going into a situation that's a mystery to me and I'm baffled. What should I do? What should I say? How should I act so I'll fit in?"

The more I thought about it, the more evident it became that there are indeed a lot of heavyweight answers women are looking for. After all, the truth is that we are still the immigrants in a businessman's world and none of us—men or women—is quite sure how it's all going to turn out. Or how we should handle ourselves while the changes are taking place. We have no past to lean on: no set rules to tell us how the game is played. All we have is a package of leftover customs that no longer apply; ideas that get fuzzier and fuzzier as our circumstances shift. The question "What should I wear?" is valid. It's a symbol; the tip of a vast iceberg of real and serious problems.

I spent the next year and a half finding out exactly what those problems are, why they exist, and how they are being solved. With the aid of my research company, Hyatt/Esserman Research Associates, we set up hundreds of interviews in every area of the country. We covered big cities and tiny suburbs, large companies and small. We analyzed scores of questionnaires and conducted dozens of focus group sessions. We talked in depth and at length to men as well as women, to get every point of view. We probed and listened to secretaries, executive managers, entrepreneurs; beginners, re-enterers, old pros; people of every age and at every stage of the career path. We learned a bookful:

- Basics are basics. What bothers women are essentially the same things that men have to figure out: how to learn new skills and techniques, advance in your field, handle conflicts and challenges, get the money and the satisfaction you need from your work. The difference is, men have a history, role models, accepted expectations. We don't.
- Sexism still exists, even though it's nearly a generation since we've

14

begun to erase it. What is more, sexism varies markedly according to industry and locale. Therefore, so do the solutions.

- Men are as uncertain in their relationships to women in business as women are to men and each other. Who should open the door for whom? Do you say Ms., Mrs., Miss, or Mary? Where does courtesy leave off and business behavior begin?

- Politics and power struggles go on all the time. They're a part of the game that can be stimulating or depressing, depending on where you stand. You can choose or refuse to play in the game. Either way, it is there and you have to be able to recognize what is going on.

- There is no single right way or wrong way to handle all of the situations that will come into your life. But there are guidelines that will help you to find the way that is right for you.

That last item is important. Nobody can hand you a book of rules that will tell you exactly what to do at every stage of your career. What works for one person can be disastrous for another. Different personalities and circumstances dictate different responses. What you need is to learn what other people's experiences have been, and then adapt them to suit yourself. Take the Roses and Raspberries story, for example. It's one of the strategies we learned about while conducting our interviews. A group of about a hundred young women in Fort Wayne, Indiana, tired of the male business community's habit of sexist discrimination, banded together to do something about it. Whenever they spotted something in the newspaper or on the air that they thought deserved comment, the women expressed their opinions by sending a gift to the newsmaker: roses for applause, raspberries for boos. Their campaign succeeded. In a light-hearted way, the group aroused the city's awareness of the fact that its prejudices were alive and showing.

The strategy worked in Fort Wayne because it's a small city, and because those women were young, unafraid, and did not intend to stay in Fort Wayne forever. It might not work for you. The point is it's not so much specific strategy that you need to know, but the basic techniques you can adapt and use. The principle in Fort Wayne was that if you band together, you can achieve the mutual support, impact, and believability that will solve your problem. That is a tried and true principle, but it is not a rigid battle plan for everyone.

15

The most successful people I know are the least rigid. They have the flexibility to take other people's experiences and advice, then add a pinch of this or borrow a cup of that to make the idea work for themselves. What follows are the basic recipes: real, personal experiences and first-hand advice that will show you how other women have worked out their problems; ideas and strategies you can flex to make the machinery of business work for you.

It's not all uphill. If you're in a field that you like and if you keep things in proportion, work should bring far more joy than despair. We found, however, that women often feel driven and unhappy because they see themselves as underachievers. They think that the name of the game is to be on the board of directors, and anything less is failure. They are misled and influenced more by media hype, nervous guilt, and outside pressures than by the dictates of their own realities. Everyone doesn't need to devote full time and energy to work. Everyone doesn't need to climb to the top of the business ladder. It's perfectly OK if you like to spend time with your family, or if a secretary's work makes you happier than the boss's. And there is nothing wrong with your reason for working; it's your reason, and that makes it right whether you are out there because you need the money to survive, because you want to be independent or augment your income, or because you need social or intellectual stimulation, have a talent you must express, or just plain want to get out of the house.

The bottom line is this: You can work or not work for whatever reason is right for you. But whatever your choice and your needs— money, status, satisfaction—one universal principle applies: If you know what you are doing and know how to get the most out of your business life, you'll enjoy yourself and succeed.

I would like to thank the many friends who contributed so generously to the making of this book. Though their names have been fictionalized in the stories they tell, their experiences and information are utterly honest. My gratitude to the scores of women and men who filled out our questionnaires and to those people who spoke so openly about their corporate politics but wished to remain anonymous. My appreciation for their in-depth interviews goes to Stephanie Barber, Beverly Barker, Paula Becker, Gerry Breitweiser, Elaine Carter, Jan Cherubin, Ellie Crawford, Morris Danzger, Dede Davies, Thomas

DeVito, Kandra Driggs, Lee Elman, Sydney Falker, Pat Finley, Joan Foden, Joan Forbath, Mary Sue Foster, Muriel Fox, Belle Frank, Leslie Gaines, Pat Gardner, Sandra Garihan, Arthur Geller, Tutty Giordano, Linda Gottlieb, Elizabeth Gutner, Gale Hansen, Janet Jamar, Elaine Karsh, Susan Kasen, Nick Kelly, Virginia Kiser, Laura Knickerbocker, Barbara Koz, Anne Kreamer, Ilene Leff, Judi K. Levinson, Peter Linden, Nancy Love, Jerry Maburn, Marion Maged, Barbara Margolis, Don McCollum, Esther Moore, Carol Morgan, Alison Moss, Donald Mulligan, Nancy Neidhardt, Mary Perot Nichols, Mary Ellen O'Connor, Philip Perrone, Jim Raniere, Joanne Roman, Virginia Russo, Marion Ryan, Toni Sacco, Marilyn Sahner, Naomi Sarna, Susan Schroeer, Charles Schwartz, Carolyn Setlow, Peggy Shannon, John Sharnik, Molly Siple, Glory Smith, Liz Smith, JoAnn Spencer, Hal Spielman, Martha Stuart, Terrie Studer, Shirley Tahan, Stewart Unger, Sandy Vohr, Irwin Weinrot, Karen Wenig, Steve Werner, Av Westin, Kathleen Westin, Fran Willis, Kay Willis, Patricia Willis, Judy Woodfin, and Jessica Zive.

THE ART OF INTERVIEWING

How do I get a job interview?

The art of getting interviews is in having determination and knowing the various ways to get an interview. The usual routes are through a business or personal contact, with the help of a job placement agency, and by answering a recruitment ad.

Of the three, the contact route is by far the most desirable. A respectable name attached to yours will almost surely get you the appointment you are after, because it implies that you are being recommended. This in turn encourages the person who is seeing you to search for reasons to hire you. The idea is, if acquaintances think enough of you to let you use their good name, they must think you have something valuable to offer. Another reason for using a mutual contact's name is that even the busiest executives will make room in their schedules to talk to somebody sent by a friend. It's a matter of courtesy and an exchange of favors.

Is it an imposition to gain entry through a contact?

Not in the least. It makes people feel good to think that they are helping. Of course, you have to ask for that help; nobody is going to walk up to you in the street and say, "If you happen to be looking for a job, please do say that I sent you." It's up to you to make the approach—to ask if they know of any openings or have friends they could send you to, and if you may use their name. Some women have told me they feel too shy to do this, or that they want to do everything themselves. I tell them they have to get over the myth of shyness if they want to get favored consideration. And that refusing to ask family or friends for help is more foolish than "nice." It is only reasonable to take advantage of the contact base that people who've been around longer than you have built up.

What if they turn me down?

This can happen. Maybe they really can't come up with anybody to send you to. Or maybe they feel competitive toward you and are trying to keep an edge for themselves. Or, less probably, they may have a grudge against you, or think of you as a total washout. Assuming that what you are asking for is within the bounds of reality, the best way to respond to a turndown is to say, "Thank you," and move on to somebody else for help.

If you don't keep asking, there is no way people can give you what you want.

How do placement agencies fit in?

Usefully, as long as you are clear about what you can do and know who you are talking to. If you can give your abilities a specific title that fits a specific job opening they are trying to fill, the agency can make a match. They are not so great, by and large, at figuring out what to do with somebody whose job definition is general and for whom there isn't a ready-made slot on their books.

You also need to know an agency's specialty. Different organizations concentrate on different fields: medicine, advertising, publishing, engineering, electronics, and so on. Further, some placement agencies are keyed into clerical and administrative placements. Others, the headhunters, deal at the executive level. It should not be difficult for you to select the area in which you belong.

What is less obvious is the agency's reputation and track record. It helps to know the caliber of their client roster and if they are an active agency, with a great many job orders coming through. But reputation is a subtle thing and difficult to nail down. You'll have to do some sleuthing. Some of the people to ask general questions of are your local Better Business Bureau and people who have been placed by the agency.

Given that the answers come up satisfactory, a placement agency is only as good for you as the person with whom you work. You must have good rapport, be able to communicate and understand each other, and have mutual respect. If you're not satisfied with the person to whom you are assigned, speak with the head of the agency. Tell him or her you would like to work with the company but with a placement counselor who is better suited to your needs.

Even the best placement agency and counselor are not enough. You still have to scout the market for yourself, rather than depend entirely on somebody else. You could wind up finding your own job, and then let the agent do the negotiating for you—at a commensurate fee.

Remember this about placement agencies: They are in business to make money. That is the only reason they are in business. The way they make money is by selling companies and employees on each other. The match is not always the right one. Buyer beware.

Can I get a job interview through a newspaper ad?

Of course. That's why the ad was placed: to get applicants in to interview. Also, reading the classifieds in newspapers and trade publications gives you clues to going rates, the number of openings in a given field, and whether a particular company is increasing its activity.

If you are at the executive level, however, you are more likely to hear about good openings before they reach the advertising stage. Really good ones never get advertised at all. Most often these positions are filled by promotions from within, by raids on other companies, or by spreading the word. After all, as an employer, which would you rather do? Read hundreds of résumés and see dozens of applicants who are more or less off the street, or zero in on people about whom you already know a lot?

When should I apply for a job?

In my opinion, it's best to wait three to five days before answering an ad, and then to make your appointment for a week or so later. Or, if you've heard about the job through word of mouth, to make your interview appointment late rather than early in the search. The reason for this is human nature. Most people don't make a decision and act on it until they're up against an actual deadline. Therefore, the last people they talk to before the crunch comes are the ones who are fresh in their minds and whom they seriously consider.

Are cold calls a waste of time?

With patience and luck, they can pay off. You can send out batches of letters and résumés or make a couple of dozen phone calls, and there is a chance that if your letter is good and your call opportune, you will connect with somebody who is intrigued by your qualifications and able to make room for a stranger. The odds are statistically slim: A two percent response to every hundred résumés sent out is considered terrific.

23

What do personnel departments do?

Their function is to find and screen the right people for the right jobs in their company. The best are indispensable. The worst are inept and obstructive. Either way, you can expect their information to be somewhat limited; they are not personally involved in the daily flow of work and interpersonal relationships.

Whether you are the boss or the applicant, you have to use good judgment, common sense, and sometimes take detours to work effectively with Personnel.

Do you mean, ignore them?

No. As employer or employee, it rarely pays to skip the organizational chain of command. If you step on Personnel's toes, they can find a way to get revenge—by "losing" records, delaying interview appointments, circulating bad reports.

As a would-be employee, one way to skin the cat and get the interview you want is to double up on your approach: Apply to the head of the company or department at the same time or before you contact Personnel. The reason for this is, if the president is interested in your letter and résumé, he can get Personnel to process you. But if your letter and résumé go only to Personnel, it can hit the wrong person on the wrong day and go nowhere. The double approach is an action-getter at best, and insurance at worst.

How does personnel know what to look for?

Wise employers save themselves time, effort, and error by taking the trouble to write up a clear job definition as a guide to the personnel department. He or she lists the tasks and responsibilities that will be required, the skills and experience that are necessary, and the type of personality that will fit in. But no matter how strong a recommendation he or she gets from the personnel department, a smart boss always interviews the candidate personally. There is a great deal of subjective judgment involved in selecting the person you are going to have to work and live with, and that is something you cannot leave in the hands of a marriage broker. The higher the level of employee, the more this holds true.

There are times when, no matter how clear the job definition and no matter how brilliantly Personnel performs, a matchmaking effort is doomed:

> I have been a public relations director of a cosmetics firm for eight years and have always found and hired my own staff. Yet Personnel and I have extremely cordial relations and there is constant interchange between us. It's a game we play, and I guarantee you the old-timers down there are onto it. Here's how it works. First I find the person I want to hire for a certain slot. Then I write the job definition so it is tailor-made to fit the person I have chosen. I send him or her downstairs to fill out the proper forms, and for the next three or four weeks I interview everybody and anybody Personnel wants to send me. After each interview I report back to them with effusive appreciation for their efforts, thank them for their concern, and give some reason why the person they sent is not quite right for the job: He lacks experience in some fine specialty, he wouldn't be happy with my pace, whatever excuse I can dream up. Along about the third or fourth week they'll send me the applicant I've already handpicked, and I call them, elated: "You have done a wonderful job, finding me this perfect person. Thank you so much! This company couldn't function without you." They have filled their mandate. I have my man or woman. And we all look good to the people we have to report to. The game is known around here as my Magic Action System.

How do you write a job inquiry letter?

Briefly, and to the point. On one page if possible. If you want your letter to open doors, the two elements it should contain are: (1) The name of a mutual contact, if you have one. This is to establish your credentials and, if possible, to force the person to pay attention to you out of courtesy to a colleague. (2) A reason why seeing you would benefit the other person or the company. This can be a specific idea or piece of information, or a generality. If you are being specific, do not give away everything before you get to your appointment. Tell just enough to make that person want to see you. And be businesslike. Use terms like "favorable results" and "mutual advantage"—not feathery stuff like, "I know it would be fun to meet you." Here's a sample:

August 17, 1980

Ms. Barbara Fields
National Manufacturing Company
1126 Johnson Drive
Lyman, Wisconsin 53000

Dear Ms. Fields:

Ann Walters of the Jones Computer Service Company suggested that I get in touch with you. She believes that in view of your expansion plans, you would be particularly interested in my expertise as a programming instructor. As you will note on the enclosed résumé, I have successfully created and executed client projects for several major national concerns. I feel certain that this background would serve you well.

It is my understanding that you are planning to increase your staff during the coming year. As you know, the supply-and-demand picture for programming specialists is tight. Therefore, I would like to suggest that we begin soon to explore the areas where I could best serve you.

I will be in your area next week and will telephone you on Monday so that we can make an appointment to discuss the possibility of my helping to fill your needs.

I look forward to a mutually favorable association.

Very truly,
Brenda Giles

Enclosure: Résumé

How about the phrase, "I look forward to hearing from you"?

It is a perfectly acceptable nicety, as long as you don't expect anything to come of it. You are going to have to call them; you are in a buyer-seller situation and as the seller, you are the one who is expected to initiate action. Many letters end with "I look forward . . ." or "Please telephone at your convenience." You have to realize that it is rarely convenient for top brass to call you. If you want to get an appointment, you have to make it easy for them to give you one.

A better way to handle a sales letter is to end it with something specific, as in the sample inquiry letter. A sentence such as "I will telephone you on Tuesday the ninth so that we can set up an appointment at your convenience" prepares the person you are writing to for your call, and lets him or her clear time on the calendar for you, if they want to. Also, it keeps you from living in the land of Maybe: "Maybe I'll hear today. Maybe they're checking me out. Maybe I should sit by the phone in case it rings."

What am I doing wrong when I can't get through on the phone to make an appointment?

If you constantly have a problem reaching certain people, there is a good chance that the problem is theirs. I do not know anybody who is good at what he or she does who won't return phone calls. Or at least have a secretary get a message back to you, even if it is a turndown.

If your calls are not being returned, you can be sure you are not the only one who is being left incommunicado. Undoubtedly there are stacks of pink message slips piled up on that person's desk, and it is not your fault.

What are the reasons some people never return calls?

- They have a problem organizing their time.
- There jobs are in jeopardy, and they don't dare make waves.
- The company is in trouble and nobody can take any kind of action. They are trying to keep it quiet, so they just don't talk.
- They suffer from pathological fear of meeting people, even by phone.
- They can't face the fact that they might have to say No to your request.
- They have a drinking problem and cannot cope.
- A secretary is shortstopping the messages.

What if they don't return my first call?

One unanswered call does not constitute rejection, or problems. There may be acceptable and understandable reasons why you don't get through the first time. One is that busy people really do have to cut down on the number of calls they respond to. Another is that you may be leaving the wrong message. Do you leave your name and phone number, and a reason why the person should call you back?

You really can't call once and let it go at that; you have to expect that you'll need to call, and call again, and make it clear that you have something important to offer.

What if I can't get past the secretary?

Brenda has been in the executive search business for fifteen years and has run into every problem in the book. She knows how to reach people without fooling around.

> Sometimes the secretary is my problem. What I do is make him or her my friend when I phone. Or else I'll stop in at the office and get into personal conversation. I give my name, and if he or she doesn't offer his or hers, I ask for it. I talk about why I think it would be beneficial for the boss to see me: I have something that would be good for the company. I'm not mysterious about what it is; I give a clue. But I don't spell out the details because I want to do the selling and not leave any decision-making to the secretary. In other words, I take him or her into my confidence just enough to create an ally, somebody who'll carry the ball into the president's office for me. I've found that if you're friendly and up front, most secretaries are like most people: They like to help.
>
> Of course, sometimes the secretary turns out to be a dragon protecting the boss. So I go around him or her. What I do is call up either very early in the morning or very late in the day, before or after official business hours when he or she won't be at the phone and my call will go directly through to the person I want to see.
>
> As a last-ditch effort, if I absolutely can't get through to make an appointment and if it is really important to me, I go to the person's office and just camp there until we meet face-to-face. I know that sometime during the day he or she is going to have to come in or go out of the reception room—for lunch, to go to the bathroom, to make another meeting. I am very courteous about it. But I persist.

When do you enclose a résumé with your inquiry?

When you want the person to have your credentials in hand, and you know that he or she is dealing with somebody who could benefit him or her. The person who reads or scans it should be able to get a fast and favorable impression of your record as it pertains to his or her needs. A résumé is your advance salesperson—the key that can open the door to an interview appointment.

You do not enclose a standard résumé when your experience has been light or spotty and you have a good contact whose name you can use as an introduction. You can, however, enclose a functional résumé that will give the person an idea of what you have to offer. A functional résumé is shown later in this section.

Tell me about résumés.

The vice-president of a garment manufacturing company talks about résumés she has seen:

> You can tell tell a lot about a person by the way his or her résumé is prepared. If it's organized and efficient, it reflects a mental tidiness. If it's impeccably clean and the typing, spelling, and grammar are perfect, you know that the person cares about his or· her work and knows enough about business to understand that this is important. I have also read through résumés that are so perfect they are literally too good to be true. I don't mean the organization or neatness; that can't be too good. I mean descriptions of accomplishments so wondrous that if true, the author wouldn't be job-hunting. He or she would be basking aboard a 150-foot yacht while pondering the latest thing in tax dodges. Often these include overblown or cliché phrases that I know have been lifted from a textbook or résumé-writing course. Could a supermarket checker really back this one up? "Continually sought to analyze information, utilize problem-solving skills, communicate clearly and effectively." I disqualify these applicants because originality and effort count with me as much as honesty. Another kind of résumé I can't stand is the gimmicky one: jumbo foldouts that belong on the Christmas card rack, giant matchbooks with each match lettered to indicate a skill, jigsaw puzzles they think I'll put together.
>
> Résumés represent what people are and do. They have to sell me on wanting to talk to the person. They have to say quality, professionalism, articulateness—a class act. Anything slipshod, right down to sloppy spelling, immediately unsells me on the person.

Give me a sample standard résumé.

The following is the work history of a person with eight to ten years' experience:

Jane Jones

100 Main Street
Norman, Ohio 09876

Home: 010-555-7348

Business: 010-555-9300

At head of page:
Name

Full address

Telephone numbers

WORK EXPERIENCE:

1976 to present: Market research analyst, Standard Research Associates, Norman, Ohio. In charge of four package goods and two cosmetics accounts, Responsible for personal interviews, data collection, information analysis. Created and implemented tabulating system that increased usable responses 15 percent.

List current or most recent job first. List title, function, company name and location, description. Include up-to-date skills and achievements most likely to apply to job you are seeking. This should be longest and most fully detailed listing.

1974–1976: Human Research Center, Norman, Ohio. Staff member of assessment team providing psychosocial evaluations of drug-addicted patients

List previous jobs in reverse chronological order.

1971–1974: Ohio Mental Health Resources, Norman, Ohio. Program developer for community educational services.

Omit very early and now irrelevent jobs such as fashion model, file clerk. Omit short-lived jobs that are meaningless or that you would rather forget.

RELATED EXPERIENCE:

Interviewer, Center for Social Research, Ohio University. Designed and implemented student research projects resulting in motivational analyses.

Include part-time or volunteer work that is applicable to your current prospecting, or that expands your scope and value.

PROFESSIONAL ASSOCIATIONS:

World Research Association
Society of American Researchers
Ohio Educational Association

Tell employer you are actively interested in your field and have contacts within it.

AWARD AND HONORS:

Honorary degree, Ohio University
AMPI Award for Excellence,
World Research Association

Spell out recognition you have received for excellence.

CIVIC ACTIVITIES:

Regional development board,
United Fund of Ohio
Voter registration director,
League of Women Voters,
Norman, Ohio

List leadership positions first: chairperson, director, organizer. Tells employer you are well connected, a doer, and believe in voluntary work for the good of the community (company) as a whole.

OTHER SKILLS:

Fluent in Russian, French, Spanish

Unrelated but exceptional or interesting abilities can click in unexpected ways. You never know what a prospect will be intrigued by or what business plans he or she may be considering.

EDUCATION:

Ohio University, B.A., M.A.; Chicago School of Health, Ph.D.; Macintosh Scholar

Give names of colleges, graduate schools. Degrees, honors, scholarships. If you are a recent graduate and lack work experience, you can include school activities such as reporting or editing for the newspaper, and special interests such as drama or photography.

REFERENCES:

On request.

If the employer is interested in you, he or she will check up. That is the time to supply references. Alert your references to the possibility of a request, and get permission to use their name.

Résumé pointers

A résumé should be as brief as possible, one or two pages, so it can be easily scanned. Choose only the information that will actually sell for you, and condense it so the reader can grasp your history easily. The time to elaborate on details is at the interview.

Always put the most important things first, just as you would in an ad that sells.

Omit personal information such as age, marital status, health, hobbies. These nuggets do not open the door to an interview and may even seal it shut.

Omit salary requirement or current salary. You need to sell yourself in person—then you can negotiate a fair deal. Specific numbers here will only categorize you, or put you out of the running because you are at too high or too low a level.

Take the trouble to write a fresh résumé for the job you are trying to get. Accent relevant experience and minimize or eliminate other background. Your old résumé probably needs updating anyway; most of us don't realize how much we accomplish and grow over short periods of time until we are forced to sit down and examine our activities for a specific purpose.

How can I keep track of it all?

If you're like most busy people, you can barely remember everything you did last week. It is wise to keep an ongoing file of jobs, responsibilities, achievements, recognition, publicity, and like material. Then you can pull the pertinent facts together into résumé (or publicity) form when you need to. You never know when that will be.

What kind of typewriter should I use?

An electric, rather than a manual, so the imprint will be evenly spaced and uniformly black. A tape or film ribbon is better than a fabric ribbon because it produces sharper, cleaner, clearer printing. Use a standard size and style of type, the kind you see used for most business letters. Avoid unusual, hard-to-read faces such as italic, oversize, and all capitals.

If you don't have access to the right typewriter, or if you aren't the world's greatest typist, go to a lettershop and hire someone to type your résumé for you. Proofread the original very carefully, so not one smudge or error slips by. Then have the lettershop or a copy center reproduce as many copies as you think you will need. Protect and save the original, in case you need to reproduce more.

How can I write a résumé if I don't have enough work experience?

Write a functional résumé, a format that focuses on skills rather than chronologically ordered job experience. This is the format of choice if you are just starting out as a young person, or have spent most of your adult life at home. Or, as I have suggested, if your job experience is light or spotty. A functional résumé highlights your abilities by category and permits you to describe your responsibilities and achievements in professional terms, such as "administrative" or "organizational" even though you have not held those job titles.

Show me a sample functional résumé.

This is the résumé of a woman entering the job market at age forty-two who has translated her life experience into business terms:

Mary Brown
110 Highland Avenue
Minton, Alabama 35000
010-555-9393

OBJECTIVE:
Administrative manager

Optional: Omit from résumé and include in covering letter instead. State exactly what position you are qualified to fill.

WORK EXPERIENCE:

Administrative assistant, Wm. Brown Co. Minton, Alabama, 1970–present. *Helped out in husband's office.*

Group coordinator, Minton Metropolitan League, 1958–1968. *Volunteer office worker for local civic organization.*

Development Assistant, State Museum Society. *Volunteer fund-raiser.*

SKILLS:

Administrative: Served as office manager at Wm. Brown Co. in charge of bookkeeping and processing sales reports. Organized and implemented travel arrangements and social events for corporate executives. Experience in purchasing. *Translates part-time volunteer work into business terms.*

Group leadership: Directed team efforts at Metropolitan League. Organized and managed subteams. Experience in public speaking.

Financial: Assisted in fund-raising for Museum Society. Knowledge of government grants. Wide contact base.

EDUCATION:

Jones Business College, 1964–1966.

REFERENCES: On request.

Shouldn't I know something about the people I want to work for?

You certainly should. You can't expect them to send you a résumé, but you can work up your own dossier on them. How and why are best explained by one of the brightest and most thorough people I know. Joyce, just thirty, is the owner and president of a national public relations firm and has had a consistently outstanding record of successes dating from her first postgraduate job at a newspaper. I must add that Joyce is a fragile, blond, Victorian type. She says she has never let that stand in her way. Those beautiful violet eyes see the world clearly and in all its dimensions.

34

I do the same research on prospective employers or clients that I expect them to do on me. If I am serious about working for a company, I'll forage for everything I can find out about them, about the industry in general, their corporate history and status, their financial standing from A to Z. Where do I get my information? I go to libraries. Archives. Search through annual reports and newspaper clips. I might run a check through Dun & Bradstreet or Standard and Poor's, or talk to my broker, my accountant, former executive employees—anyone who might be accurately knowledgeable and have a line on them. By "accurately knowledgeable" I mean you have to take information from some sources with a grain of salt. There may be disgruntlement or jealousy involved, so you have to examine who is telling you what, and why.

Certainly as a job applicant I would find out how many women have moved up in the hierarchy and how high. My entire future may not lie with that company, but I'd want to know just what I could expect to get out of the job.

Somebody once asked me if I never took anybody on faith. I told them that faith plays a part—you have to trust your instinct too—but facts are something you can rely on as backup. I see no point in casting my lot with people who sound nice but who are in fact on the verge of bankruptcy or who are known by insiders as swindlers. Investigation can save you from a nightmare.

There's something else all this homework achieves that works in my favor. I find that prospects are always very pleased and impressed when they discover that I am interested and businesslike enough to take the trouble to find out who I am talking to. And it helps immensely in making conversation at the interview.

How can I make conversation when I'm so nervous I can barely speak?

Try these techniques to help you relax at an interview. Take several deep breaths just before the meeting, the way actors do when they are going on stage. Meditate, if that helps you. Focus on the positive: how well you look, how prepared you are, on the success you are about to have.

These are behavioral techniques, and they work. Try one of them this minute and see. Pretend you are about to be interviewed and focus on everything negative about yourself that you can think of: your nervousness, shyness, ineptitude, uncertainty. Terrible, isn't it?

Now start trying to sell yourself to your imaginary boss. Get the point? If you focus on nerves and shyness, you will be nervous and shy. If you concentrate on your inadequacies, you will come across as inadequate. But if you think, "I know what I am doing and I am good at it," you give yourself a productive kind of self-fulfilling prophecy. The choice is yours. Like anything else in this world, you just have to be aware of what you want and work at it until you get it.

It is worth your while to do whatever you have to do to appear poised, collected, and confident at an interview. The last impression you want to convey is "typically female; can't handle pressure."

Am I the only one who gets nervous?

Indeed no. We are all scared at one time or another. It may comfort you to understand that the person who is hiring you may be out of his or her element, unskilled in interviewing techniques. He or she is on the line, as you are, and is having some anxious thoughts. "If I make the wrong decision and hire somebody who's wrong for the job or who causes disruption, I'm going to look bad to everybody. My neck is on the block and I wish I were sure of what to do. I have to weigh so many tangibles and intangibles, and take so much into consideration . . . and I am out here all alone. The only thing I'm dead certain of is, I'm in for another sleepless night."

When there is tension in the air it's contagious, no matter who starts it first. You need all the self-confidence techniques you can muster to keep from becoming so unnerved you wind up babbling like a schoolgirl.

How can I prevent nervous babbling?

Rehearse your act before you go on stage. Plan what you're going to wear so you don't sit there wishing you'd worn the suit that's back home in the closet instead of the outfit you threw together in a last-minute rush. Prepare the scenario from "How do you do?" to your exit line. Write a script containing all the questions and answers you can anticipate, and practice your role aloud over and over again. Use a tape recorder and play back how you'll sound. Enlist a friend to help you with your dry run—somebody who will bounce unexpected ideas and dialogue off you, and who will give you useful criticism. Don't be impatient or embarrassed about rehearsing. Thorough practice is what gives great actors, orators, and successful interviewees the self-confidence that makes them shine.

Is there such a thing as overconfidence?

Yes. Sometimes it's due to carelessness, and sometimes it's arrogance. It can show up in your manners as well as in what you say and how you say it.

A pleasantly firm handshake, easy eye contact, and erect posture are as much a part of your packaging as your wardrobe. They show confidence and poise. It is bad manners and a turnoff to smoke without permission, chew gum, spit, cuss, or put your feet up on the desk. Not that I believe there is any danger you will commit such transgressions. These comments are merely a reminder that the first impression you make on your prospective employer is as vital as all the rest of your interview.

Mark, the executive vice-president of a large insurance firm, talks about the most overconfident, arrogant person he has ever interviewed:

She was a slim, well-groomed, quite attractive young woman named Jacqueline. She'd been recommended to me by a headhunter as the fair-haired wonder woman of insurance. Her résumé looked good; she'd had four and a half years' experience in a number of facets of the business, and I was eager to meet her. Jacqueline sounded like the very person I wanted to hire. She came in, we shook hands, said all the right things to each other, and the minute the amenities were over she turned killer. "Mark," she said, "I'm delighted that you made this appointment with me because I have watched this company and I know exactly what is wrong with your operation. I want you to know that I am very enthusiastic about coming in here and straightening out the organization. There's just one thing we should get clear at the outset. Your company has been very unfair in the past about promoting and paying women the way they should be promoted and paid. Let's be frank with each other. Do you still feel that threatened?"

Threatened? Hardly. Jacqueline needs a lot more seasoning before she can begin to be a genuine threat to anybody. Right now she is just a pain in the neck, flailing her way through life, demanding fictitious rights. That way, when she is inadequate in her job, it is all somebody else's fault. She implies that she is better than other people; there are no other possibilities. Do you know why you keep running into the Jacquelines again and again? Whenever somebody disagrees with them, they deride and discard them, and then move someplace else . . . until that place becomes troublesome, too.

With just a few sentences this woman managed to get my hackles up and lose me forever. I handled it by pressing the buzzer for my assistant, whom I asked to talk to Jacqueline. I said I'd review the notes later. My assistant knew perfectly well why she was called in to take notes. I no longer had any use for this person.

Jacqueline made three blatant errors in her opening speech:

1. She addressed her interviewer by his first name without his invitation to do so. If there is any first-naming in an interview or new-job situation, it is initiated by the person in charge, not the employee. At that, only with permission. "May I call you Jacqueline," would be appropriate. Or, "Ms. Smith . . . ?" and then a pause so she could say "Please call me Jacqueline," if that is what she wished.

2. "I know what's wrong with your company and I'm going to fix it" was an arrogant assumption on Jacqueline's part, and a flaming example of countersalesmanship. Immediately, she made Mark wrong. She failed to assess the ego and personality that had gone into the company's efforts, and Mark's knowledge that the company had a disaster on its hands. Mark knew he had a problem, but he didn't want to be told that by somebody coming in from the outside. Jacqueline should have waited until well after she was hired, and then worked within the structure to try to improve the operation. What she could have said at the interview, after she had sold Mark on her qualifications, was, "You may have some problems that I could help you solve."

3. "Your company has been unfair to women." Jacqueline not only accused Mark and made him wrong again; she made an assumption based on hearsay. The fact is, to call Mark's company unfair was to rewrite history. Jacqueline threw up the charge as a decoy she could blame if she failed . . . a consequence she insured by her abrasive hostility. Catch 22, self-inflicted.

What questions do they usually ask at an interview?

Questions that will make you reveal whether you would be an asset to their organization. Be prepared to answer the following:

Question	Reply	Analysis
Tell me about yourself.	(If you have a solid track record): I was a production manager and then cost estimator for the Jones Publishing Company for four years. When the company began to founder, I crossed over to one of our suppliers, Arctic Paper. In both of those jobs I created and implemented systems that reduced overhead and at the same time increased sales by 5 percent. In my two and a half years at Arctic I also brought in ten new accounts that generated $20,000 worth of new business for the company.	Stress contributions and achievements that interviewer can relate to benefits for the company. Be truthful; they can and probably will check up.
Tell me about yourself.	(If you are a beginner): I have a strong affiinity for the printing and publishing business and want to learn to be the best production person in the field. My goal now is to find out everything I can about the industry by working very hard in as many phases of it as I can. I should add that I have always been able to work well with other people, and to direct and lead them, as my college and volunteer	Express serious commitment to your career and your willingness to work hard to reach your goals.

Question	Reply	Analysis
	work shows. I think that experience fits in well with your needs.	
Why did you leave your last job?	I haven't actually left it yet, although they know that I plan to as soon as I find the appropriate niche. I'm leaving because it is a large company, and my style is more personal.	Never place blame or criticize other people.
Why do you want this job?	This is an outstanding company, and of course I want to be associated with the best. I believe I can learn a great deal and advance my career by working with your people. At the same time, I feel certain that my skills and experience will contribute to your company's growth.	Flatter your prospect without going overboard or sounding unctuous.
What do you see as your greatest strengths? (or) What do you like to do best?	I think what I like to do and am best at doing is in the area of analysis, scheduling, and cost accounting. More than that, I enjoy organizing teams of people by applying these disciplines so they work efficiently for the company, and so the teams can work cooperatively and satisfyingly for themselves.	Keep your answer relevant to the job you are seeking. Be as specific as you can.

Question	Reply	Analysis
What would you like to be doing five years from now?	My goal is to become vice-president in charge of operations.	Talk in career terms, not personal (marriage, children, travel) so your answer becomes a benefit for the company and shows your commitment to work.

Will I have to fill out a job application form?

Most likely. You may feel that some of the questions are discriminatory, but in fact it is perfectly legal for prospective employers to ask your sex, marital status, height, weight and even your age— with two provisos. One: they have to ask those questions of everybody, male and female, who applies for the job. Two: they must use your answers for genuine screening purposes only. If your height or weight mean you cannot do the work safely or well, that is a legitimate reason to turn you down.

Will they test me?

If they know what they are doing, they will test and probe as much as they can.

Marlene is the editor-in-chief of a weekly newspaper, and she has been around long enough to know there are ways to sift a person for flaws:

Certainly I test people for their technical ability. I scrutinize their work samples carefully, and sometimes ask them to submit a sample that is tailored specifically for our publication. But there are other less tangible measurements, and often I have to trust my intuition.

When I'm hiring a managing editor, for example, I know that this is a very sensitive position. The person has to be able to get along with other people in various levels, to get their respect and cooperation. This includes art directors and writers, creative people—not the easiest in the world to get along with. An effective managing editor can't come across as aggressive or obnoxious; a dictator just isn't going to work out. So the personality is important. So is organization and efficiency. How do I find out if it's there? I'll take them through some problem that they would have had to solve in their previous job. I might ask, "What kind of system did you use? How did you follow manuscripts in and out of the plant? What sort of plan did you have? How did you set up your files so if anyone wanted to put their hands on a particular manuscript, they could locate it right away?" It's not that I care what the system was; I'm testing to find out if that person did have a system, checking his or her attention to detail.

Do some interviewers rely heavily on intuition?

Yes, Phyllis, the sales director of a radio station in the Northwest, is another person who has had years of experience interviewing and hiring people. She has come to believe that there are no objective indicators worth relying on fully.

It's all in the gut. You have to develop antennae that tell you this person has energy, an attitude. He or she is positive, cooperative, succcess-oriented. I listen a lot for the signs: tone of voice, willingness, spirit. Of course, antennae can be wrong; you never really know a person until you live together. Still, I know what I want: somebody who is loyal, works his or her behind off, never says, "No, I can't or won't do it," and whose appearance and manner will reflect creditably on the station. Little things sometimes are a tip-off: bitten nails, overweight, something in the eyes or speech pattern, mysterious gaps in a résumé. Neurotics I don't need. I remember one candidate who was by all yardsticks a real workhorse and an old pro. She came loaded with newspaper clippings, letters of recommendation, all the right credentials. But there was something I couldn't put my finger on, something not quite right. I saw her four times, mostly because everyone else at the station was urging me not to let this one get away. I was still dragging my feet after the fourth interview. One reason was, her résumé had two two-year gaps during which she said she'd traveled. It didn't add up; you'd have to be independently wealthy just to travel for two years when you felt like it, and this person let me know she was hard-up for money. The fifth time we met, I invited her out to dinner, and that is when the truth came naked. Even though it was an interview situation and she knew it, once liquor became available she could not control her drinking. At eleven o'clock she stumbled off, sloshed to the gills. And I went home relieved that my decision to hire or not hire her was now crystal clear.

Are looks important?

They certainly are. A good appearance can get you through a great many doors that stay closed for people who look sloppy or out of place. The right clothes and accessories, immaculate grooming, an alert and self-confident bearing go a long way to make you an attractive commodity. People are drawn to the look of success, the executive image. It tells them you are a person in control, an authority, someone it would be pleasing to know and advantageous to do business with.

What you wear is a symbol for what you are. People do read books by their covers, and how you package yourself can make a favorable impression. Or it can turn people off. There's an idea that if you're smart enough it won't matter how you look. Life does not work that way. A poor appearance is points off. Even a genius who gets 90 percent for her brain loses 10 percent of her effectiveness if she looks unappealing. The more unappealing, the more points you lose. Like it or not, what you wear affects how people perceive and react to you.

A professional look commands respect. A careless appearance tells people you don't think enough of yourself or of them to make an effort.

How can I be sure what's the right thing to wear?

Check out the territory you are in. Acceptable styles vary widely from region to region, industry to industry, position to position. Where southern California decrees jeans, New York says suits are the thing. Bankers dress differently from musicians. In an ad agency, anything goes for an artist; an account executive must come off more starchy.

The object of the game is to fit in. If you don't—if you insist on being the fringed-leather maverick in a button-down world—you will just have to work harder to prove your worth. It's a law of nature that swimming against the tide is a lonely and difficult route. Better to give yourself the plus of looking like a winner than the deficit of a questionable appearance.

I once watched a woman from one of my workshops decide what she would wear to a job interview. Sylvia, thirty-six, is trim, quietly blond, and supremely collected. She is one of those people who can tuck a blouse into her skirt and it doesn't dare pop out. Or tie a scarf at her neck so it stays just where she draped it, all day. Sylvia's mind is as orderly as her appearance. When she heard of a job in the financial department of a big company in Atlanta, she prepared for the interview thoroughly. The first thing she did was ask the executive recruiter for a description of the person she'd be talking with. The answer was, this is a very serious man, analytical, detail-oriented, purposeful. Next she visited the company's corporate offices to check out the atmosphere of the building and the type of people who worked there. She could see by the furnishings, the paintings on the walls, and the executive style that this was a contemporary but conservative organization. Now Sylvia knew exactly what to choose from her wardrobe. A look of subdued elegance was the key. This is what Sylvia put together for the interview:

Gray flannel skirt	Natural makeup base
Medium blue silk blouse	Blusher
Black velvet blazer	Rose-colored lipstick
Single strand of pearls	No eye shadow
Black pumps	Black leather briefcase, discreetly monogrammed

What if they ask things I don't want to tell?

Everybody knows by now that it is illegal for employers to use the answers to certain questions to discriminate against people. However, your job at an interview is not to look for discrimination; it is to get them to want you. If they ask your age or your marital status, if you plan to have children, or who takes care of your children, you can assume that they are probing to find out how dedicated you will be to your job. You can answer in a number of ways. Directly. Or with a probing question of your own: "Do you mean that you are wondering how much time I can give to the job?" Or you can deflect the question with a gentle nudge sideways: "I don't think people should bring personal matters to work with them, do you?"

Here are some other answers that work well:

Q: *Are you married or single?*

A: *I am married.*

If you are in mid-divorce and say so, they will anticipate that you will be in a stressful period, with frequent requests for time off to see your lawyer. You can remove that negative factor by answering, truthfully, "I am married."

| Q: *How long have you been divorced?* | They are trying to find out if it's true you are in mid-divorce. Tell them the papers have all been settled, and there will be no further problems. |
| A: *The situation is no longer a problem.* | |

| Q: *How will you take care of your children if they become sick?* | They understand that you are single and want to be sure that absenteeism because of child care will not be a problem. |
| A: *I have made arrangements with a sitter and a backup person in case of emergency.* | |

| Q: *Do you plan to have a baby?* | If you tell them you plan to have a baby soon, it is the same as saying that you plan to be absent from work immediately. Wait until after you have proved yourself on the job, and they can accept your announcement. |
| A: *Not in the foreseeable future.* | |

| Q: *How will you be able to live on this salary?* | They are expressing a pious concern about something that is not their business. Thank them for their interest and assure them that their conditions are satisfactory. |
| A: *It will not be a problem for me.* | |

What if they try to find out if I'm "available"?

If the questions are put in such a way that you feel they are to find out if you are game for sexual skylarking, deflect them just as gently. Make it clear that your interest is in working, and that is why you are here. You can make your point just as clearly by changing the subject or by shifting the conversational focus onto somebody else. An answer like, "They say the number of women in executive positions will double within the next two years. What do you think?" does the job, and doesn't leave egg on the other person's face.

Sexual approaches from an out-and-out lecher who won't let you off the hook take more direct handling. Some suggestions: "That is not why I am here." "I have a very strict rule never to mix business

45

with personal matters." "I am not interested. Shall we proceed with the interview or would you rather I leave?" You have been definite and have left the door open for productive discussion, now or in the future. Remember that even a lech can bad-mouth you to somebody else. You never know where he or she will crop up again.

Are there other times to avoid making direct answers?

Yes. When you don't know what you are talking about. Actually, you can answer directly by saying, "I don't know," and often that is the smartest thing you could say. It shows you are honest and a realist, and are not trying to fool people by coming on as the omniscient Wizard of Oz. Other times, you may be called upon for an opinion or decision that is not within your grasp at the moment. If "I don't know" is simply not the politic reply, it's OK to do a little soft-shoe. There is nothing dishonest about saying, "May I get back to you on that?" Or, "I'd like a chance to think about that and get some more information." You are far better off to defer your reply than to try to fake it and be wrong.

Should I say that I have other job offers?

That's a hard question to answer. Personally, I like to hire people for middle management positions who have other job offers. It's human nature to want people who are hard to get, especially in sales. When somebody tells me, "I want to be fair and let you know that I am considering other companies," I know that they're not in a survival situation, that this job is not their rock-bottom line. Other employers feel differently: They want to believe that they are the one and only. I think it has something to do with their need to have subordinates in their power, and their fear of knowing they might lose out to competition.

What information should I volunteer?

It's a good idea to clear away any possible doubt that you have goals and will travel, if that is how you see your future. Remember, you are asking this boss and his or her company to make a very real investment in you. He or she deserves reassurance. "My husband is completely in accord with my working full time and for an entire career. I have an excellent housekeeper who sees to our meals and whatever else is necessary, so that long hours or travel are no problem. We don't plan to have children, so I'm free of baby-sitter and sick-child problems. My husband also understands that this job is important to me, and has said he will cooperate if the question of transfer comes up." Let them know just what they are getting.

There is no point in inventing fiction. If the fact is that you need to be on call for your children, can't travel or relocate without upsetting your family, or don't want the headaches, long hours, and hard labor of an all-out career job, say so. You will do yourself and your employer a service. If you get the job, they will know how to use you best and not expect the impossible. If you are not hired, you are free to go job-hunt at a place that can use your abilities.

Should I say, "I want to be in your chair"?

No. That is a direct threat. If being in the boss's chair is your ambition, now is a good time to find out if it is possible to achieve, or if a job with this company is dead-end. Instead of threatening, use the opportunity to ask the kind of questions that will tell you how far you can go.

Then it's all right to ask them questions?

Definitely. You need to have a clear definition of your job and its responsibilities. You should know what a typical day will be like. Who the people are you report to and what the chain of command is. Will you be going in with a backup staff. What will your future with the company be. Ask what their policy is about moving people up, and what are the criteria. Find out where your predecessor is now, and how long it took him or her to be promoted. If you have an inkling that there is chauvinism afoot, ask if there is anybody you'd be associated with or reporting to who objects to working with women. You'll also want to learn something about company philosophy: what kinds of customers they do business with, what plans they have for expansion or change, where the company intends to be five years from now.

By all means, ask if they have any further questions about you. And inquire when they will make their hiring decision, so you will have a timetable to go by and not be left hanging by your thumbs.

It may take more than one session for you to find out everything you need to know about each other. The more interested you are in the job, the more effort you should make to learn as much as you can before you plunge into the marriage. This is something Cynthia, a top-notch hospital administrator, failed to do. She spent the next two years of her career regretting it:

> I was bored with California and wanted to move someplace else. Houston is a major medical center, so I put out some feelers and lined up several interviews in short order. It wasn't hard: When you've been around a few years, people in the field get to know your name, and I've been a hospital administrator since I was thirty-five. Long enough. The second person I went to see was the new director of a small but growing hospital. I thought, here's a situation where I could really make a difference, leave my own imprint. The director was eager to find somebody with my qualifications and said as much. He also told me I'd have a wonderful staff to work with, the latest equipment and anything else I needed at my fingertips. Plus his complete cooperation. We did the usual dickering over salary, I got what I wanted, and went to work one month later. That's when I found out what a super salesman the director was. It turned out that I didn't have the authority I'd been led to believe I would have. The fact was, he really wanted to do my job too. As a result, I had to report every move I made to him, and the people under me found themselves taking directions from both of us. It was very confusing to them, counterproductive in terms of hospital efficiency, and frustrating as hell for me. He really hadn't defined his own or my functions clearly and, in my opinion, didn't know what he was doing. It was a two-year fiasco and I have myself to blame for getting into it. I misjudged him because I didn't ask enough questions, didn't check him out with other people, didn't take enough time to find out about his personality and abilities. He did a sales job on me and I fell for it.

What if you don't like the boss but need the job?

Your need will rarely be so desperate that you don't have choices. It's dangerous to leap into the first thing that comes along out of panic. Too many people have plunged into disaster because they had no money coming in and their bank account was shrinking, or they saw a tight job market and thought they'd better grab anything that was available. They would have been in a far better position if they'd said, "I'll wait till the right job comes along," and borrowed money to tide themselves over for six months. The right job usually does come along, particularly for people with skills. What usually happens is, two or three offers come along at the same time. Then their only problem is to make the right choice.

What does it mean when they hire you without checking your references?

One of two things. Your record and the impression you've made are so terrific there's no question about you. Or they are snatching at you for some unstated purpose. When somebody hires you quickly, without asking the right questions, be suspicious. Why are they so desperate? Is this a company where morale is so low the staff whirls in and then out again through a constantly revolving door? Do they want to hire you simply because you fill a minority requirement? Is there always a slot open here for the company bedmate, and it's your turn next? When in doubt about somebody's motives, check it out. An early fact-finding mission can save you many demoralizing months.

Should I accept a job for a trial period?

Yes, if you have no other job in the offing. A trial period will give you a chance to see if you'll really like the job, at the same time it gives the company a chance to see if you'll fit in. It's also an opportunity for you to negotiate your salary. You can say, "All right, I'll take the job at seventeen thousand dollars for the first six months. Then, if you think I'm doing good work you can pay me the twenty thousand dollars I really need. And if it doesn't work out at the end of the trial period, we can part company with no hard feelings on either side."

The most you will have lost is six months in the job-hunting market, but you will have been paid well for your time.

What can you tell about a boss before you take the job?

People give off messages all the time. You can tell a lot about a person by his or her office. Take note of the decor. Is the furniture or carpeting shabby, the drapes or blinds dilapidated? Are they tasteful? Cheap and sloppy surroundings usually reflect a cheap and sloppy occupant. Even company-issue decor bears personal signatures in the accessories: photo displays, artwork, gimmicks. Check them out. Is the place cluttered? Compulsively neat? You're entitled to make private judgments at this point, and you probably will be right. To give you an extreme example, if you saw that the boss's desk was on a raised platform, you'd be smart to run for your life. This is a person whose need to dominate is hanging out there like a red flag.

Listen with everything you've got to listen with. Is this a windbag you're casting your lot with? Can he or she ask and answer questions directly and quickly, or is his/her mind in chaos? Does he or she seem cheerful, upbeat, energetic? Remember that every company or department is the length and shadow of one person, its head. His or her strengths, weaknesses, and personality affect everyone in it.

Are you talking to a Hitler type? A milquetoast? A groaner? Somebody who would love to lean on you as a mother? If any of those qualities aren't your style, forget this job and look for another. You'll have nothing but trouble here.

There is a chemical click that takes place when two people are right for each other—in business the same as in social situations. Pay attention to it, because you are going to be living with this boss most of your working hours. If you are one of those women whose intuition is usually right, go with it. Trust your instinct that this is a person with whom you can develop a good rapport. Or not. It's an important quality, from your point of view. A man or a woman you can talk easily with and who interests you as a person will go a long way to making your job a pleasant one. When the inevitable office politics crop up, or when you have conflicts or business problems to solve, you want someone you can be comfortable about going to. Otherwise you will be in an isolated position, and isolation is a fast route to frustration and nonproductivity.

Keep your eyes and ears open outside the boss's private domain. Is the office atmosphere happy? Do people talk amiably to each other? Do they seem brisk, eager, joyful? You can even tell something about a company by the way the receptionist or secretary answers the phone when you call. A pleasant voice and warm manner is more than good box office; it's a clue to the atmosphere he or she is working in.

Incidentally, a pleasing telephone voice and manner is something a good boss is on the lookout for during the hiring process. Check it out when you are doing the interviewing.

What are some common oversights in interviewing?

Judging by the number of gravel-voiced grouches who answer telephones, I'd say that listening attentively is one of the most common.

Another mistake interviewers frequently make is hiring out of wanton eagerness to get help. I've done it myself. Sylvia, a partner in a Pennsylvania accounting firm, says that she has done it again and again:

> Why can't I learn my lesson once and for all? I'm always so up against time, and I get so impatient interviewing applicant after applicant, that when somebody who might possibly fill the bill comes along I practically push them into the job. "This has got to be the one," I say to myself, and then proceed to do all the talking, to make sure I get the answers I want. Instead of asking what kinds of systems they've used, I'll say, "Do you like detail work?" or "Do you get along well with people on the phone?" Of course they give me the answer I want to hear. I did it again just last spring, when I was desperate for an office manager who could straighten out certain problems we were having. A woman who had just graduated from business school came in to be interviewed, and I gobbled all her textbook answers as if they were candy bars, never once stopping to ask her the right evaluative questions. She seemed so enthusiastic and assured, I reasoned she'd fit right in. Wrong! She came to be known as Sylvia's Disaster Number Twenty-six. Within two months after I hired her every employee was grumbling under her stern hand. She reorganized the work flow so that whatever had worked before was gone, replaced by new systems that were totally unmanageable. The place was in a shambles and I was right back where I started, only worse.

What are the mistakes women make at interviews?

They put themselves down instead of selling their assets.
They are vague about their goals.
They have a feminist chip on their shoulder if the boss is a man.
They act as if it is demeaning to work for a woman.
They jump the gun and disqualify themselves.

Jump the gun?

They ask questions prematurely about details that should not be discussed until after they are offered the job.

Anybody who asks, "What are the hours?" marks him or herself as an hourly laborer, not a salaried career person. "The hours" are as long as it takes to do the job. The only appropriate question is, "What time would you like me to come in tomorrow morning?"

Leave questions about salary and fringe benefits until after you have got them to say that they want you. If you don't get the offer, you will have nothing to reject. If you do get it, then the balance will be on your side and you will be in a good position to bargain and negotiate.

What if they ask how much I need or what I'm making now?

Be circuitous. If they talk about salary, say, "That's only one of the many factors to be considered." And drop the subject until they offer you the job. If they pin you down about your present salary, tell the truth. You can tack on a comment about the increasing cost of living or your potential value to this company, if you want to indicate that it's not enough. Do you know that some people lie when they answer this question, to try to jack up the ante? Don't do it. You are sure to be caught, and the lie will put you out of the running.

What if the subject of money never comes up?

It means one of two things. Either you are not being considered for the job. Or they are interested in you and will ask to meet with you again.

Does that mean I might have to go through two interviews?

Maybe more than two, if you make a good impression and the position is important to the company. The higher up you go in management, the more carefully they will have to consider you as a candidate, and the longer it will take them to make a decision.

Also, the longer you should take in accepting their offer. You want time to think about all the advantages and disadvantages, and you want to let them know that this is an important move to which you are giving serious consideration. If they really want you, they will be more eager than you at this point for your answer.

Sometimes a second interview will be with different people than you saw the first time: other executives who must also approve you. Carolyn, a good-looking blonde from the Midwest, was amused and a little rueful when she discovered who her second appointment was with:

> My kids were grown and my husband had said, "OK, now you can get out of the housework you say is so boring and get a job if you like." That's all I needed to hear. I whipped up a résumé based on ancient history and guts—a sales job when I was in my early twenties and four years of travel in between college semesters—and talked my way into working for a guy I sort of knew. He owns a travel agency in town. One of the things I knew about this man was that he has a reputation for philandering. His last three assistants were friends of friends of mine, and I'd heard there was plenty of fooling around in and out of the office. Apparently his wife had heard it too, because the day after he said he'd hire me, he phoned and asked, "Would you mind coming into the office one more time, please, before we settle our arrangement? There's somebody else who would like to meet you." I trotted in and the somebody else was his wife. I can't remember exactly what she asked me, but it was nothing of any consequence. She just wanted to get a good look at me to see if I'd be another "other woman." I passed muster and got the job, but I'll tell you the truth: I wasn't sure whether to be pleased or miffed. Obviously she thought, "Hmmm. Over forty. Not sensational-looking. Perfectly safe."

What if they hire me as the token woman?

Take the job, if it's your chance to get into management and you are sure the people you will work with aren't going to be antagonistic toward you. Back when government regulations first came out and erased ostensible sexist discrimination, more than one woman took advantage of being the token. They walked into executive jobs they were less qualified for than their male competitors, just because they were the right gender at the right time. Those days have passed; now you must have the right training as well.

Before you get yourself into a situation that you know is tokenism, find out if the waves are going to part or if you will drown fighting a fruitless battle. Talk to the people who are hiring you and ask them who you'll be working with. Try to talk to your prospective colleagues in advance, too, to find out if everybody is going to be against you because you are a woman, or if you will have some allies. The significant questions are, "Who will go to bat for me if I'm thwarted by the company in doing my job? What will happen if a customer says he won't work with a woman? Will I be thrown to the wolves or will somebody help me solve the problem?" You have to know ahead of time that there is some way for you to flourish in a potentially hostile environment. And you have to understand that if you have nobody on your side, in a situation that is going to be strange and new for the company, the job may be too tough to warrant taking on single-handed and you'd be better off turning it down.

What does it mean when they tell me I'm wonderful but I still don't get the job?

Almost everybody who has to turn people down tries to make it easier by saying something nice to the person. They may or may not think you're wonderful. Just the same, hearing it makes you feel better about yourself. Even if you don't hear it, keep in mind that the turndown was not a personal rejection. You just weren't right for that particular job at that particular time. Or, for all you know, the job was already wired for somebody else and you were sent in as a ringer.

A turndown is one thing. Repeated turndowns are another. If you keep losing out again and again, you had better start to figure out why. All ten people who said No are probably not wrong. Try to assess yourself. Ask two or three of the people who turned you down for help: "Do you think I need more training? Does my résumé look wrong? Do I come off badly in an interview? Please be honest; I am looking for helpful criticism. If another opening came up in your company, would you consider me for it or not?"

If you are consistently losing out on jobs, you have got to find out what makes you Number Two. Analyze yourself honestly and realistically, and do whatever you have to do to bring your qualifications up to snuff. Work at it from a positive point of view, not as a defeatist. Keep your self-confidence high. That is the key: When you have a good opinion of yourself, you can convince other people to believe you are good. If you walk into a new situation thinking, "This is going to be another success," the chances are that is what you will come out with: another success.

JOBS AND THE MARKETPLACE

How much does luck have to do with success?

Somebody has said, Luck is when opportunity meets preparation. You have to be ready for what you want to do. You have to keep your eyes open for the chance to do it. And you have to go after the chance and capture it. Luck is opportunity and determination, plus ability. It is placing yourself in a target position and being ready to take the leap.

The other side of the "luck" coin is to have specific timetables for your goals so you are not subject to the roll of the dice. With goals, you can strategize and influence the dice to make things happen, so that you reach your objectives sooner.

How long should you stay on a job before you move on?

About two years. You may find sooner that you're in a dead-end spot: You're not advancing in your career, you can't make enough money, you don't enjoy what you're doing. Move on. But don't make a practice of moving on after a few months here and a few months there. A résumé with a series of short job-hops will make you look erratic and unreliable—qualities that prospective employers will shun. You need a résumé that says you have had good training and experience, fit in well where you have worked, been a valued contributor to previous employers.

When you change jobs it should be for good reason. You have to know where you are going and why, and you have to make it clear that you are a goal-oriented person, not a grasshopper.

How do I set up work goals?

One way is to start with your long-range objective and work backward, to see the steps you must take to attain your ambition. You might decide that what you want five years from now is to be an editor at a news magazine. The way to make the leap from here to there is to set up realistic, short-term goals that will get you where you want to be. Think:

Q: *What would I have to do, starting right now, to move in on my five-year plan?*

A: Start to get news-reporting experience.
Three-month goal: Get any job available at a news publication, to learn how the business works.

Q: *Where should I be after the first year?*

A: In a more responsible job at the publication.
One-year goal: Move up to the editorial department.

Q: *What should I be doing two years from now?*

A: Focusing on a specialty.
Two-year goal: Develop an area of expertise such as business or politics, and start to gain recognition in that field.

Q: *Three years from now?*

A: Focus on my special area of news coverage.
Three-year goal: Become a columnist covering the news within my area of expertise.

Q: *How will I reach my five-year objective?*

A: By being the business or political editor.

Must I have specific goals?

It is certainly advisable. But you must do what works best for you.

The key word in that sentence is "do." If you sit around and complain, blaming your parents, your health, sexism, society, and the world at large for your nowhereness, that is where you will get: nowhere.

Sometimes you don't plan what's coming next, and you make giant strides anyway. That happened to Gini, a bright young research analyst. The company she worked for lost its major account and had to let Gini's entire team of researchers go. She was devastated. "Where can I go?" she asked the president of the company. "There just aren't any jobs like this around, and research analysis is the only marketable skill I have." The president answered, "That's not true, Gini. I've been reading your reports for the year and a half you've been here, and you happen to be a very good writer. Losing a job is no fun, but this could be your chance to move into another field, one I'm sure you will excel in. I'll be happy to place some calls to some people I know and help you get started."

Very often it takes someone else to help you see what the next step should be. Don't be afraid to ask for help when you need it.

What are the best fields for women these days?

If "best" means the areas where you can reap the most prestige, pay, and potential, the hot fields of the eighties are those that are not yet crowded with women at the top. Science, technology, politics, government, finance, law, medicine—the list is limited only by imagination and drive. Then there are the usual women's fields: nursing, teaching, and other support services. These areas are easier to get into and less resistant to female leadership. But there are two major drawbacks to working in a women's field. You can get lost in the crowd. And your hard work and devotion earn small rewards.

Is finance a good field if you're money-oriented?

Yes, but it's difficult. There is something interesting about money and women in business. The closer you are to money, the more established the male enclave is at the top, where there is direct, hands-on control of big money and risk-taking. That establishment sees women as intruders and rivals. This is one reason why women have progressed slowly into the executive ranks of high finance, in the realms of banking investment, venture capital management, and the stock and commodities exchanges. Another reason it's hard is our lack of training and experience. It is true that you hear of female superstars: women with seats on the New York Stock Exchange, partners in important law firms, board members of Fortune 500 companies. The percentage is small and the movement into high-paying, powerful positions is gradual. It takes a strongly motivated, thoroughly professional woman to achieve recognition on male turf.

What is professionalism?

Knowing your job.
Knowing the answers.
Having a strong contact base.

Keeping deadlines.
Being organized.
Having the flexibility to meet new situations.
Showing self-confidence.
Harmonizing with people.
Having goals you can realistically expect to meet.

What kind of job should I look for if I don't know what I want to do?

My parents sent me to a good liberal arts college, then supported me while I took a year to find myself. Now I have to get a job, and I haven't a clue. I'm not trained for anything special, like dentistry or computer programming. I have no talents, like singing or painting. I'm lost. Where do I begin?

Almost anywhere that is realistic. The point is to get started, so you can get your career moving. One way to start is to check with a career consultant, through a private organization, a woman's group, or a university. These people are trained to probe for your areas of interest and then label them in terms of the business world. Your interest in animals may translate into the veterinary field, or a fondness for gardening could become an affinity for botany or the florist business. A good consultant can also tell you the supply-and-demand picture in various fields, and help guide you to a position that fits your needs realistically.

Even if you begin in a field or type of job that turns out not exactly right for you, you'll be giving yourself the opportunity to find out what it is you do not like. You will also place yourself in a position where you will meet people who can give you ideas and leads. And you will have a chance to learn business skills while you are learning about yourself.

With no strong drive or concrete goal, what you need most is an open mind and a willingness to explore. Then you can pick anything in this world that you want and, if it's realistic for you, go after it.

Some people are born knowing exactly who they are and what they want to do. Others have to figure it out as they go along. Marion spent nine years in the work force, in three different jobs. Each job led her to be more specific about her career goals. This is now her tenth work anniversary, and she is able to be very precise about what she needs:

I am looking for a job in human resource management. It must be in a company where there is an opportunity to create new programs. It has to be in a Fortune 500 company, and the company has to be located in New York City. My friends say I am the only person they've ever heard of who has a job target with a zip code!

Does my personality have anything to do with the job I should take?

Yes. You really have to know yourself: your energy level, your frustration threshold. Some people find that pressure and deadlines spur them on. Others function better in an easygoing atmosphere. The copy chief of a Chicago advertising agency told me a story that illustrates perfectly how the right person can get into the wrong slot:

Somehow I missed the fact when I interviewed her that Gwen was accustomed to the slow pace of a longer-range operation than advertising. She'd been with an industrial magazine where her job didn't depend on coming up with tomorrow's ideas yesterday, eight times a day. I could see that she wasn't working out here. She was missing deadlines, her ideas were stale, she looked pale and nervous. I called her in and said, "Gwen, you are a very capable and cooperative person and I enjoy having you in my department. But I'm afraid that it's not right for you. I'm transferring you to our catalog division, where I think your talents will be better utilized. Trust me and try it, will you? I know it's the right thing for you." She broke down and cried, feeling that she'd failed and was being demoted. I did my best to reassure her, and she agreed to give the catalog division a two-week try on my say-so. The two weeks have become two years, and Gwen is doing a whizbang job. She is now second-in-command in her department and has her old energy back. It's the right place and the right tempo for her personality.

I helped Gwen because I knew she had potential and I understood why her work was lagging. But I've had other people I've dismissed because they wouldn't accept the facts of life. In business, the demands of the corporate machinery are what pay your salary and that is what you must adjust to. You are measured by how well you fulfill your responsibilities. I might add that you can measure yourself by how happy you are in your job.

61

What are some specifics I should consider in accepting a job?

1. The Size of the Company.

You have to know yourself to know whether you would be better off in a large or a small company. If you must have informal, personal contacts all up and down the line, like to know that there is a great deal of flexibility, and want the freedom to choose your own options, you probably should work in a small company. A large company would be a good choice if you are a person who works well within bureaucratic bounds, enjoys hierarchical privileges, and likes to know that if you do your job well you can be pretty certain of scheduled promotions and raises.

One question to ask yourself is, Are you happy being accountable to other people or do you have to write your own rules? Large corporations are necessarily structured as bureaucracies, with tables of organization and channels of command that can flex very little. Otherwise there would be chaos. Large corporations require conformity to rules and, excepting within departments, tend to be impersonal. In some large companies, you may never even meet the president and other higher-ups.

Small companies are usually more loosely organized and entail more personal relationships. They let you learn more about all facets of the business. You can move faster from a support or advisory position into executive management. You can express your individuality. You can be a big fish in a small pond and reach star status in a short time. The drawback to working in a small company is that the owner's style usually sets the tone for the entire organization. If you don't get along with that person or don't like his/her style, you probably won't get very far—unless it's a company that is moving into new fields and you can carve out your own area. At that, if the company is very personally dominated, the owner will probably want to control everything and not part with much authority.

2. Hours.

Consider whether the company's hours fit in with your own and your family's lifestyle. If not, would the company give you leeway to make an arrangement you could work with? Be realistic about whether you can adjust to a job that means working nights and week-ends. What arrangement could you make to take care of personal matters such as trips to the beauty salon and the butcher, courses of study, chauffeuring the family?

3. Money.

You have to be sure that you will earn enough to meet your needs. Sit down with a pencil and paper and really work out how much you will actually take home after deductions. Are the fringe benefits good enough to take care of your medical costs, travel and entertaining expenses? How much will it cost you for transportation and meals out? Do enough research to be sure of the company's history in terms of giving raises: How much can you look forward to, and when? Think about whether taking this job will make you worth more on the market after you spend a couple of years gaining expertise.

4. Lifestyle.

How will this kind of work affect your personal life? What will happen if you earn more money than he does? Will he be willing to help with the household, the children? Can you keep up your interests in theater, travel, sports, clothes?

5. Location.

Some people love cities and hate small towns. Some love the sun and can't bear winter. Other people feel just the opposite. If you are sure of your preference, target your location requirements accordingly. But be careful that mere fear of the unknown doesn't make you rule out a good opportunity. You may have to actually live and work someplace to know whether you love it or hate it.

Another factor is supply and demand. Is there a need for your business or service? Is the region already clogged with people who do what you do?

Investigate the cultural and economic climates before you move to a new location. If you have children, find out what the school system is like. How is the housing situation? Will property and income taxes kill you? How is the transportation, for local commuting and for trips out of town?

The fact that you are a woman is something else that you should consider. In general, large cities offer more opportunity for women aiming at senior management because female executives are not the strange new animals they are in small towns. In major metropolitan areas, it is accepted that you will go for the top; you have already had predecessors who have paved the way. Further, there is more money in the big cities, and therefore more of a pie for you to carve your slice from. Of course, living expenses are higher, too. You have to be sure that your salary will cover your costs.

My advice, if you are not absolutely certain where you belong, is to explore, as Helen did when she found herself at age forty, fresh from a divorce and yearning for a complete change of scene.

I was free at last. Single. Some money from the sale of the house. No one to report to, no children and schools to tie me down. I could leave my legal-secretary job in Chicago anytime I wanted, and trade that terrible climate for a new life of sunshine, sailing, and relaxed hours. I thought, "It would be heaven to be with people who work to live, for a change. That's what it's all about." I was heady with the idea, but not so far gone that I'd kick over all the traces. I am not exactly an heiress and I do have to keep a paycheck coming in. So what I did was take a month's leave of absence, so I could really taste the town in Florida where I wanted to live.

It's a good thing I did it that way. The town was just as pretty as I remembered it from my visit a couple of years before. I set up about twenty appointments for the job-hunt part, and scheduled the rest of my time for sightseeing, trying the restaurants, counting the homes and apartments I might be able to afford, checking out the activities that might interest me.

I really tried. After ten days my rainbow began to melt. Not one single job was open, one reason being that there weren't very many to be had in the first place. The pay was a fraction of what I'd been living on, even taking into account the lower cost of Sunbelt living. I ran out of restaurants, shops, movies, and art galleries in about five days. And I was getting extremely antsy. But I stayed on, knowing it takes more than ten days to become accustomed to a new environment and a different pace. At the end of three weeks I knew for sure: Small town life was not for me. At least I'd given it a try, gone in with a completely open mind, and lived as much as possible like a real citizen. I couldn't wait to get back to the hurly-burly of Chicago.

Would moving from a small town to a big city get me a more important job?

Not necessarily. Claire's story is the flip side of Helen's. She is a widow who'd been a teacher most of her fifty-five years, and who had spent her entire life in the same Southwest suburb. She began to feel embarrassed when her daughter, a Washington attorney, wrote home about her big salary and the power circles she moved in. Claire thought, "When I was that age I didn't have much ambition and the opportunities weren't there. But it's decades later and here I am, still doing what I've always done. Suddenly it doesn't feel right anymore. I want to do something more interesting, more impressive. I'm going to pick myself up and move to another city where the lights are brighter."

Claire sat down and took stock. She listed her assets and liabilities, the pros and cons of moving. She was surprised by what she discovered. Her house was nearly paid for. The local tax rates and cost of living were modest. She was due for a retirement pension at age sixty-two. It looked as if maybe she shouldn't move after all. Besides the financial benefits of staying in place, Claire really liked her hometown and her place in it.

Still she was dissatisfied. "This is madness. I am going to get out of teaching, hell or high water. Where is it written that I must wait around seven years to get a pension? I could die in the same old saddle, of boredom if nothing else. On the other hand, I'm not keen about trudging around town looking for a job, even if there were a decent one here for a fifty-five-year-old to look for. It is time for me to clear away the cobwebs and start to think fresh."

The upshot was that Claire, who had always had a zest and flair for baking, took that affinity and skill, and gradually built up a bakery. She started in her home, with local stores as clients. They were happy to order from a resident. Her business now employs forty people and is still expanding. What is most important is that Claire moved off the treadmill onto something she truly enjoys.

Do I need a degree to get into a career?

Some people need a college degree to get a job, some get along very well without a degree, and others get along but feel inferior because they don't have educational initials after their name. The fact is, a college degree can be important when you first go to work. At that point, your academic record is the only concrete thing for an employer to look at. After you've held a job for two or three years, the importance of your degree drops to about 20 percent in value; it's your demonstrated achievements that count.

Which degrees you need depend, in part, on which field you are going into. Obviously, you must have a graduate degree for medicine, law, architecture, or engineering. If you are going into something like sales, advertising, or travel, the need is less obvious. A lot depends on the company that hires you. Some large corporations require a college degree for sales or secretarial work—their personnel departments need ways to pigeonhole the thousands of applications they receive. At a small company you may be able to win a job on nothing more than basic skills. Then, once you have proved your ability, the job becomes your degree: the credential you need to move onward and up.

Why are more women getting their master's degree in business administration?

Because it gives them a competitive edge. An M.B.A. in the eighties is what a bachelor's degree was in the sixties: proof of knowledge. But there is this difference: An M.B.A. is proof of specialized knowledge in business data, analysis, and decision-making techniques. And there is no doubt: This is the age of specialization. An M.B.A. is also proof of your seriousness about a career. Nobody would take on the grueling hard work of getting an M.B.A. unless they meant— well, business.

Very few women used to go for an M.B.A. In the mid-sixties there were about five hundred who had earned the degree. Ten years later that number swelled to nearly five thousand and by 1980 there were about ten thousand women M.B.A.'s. Clearly, the dramatic increase is directly related to the women's movement into the ranks of high-paying jobs. These ranks, as we know, are not only highly competitive, but also increasingly specialized and subspecialized. An M.B.A. from a top-rated school can give you the leg up you need to break into those ranks. It is a credential employers are accustomed to look for in considering well-trained, goal-directed men.

Some caveats are in order:

1. An M.B.A. from a top-rated school is an extremely valuable commodity. A degree from a questionable school is not a good credit to have on your record. Check out the school's credentials before you commit yourself to two years' hard work, and a cost of $800 to $20,000.

2. Your M.B.A. can be the passport to an impressive entry salary. If you are at a good school you will be wooed by high-powered corporations to come aboard at an entry salary in the $20,000 to $30,000 range. But you will have no insurance policy on continuing promotions. You have to face the fact that women often are passed over in favor of men. And that women execeutives' salaries still average one-third less than their male counterparts.

3. You can learn skills such as marketing analysis, accounting, and management counseling. But an M.B.A. is only as good as you are. You still have to display initiative and enthusiasm, interview well, know how to dress, and give the image of someone who will harmonize with an organization. An M.B.A. is a great source of self-confidence. It is also famous for promoting arrogance, a quality that can close doors in your face.

What if I have no time or money for college?

There are ways to earn credentials without four years of college or graduate school.

Most colleges now give credits to mature individuals for life experience, which will help earn the credits you want for your career if you need a degree.

You can take advantage of financial aid programs, many of which have been created specifically to help women. Ask your local office of the National Organization for Women (NOW), or the women's studies program at a nearby university for a list of the programs you may qualify for. You may be eligible for a grant or scholarship through a state, federal, or university student-loan program. Professional organizations and civic groups often have scholarship or loan funds, as well.

Or you can create your own credentials. A woman I know with a talent for research could not get a job because she had neither a degree nor recent work experience. So she invented her own market research study—did all the legwork, assembled and analyzed the data—and produced a very professional study. With her self-made dossier in hand, she was able to approach local research organizations with concrete evidence that she knew procedures and could produce professional results. She reentered the job market, after an eighteen-year absence, with a $16,000 salary.

What is a reentry job?

When you return to the job market after a period of not working. Many women who have completed raising their families are in the reentry position. Often they take courses to brush up their skills, join discussion groups to catch up on what's new in the business world, or talk with career consultants to pinpoint how they can translate their life experiences into career assets. They find that community service volunteer work and even homemaking translate well into paying jobs. For example, the years you spent hostessing your husband's business functions could look like this on a résumé:

> 1965 to present: Organized business meetings for corporate executives in Chicago, Atlanta, Washington, D.C. Developed wide contact base. Excellent organizational skills.

An interest in horticulture can lead to work as a floral designer. Proficiency in helping people translates into sales, personnel, or social service work. Other areas that may be low-paying but provide an opportunity for women to reenter the job market include:

AFFINITY	JOB TRANSLATION
Money management	Bank teller, clerk, collection worker
Personal relationships	Employee benefits assistant, paraprofessional nurse, teacher, social service aide
Service	Airline reservations agent, insurance adjuster

What does "line job" mean?

One definition is, a job that puts you in line for the top; senior management, president, chief executive officer . . . the boss.

Line jobs are the least dispensable in economic hard times. They are the positions of leadership, influence, power, and authority. They are directly connected with the heart of business: manufacture, sales, and management.

You can't always tell a line job by its title. A salesperson, lawyer, accountant, or other technician may or may not be in a line position. It depends on what influence dominates the company.

Age or seniority in the company have nothing to do with whether you are in a line job. Margaret is thirty-four, and she is definitely in line for high executive rank at the insurance company where she works. She has the ability, the direction, and the attitude that spell success. One of her most important assets is that she takes responsibility for doing whatever needs to be done without whining, "This isn't my job, it's not what I'm paid to do." She understands that there are plenty of people competing with her for promotion, and that she has to work hard to get to the top. Balancing this is the fact that there aren't many people who will argue with you when you are in a line position; they are all working on the same problem you are.

I asked Margaret how she got her start:

I came to this company just after college graduation. I was part of a minorities program in which I was moved around within the company so I could become oriented to management. After my learning period, I became the executive assistant to a senior officer, and in that position I had a great deal of exposure to various line functions. My next steps up were managerial—always in line jobs. I was in policy administration, then became a regional manager, and I am now a strategic reorganizer at corporate headquarters. I have been told that my administrative strength lies in my abilities as a problem solver, the care I give to preparation, my powers of observations, and my excellent memory. As a matter of fact, I do have an excellent memory, but I never rely on it. I dictate everything into paper, so the facts will be on record.

What is the opposite of a line job?

A staff job. Support positions such as secretarial, personnel, and publicity help to get a product or service in and out of a company efficiently. These jobs are of an advisory rather than executive-suite nature. They can make or break a company, and are the first to be chopped out of the budget when money is tight.

Should I avoid taking a support job?

Not at all. You can make very good money and a name for yourself in a support job. You can use it to get your foot in the door and later switch over into a line position. A staff job can be the rung on which to learn the business, gain experience, and attract favorable attention to yourself. Or it can be an extremely satisfactory end in itself. The better you are in support, the better your superior will perform, and the more important and rewarding your job will be.

Is secretary a support job?

It is. To be a good secretary is to be invaluable. It is also a natural outlet for a woman who enjoys the role of helper and nurturer. What is more, secretarial work in the executive suite can pay very well and is an increasingly desirable, respected position. It's quite different from the late seventies, when many women shied away from the label "secretary." These days, good secretarial skills are more and more in demand.

Settling down into a secretarial slot can hold you back, however, if you are in a large corporation and want to move on to senior management. Support functions are outside the executive structure, and in most bureaucracies, the structure is rigid. Secretaries serve and assist, they do not make decisions.

If you are in a secretarial career, I suggest that you step back from time to time and reassess your goals. Do you want to have power, control, influence, authority? Then you must work where it is possible to become head of the department, not merely secretary to the department head.

It is possible to move out of the secretarial groove into management. If that is your intention, you should find out if your goals are achievable. Check it out. Speak to your employer. Find out what has happened to your predecessors. Ask where they are now. Ask if it is possible for you to cross over from secretarial to management. Do not live on pipe dreams.

Be specific, be realistic, and be purposeful. That is the best way to get everything you want from your job with a minimum of needless disappointment.

What about selling?

More and more women are finding that sales is the perfect slot for them, as a first job or as a career. For one thing, it is often a good route into management: Nobody knows more about a product, its manufacture, and its market than a salesperson. Without him or her, that product or service might as well not exist.

Selling is a wonderful way to build self-confidence. It teaches you to stop focusing on your shyness and to concentrate on benefiting other people instead.

It has immediate, measurable rewards: contracts, commissions, the triumphant feeling of success.

Selling involves you with ever-expanding networks of people: men and women who will be your friends and contacts when you want to reach further goals.

Do I have to work for somebody else?

At least at the beginning of your career, it's a good idea.

You may be one of those people who marches to her own drum, who cannot bear conforming to someone else's rules, who feels hemmed in and defiant unless she can be a free spirit. That is typical of the entrepreneur. But to be a successful entrepreneur, and to be successful sooner, you should apprentice first. Too many people have failed because they skittered blithely into self-employment without serious real-life preparation.

For most people, it is imperative to take the time and put in the effort to get a thorough training at somebody else's feet. This enables you to gain an intimate understanding of the detail of your field and business in general. A job placement executive puts it this way:

> Every month at least one eager young woman comes to me who wants to start at the top. I'm talking about brilliant women, obvious achievers with superb graduate school credentials. Either they want advice on starting their own business, or they are looking for a thirty-thousand-dollar-a-year entry salary. I can't place them anywhere. The only thing

I can do for them is to tell them to come back when they have experience. I remind them, with a twinge of disloyalty to the corporations I work for, that they can get that experience on somebody else's payroll. It's like taking money for going to school.

One of the women I advised not to strike out on her own falls into a different category. Eleanor has been out of school and working in publishing for twelve years. At the time we met she was the architectural editor of a well-known magazine. She'd paid her dues, she knew her job, and she was frustrated to the point of anger and depression. She told me, "This job is absolutely dead-end for me, and I have to get out of it. I can't stand having to account for every move any longer. Besides, it's stifling my creativity; I've gone way past the stage of describing the charms of center-entrance Colonial homes. What I want to do is some serious architectural analysis and criticism, and there is no room for that kind of thing in a popular magazine."

I said, "I appreciate how you feel, Eleanor. Let's look at your options. You could quit the magazine and be a free-lance architectural writer. However, the outlets for your specialty are limited. Could you earn enough to keep on paying your child's school costs as well as your own expenses?" She thought not. I suggested, "You could get a job at a small, serious magazine that would let you express your architectural ideas. But small magazines pay less than what you're earning now, and you would have a money problem."

Eleanor agreed that that option was out of the question for financial reasons, and reminded me that she would be fighting a company system even at a small magazine. The solution was in the third alternative I presented. "The trick for you is to be assured of the money you need and to express your individuality at the same time. A realistic compromise would be to keep your present job and, instead of fighting it, apply your energy to something that will satisfy your needs. If you write a book on architecture at the same time you're drawing a paycheck from the magazine, you can use your professionalism the way you like."

I am pleased to tell you that this way of working turned out to be just what Eleanor needed, and she is now producing her second architectural book while continuing to receive steady income from her editorial job.

Is it bad to be a job hopper?

In your father's day, any move was called job hopping. Then, stability and security were more important than doing good work and fulfilling your needs. Although the phrase "job hopping" is still pejorative—it means diddling at this or that for a short time and never doing anything well—today's "mobility" is both acceptable and desirable. It is the new freedom. It is permission and opportunity. It is the liberty to switch jobs or careers, and take what you have learned up the ladder with you.

Tell me how to get a job on nothing but guts.

I'll tell you how Barbara did it. She bluffed her way in with the help of a canny adviser, a scantling of knowledge—and guts.

I had been trained as a kindergarten teacher and I knew, one season into the land of clay modeling and milk breaks, that it was not for me. What I wanted was a glamorous adult-world job. I went after one and got it. For two years I worked for a product designer and learned everything I could about publicity: how to write releases, how to set up pictures the newspapers would consider fetching, how to make the right lists and phone calls—the technical details.

"So much for my adult-world education," I thought. "Now I want the glamour part. My next job will be with a national magazine."

I knocked on doors. I hit every magazine in town. I kept at it until finally one editor said he was looking for help. He asked if I could handle their publicity. I did a little soft-shoe and told him I'd been in publicity for the past two years. He said, "I am very eager to talk to you about your ideas and I'm terribly sorry that I have to rush out to an appointment. Would you mind coming back on Friday?" I lit out of there, dashed to the nearest phone booth, and put in an SOS to my friend Mike. Mike is an old old pal who used to do publicity for a circus. He once told me that if I ever needed help to come to him. Unquestionably the time to gobble up his offer was at hand. I babbled the events of the day to him and gasped, "I am terrified. I haven't an idea in the world. What do I do now?" Mike said, "Go to a newsstand, by a copy of the magazine, and get it and your fanny over here pronto. We'll figure something out."

Mike is marvelous. He knows how to make you stretch. We sat down and he turned to a story in the magazine on potato farming. "Look this article over and work up a publicity idea for it," he commanded. Idea, idea, where are you idea? Ah ha—I'd been to a wine-tasting party the week before; how about a potato-tasting party? "Great," said Mike. "Now what would you do with this article by a

73

professor at the university upstate?" I said that for starters I'd make sure the university had plenty of reprints to distribute to its alumnae, so the magazine's name would get around in the right places. Mike applauded, and then we went through the magazine article by article. Between the two of us, we had at least one idea for every story, and I was ready for the Friday interview. Then Mike gave me some good Irish advice. "Don't let the editor ask you any questions. You start the interview by instantly asking him a lot of questions. Turn to the potato story and say, 'What kind of party are you having for the potato farmers?' Then flip to the professor's piece and say, 'What have you done about this? Do you have reprints at the university?' And listen, Barb, if the son of a bitch tries to chase you around the desk, just tell him that is not what you are there for."

I kissed him. "Mike, you are a doll. If I get the job I will send you red carnations. If not, they'll be dead-white."

At the interview, I followed Mike's advice to the letter. The editor said, "Nobody's giving any party for the potato farmers, and I thought of getting reprints to the university, but there's no one here to take care of it. I can't do publicity and be editor, too. That is precisely why we need you."

I sent three dozen red carnations to dear Mike. He had got me to define the job to the editor. From there on it was up to me to come through.

Should I take a job where there is somebody I hate?

I have just been offered a wonderful job. It's for a charitable foundation, which is definitely my field, and the director has asked me to come in as a division head. There is one problem. The other division head, with whom I would have to collaborate on a daily basis, is an absolute bitch. She is rude, she is arrogant, she is trouble. I know that if we clash there will be no way I can confront her or let the director know there's a problem: She happens to be his lover. I'm dying to take the job and I'm also afraid of it. What should I do?

If you feel that strongly and can foresee trouble, you might be wise to turn down the offer. You're good enough for that company to have sought you out; you are probably good enough so that other companies or foundations will want you, too. True, you may have to wait for a long time until another desirable opening comes along, but that's the chance you'll have to take if you want to insure good working relationships.

If you decide to take the job, there are ways to handle it amicably.

• Detach yourself emotionally from this person. Keep in mind that it is her personality that is the trouble, not what you might say or do. Be objective and don't personalize; remember that the reason you are there is to get a job done. Keep the foundation's welfare as your primary goal, and a personality clash as just one of the elements you have to work with.

• Remember that projects are team efforts, not solo displays, and do everything you can to help that other person do her job well. Your joint accomplishments will make you look better in the long run.

• Make sure that you get whatever credit is due you. Your colleague will have the boss's ear anytime she wants it, and his sympathy as well. Get yourself on record at all times. Send memos and reports to the director, with carbons to other appropriate personnel, so nobody can say you are being sneaky.

• Cultivate a good rapport with the director. Just because he has an office wife doesn't mean you can't be his office friend and respected employee.

• Never put that other person down, to her face or to anyone else. The word will get back. You may be tempted to let people know she is wrong and you are right. Don't do it. One drop of antagonism is all the fuel she will need to light a fire that will cremate you.

Supposing we cross swords and I win?

Even if she gets fired and you are promoted, the chances are you will lose in the end. The reason for that is, sometime in your career you will undoubtedly meet again, and she will remember the time you stung her. It may take a week or it may takes years, but she will remain your enemy, waiting for a chance to even the score.

This is exactly what happened with two city planners who, five years ago, worked at the same governmental agency. Frances had got her job first, and as soon as she could, hired her friend Irma as as her deputy planner. Irma tells it this way:

> As soon as I was in the job I could see how unfairly Frances operates when she's in a position of command. She gets other people to come

75

up with all the ideas and do all the work, and then grabs all the credit. For instance, it was my idea to get a federal grant for a housing rehab program, and it was my spadework and follow-through that made the program successful. To hear Frances tell it, which she did over and over again to the press, the mayor, and everyone else in the office, the whole thing was her baby from start to finish. I might as well not have existed. We'd go to meetings and it would be the same story, whatever the program we were working on. After a year of this, I quit in disgust and went into the private sector. Needless to say, there was nothing left of our friendship. We never spoke again until last month, when I was hired by a commercial development firm to head up an important new project. My first act was to fire the relocation expert I'd inherited with the department—Frances.

ENOUGH MONEY:

You and Your Paycheck

How important is money?

It's as important as you think it is. Different people have different points of view:

"To me it's what working is all about."

"Money is a necessity. It's what pays the rent. I do whatever will earn me a living."

"Money is what I can never have enough of. They used to tell me it was something you never mentioned. Now that I'm into earning, I eat, sleep, dream, and live for it. I love money."

"Money is what buys you the things you want. That can mean school for your kids or it can mean a thirty dollar bottle of perfume. If you want nice things you have to pay for them, and that usually means money."

"Money is the measure of your worth. It is the award, the recognition, the sign that you are good at what you do."

"Money? I'm not sure. It's important if you don't have it and a convenience if you do. I don't think about it very much."

"For years I compared myself with other women. I thought I was in good shape because I was making more than my friends. Then it dawned on me that I wasn't making money, I was making *female* money. The world has both men and women in it, and I'd been restricting myself to the lower-paid half of the population. Why not compete with the other half? That was the turning point. I began to take risks, dare to lose, charge big money for doing big jobs. It made all the difference. My goal this year is to take home one hundred thousand dollars. Four years ago I was grateful to come out with thirty-five thousand dollars."

Is attitude important?

Yes. A negative attitude can keep money away. Some people deny themselves financial success because they think poor. When they make money they're sure it is all a mistake, they don't deserve it, it's going to vanish. They are forever on an austerity kick, think like hidebound bookkeepers, won't invest in their own success. They settle for third-rate everything: office, clothes, staff—the totems of power that people respect.

Like it or not, money attracts money and symbols count. In the business world you will always have to compete with people who have more money than you do. The trick is to appear as successful as they, and not deal yourself out of the race.

Am I wrong to work in a low-paying field?

Not necessarily. Making money is not everybody's top priority. Here are three other points of view:

Jane, free-lance writer: I could write advertising copy instead of magazine articles and get paid lots more for doing less work. But I wouldn't be happy. As it is, the fact that I get paid for doing what I love to do seems almost obscene to me. The fact that it isn't a lot of money is not important. What knocks me out is that people pay me to do what I feel like doing. I feel spoiled.

Sheila, bookshop owner: I feel I'm providing my customers with something worthwhile at the same time that I'm indulging my love for books. Don't misunderstand: If I didn't have to earn money I'd be at home reading. But I do have certain financial obligations, so I meet them in the way that pleases me best.

Katharine, medical school student: My next step could be to train as a specialist, then go into private practice where I could make huge amounts of money. But the part of medicine that attracts me is research, which doesn't pay awfully well but has its own rewards. What I intend to do is go into research, and make sure that I marry a man who is headed for the big time. In plain language, I intend to have it both ways.

As Katharine points out, doing what you truly want to do may mean earning less money than you would like to have, but it may be worth it to you for the personal rewards.

How can I augment my low income?

Moonlight. Practically everyone does it at one time or another, if they work for a company that permits moonlighting. They type, do research, bookkeeping, tutor, sell real estate, give music lessons, sell on commission. Moonlighting has another advantage besides added revenue. If you do enough of it, you may be able to deduct a portion of your personal overhead at tax time. It's a good thing to check out with your accountant or an Internal Revenue Service agent.

Moonlighting is easier to swing and makes good sense when you are at the building stage of your career, especially if you are young and single, with the strength and time for a double load. About five years of that is enough for most of us. By then you should have perfected your skills so you can charge enough for what you do and devote all of your time to a single career.

Can moonlighting help to advance your career?

It can. For Karen, a twenty-eight-year-old art director, moonlighting meant a giant leap forward. This is how she describes what happened:

I have always been a timid, quiet person. Unassertive, I guess you'd say. I just hate making waves, even when people tell me I should. I was brought up that if you are gentle and courteous, people will be gentle and courteous back. It's hard to shake that training, and be any less of a lady than my mother taught me to be.

You can understand why I chose a nice, safe, quiet woman's magazine to work at, and why I buried myself there. It was such an easy, proper, well-bred, convent way of life. We were all women, we were all low paid, and we were all doing exactly what was expected of us. For the first five years it never occurred to me to do anything else. But as I learned more about my craft, I could see that there were other, more interesting places where I could be an art director. I knew that if I were in television I could experiment and open up my creativity. But television is so cutthroat; it scared me. I think the more money there is in a field, the more competitive it is. The way I got over my fear was to move into television gradually, by moonlighting. I began to talk to people in the professional club I belong to and got friendly enough with a couple of the ad agency people to ask if I could watch them work on their commercials. One of them accepted my offer to help at no charge, and it was wonderful training. Not just in technique, but in learning to be comfortable with a different breed of professional. Eventually I got to the point where I could moonlight some TV assignments of my own, and that gave me my real start. A year ago I moved from the magazine into the full-time job I have now at a TV production house, and I feel like a caterpillar released from its cocoon. I am spreading my wings, daring to fly. And do you know what's the greatest release of all? I've found out that its OK that I'm not just like my mother.

How can I tell what I should be making in an entry-level job?

Do some research. Find out what the going salaries are in your position. Read newspaper ads. Ask somebody at a job placement agency. Make discreet inquiries among your friends. Really dig in and find out before you accept the first salary offer you hear. People can take advantage of you if you are naïve or uninformed, and you will have only yourself to blame.

How do I know if I'm being paid fairly?

First, be honest with yourself. Do you deserve more than you're getting? Do you do your work better than others who get paid the same as you? Can you prove that this is so—by the number of sales you make, the volume of material you produce, the profit you add to the company?

Second, be sure you know what fair pay is before you holler "foul." One way to tell is to check out what's par for the course. Look at the newspaper ads that describe your kind of job: What are the salaries mentioned? Talk to colleagues in companies similar to your own. Ask somebody who's recently left your company and doesn't mind telling what he/she or others have earned.

There is one person you should not ask: the head of your company. He or she will not reveal payroll details and will probably resent the fact that you are probing.

What are fringe benefits?

Rewards and incentives outside of salary. At the executive level, where you may be heading, fringe benefits may include all or some of the following:

Expense account	Club memberships
Health insurance	Union dues
Dental insurance	Subscriptions
Bonus plan	Legal insurance

Profit sharing

Pension or retirement plan

Life insurance

Tuition refunds

Company limousine

Automobile insurance

Company car

Use of company plane

Use of company apartment

Stock options

These represent nontaxable forms of income for an employee, and tax-deductible expenditures for employers. In executive echelons, fringe benefits are rarely given out automatically as a complete package, but are used as bargaining tools: items to be negotiated when salary is discussed.

Can benefits be bad for you?

Yes. They can make you believe you are locked into the company because they take such good care of you financially. They can make you cling to a job just because there is a pension in your future. They can make you afraid to take a chance and move someplace where the fringes are fewer and career opportunities greater.

What should I ask about my fringe benefits?

Everything you can think of. You need to know exactly what it is you are getting.

Find out if major medical coverage is part of your health insurance, what you are covered for, and how much the plan will cost you.

Ask how much you can collect on your pension fund if you leave the company before retirement age, and if there are strings attached.

Ask what your bonuses are based on: dollars, performance, seniority, or what. Pin down the specifics. You'd be amazed at the variations among bonus plans.

What are bonuses based on?

Different things in different companies. Here are the answers five employers gave to that question:

Company A: I give my support staff bonuses on the basis of performance evaluation. Each person is reviewed every six months. What we look for is the ability to work well with other people, and willingness to put in extra time and take on extra loads. We reward people who

83

are conscientious. When you come down to it, performance evaluations are really a matter of subjective judgment; the evaluations depend on who is making them. It's not the best method, but it's the best we've been able to come up with.

Company B: I usually give my people 15 to 25 percent bonuses at Christmastime. By March, everyone's forgotten the handout and is grumbling again.

Company C: We don't give bonuses in the traditional sense. We give shares of stock. It's my feeling that this is a stronger incentive because it makes people work harder so their stock will be worth more. Stock sharing also gives them a feeling of loyalty: "This is *my* company. I own a piece of the rock."

Company D: Every time an employee drops a hint into the suggestion box, he or she gets a bonus. Every time they turn in a good job, even if it's nothing more sensational than what they're being paid to do in the first place, they get a bonus. In addition to cash gifts, we send them to school. We pay for child care. We are Big Mother, rewarding and motivating from cradle to grave. We see to it that our people's lives are vested in this company. If they are any good at all, we want to cement them to us forever.

Company E: Our bonuses are based on a profit-sharing formula. At the end of the year we distribute a share of the profits we've made to each of our executive and administrative people. How much is based on their salaries. We feel it's an excellent form of incentive to help make the company's end-of-year profits greater.

What is a profit-sharing retirement fund?

Money saved or invested for you each year by the company out of its annual profits. In some cases this is augmented by voluntary contributions from your salary. The money is returned to you when you retire at sixty-two or your retirement age, or else when you leave the company, depending on how the company has structured its plan. The advantage to you, if you must wait until retirement age, is that then you will probably be taxed at a lower rate on the income than if you received it during your earning years. In effect, a retirement fund is forced savings for you; funded by the company as an employee incentive.

Profit-sharing retirement funds are strictly governed by federal regulations. Companies are permitted to earmark up to 15 percent of their annual profits for profit sharing by their employees. And employees become vested—that is, entitled to participate in the plan —after eighteen months or more on the job.

What are stock options?

The right to buy stock in your company any time during a specified number of years at the market value it had when you joined the company. Stock options are offered to high-salaried executives as an inducement to join a firm, and as an incentive to improve the company's financial picture so their stock will be worth more.

The reason stock options come under the heading of fringe benefits is that the profits on stock are known as capital gains and are subject to a lower tax rate than salary.

How often should I expect salary reviews?

If you are in management at a large company, you can expect a review once a year; more often if you are in a lower-paying position. Small companies usually schedule salary reviews informally or not at all, leaving it up to you to initiate the subject.

How will they review my salary?

Probably under one of two systems if you are in a large corporation (a company that has 250 or more employees). These systems determine your salary based on evaluation of your job performance.

1. *Grading.* Under this system you are given a grade number according to the responsibilities you are assigned. Grade scales vary from company to company, and from company to government agencies. In one company, for example, a market research manager who is responsible for supervising five staff members, handling three million dollars' worth of merchandise, and producing twenty studies a year, may have a grade number of 24. In this hierarchy, a 24-grade manager earns $30,000 a year. When his or her responsibilities are increased by another two staff members or an additional million dollars' worth of business, the grade goes up to 25, with a commensurate salary increase.

Your grade also indicates how many weeks' vacation you are

entitled to, what kind of office you get, the size of your expense account and seminar budget, and in some cases, whether you receive a bonus for performing at the top of your grade level.

2. *Management by Objective*. This system evaluates your performance and salary level on the basis of your own work objectives. It calls for a quarterly conference with your manager in which you set down the fifteen or twenty specific goals you plan to reach within the coming three months. Depending on your area of responsibility, these may be:

    a. Increase sales by a certain volume or dollar amount
    b. Hire a certain number of minority personnel
    c. Design and implement an improved filing system
    d. Install new telephone communications.

At the end of each quarter, you and your manager review the status of each of your objectives, checking off the ones that you have accomplished. Together, you examine the objectives you have not reached, to discover what the problem was and to find ways you could reach your goal during the next quarter. The results of your performance evaluations are filed in your personnel record.

What can I do about the fact that I'm never offered a raise?

Ask for one. Even if you're one of the generation of women who were brought up to believe (a) it's not nice to talk about money and (b) your virtue will automatically be rewarded, you have to realize that's not the way it is in business. The fact is, your boss is more interested in his or her profit picture than in yours. It may be true that more pay will encourage you to work harder, but you can't expect him or her to focus on that. You have to point it out. You have to ask for what you want, and bear in mind that the worst answer you'll get is No or Maybe. At that, your request counts for something: It will lay the groundwork for the next time you ask.

Why do I cry whenever I have to ask for a raise?

Most likely you cry, shake, and lose control of your voice anytime you ask for something for yourself. It's a reflex that comes from being trained to believe that it's not nice for women to ask.

Think it through realistically. Who said it's not nice to ask? Your parents or fifth-grade teacher? Probably. The person you're asking? Probably not. That person is entitled to know what you need, and the only way he or she can know is if you tell him or her. The alternative is to leave that person in the dark while you slouch around and grumble, feeling neglected because he or she didn't think of handing you a raise.

It is not begging to ask for something you deserve. It is recognizing your own worth and stating it to the person who benefits from what you do. You are not panhandling. You are trading hard work for reward.

When is the best time to ask for a raise?

Right after you've done something terrific: saved the company money, come up with a profit-making idea, brought in new business. Ask when your boss has time to listen to you and is in a good mood. Do not ask when he or she is tense, moody, hung over, or choking on business reverses.

Evaluate your boss. This may be a person who likes thinking time. If so, it's wise to send in a memo first, rather than hit him or her over the head with a sudden request. Or just say that you'd like an appointment to discuss your salary. Most people don't like surprises.

Do not ask when your boss is in trouble, business is rotten, or you have just made an obvious mistake. Wait until the trouble has blown over and the atmosphere is favorable to you.

What should I say?

The way to ask for a raise is to sell the person you are asking on why you should have one. Present your request as a benefit to your employer. Spell out in specifics what your accomplishments have been, your productivity, your value to the company. Think of yourself as a package and present your case with a price tag attached. Whether the person you talk to has the final say-so or has to go to a higher authority to get the OK, you need to feed in all the ammunition you can muster.

Lillian is a good example of how to ask for a raise:

It was ironic, working in an industrial relations firm and not being given incentive raises as a matter of course. Nonetheless that's how it was. So I made a date to discuss a salary increase with my boss, Dorothy, and went in armed to the teeth:

LILLIAN: Dorothy, I have worked as your assistant for eight months, and I think that we've been a very good team. I'd like to talk to you about my salary.

Broaches the subject of money directly, openly, without apology or fluster.

DOROTHY: Certainly Lillian. What's on your mind?

LILLIAN: It's time for me to have a raise. I've proved my capabilities to you, and have gone beyond the line of duty. The new system I created has meant money in the company's pocket. I think that is worth a 15 percent raise.

Establishes her worth in terms of profits as well as basic ability.

DOROTHY: I agree with you, Lillian, that you are good at what you do and your contributions are worth money to us. You should have a raise, but why 15 percent? You know that would be a burden on my budget.

LILLIAN: It's a fair figure. Actually, I'm worth three thousand dollars more on the market. But I like working with you and I'd stay on for a 15 percent increase.

Presents factual, re-searched figures. Implies without threatening that she would go elsewhere for more money.

DOROTHY: It probably is a fair figure. But you have to think of my side of things.

LILLIAN: I have. First, the system I put in brought forty-two thousand dollars in added revenue to the company. I'm asking for a small share of that. Second, you would probably have to pay three thousand dollars more than I'm asking to re-

Drives home her bargain with solid information. Omits the fact that she has a sick mother to take care of, and sticks to facts and figures.

place me—if you could find somebody who's already trained in how this department works. Third, a 15 percent raise takes into account the cost-of-living rise that's projected for the next six months, which means you won't be hit with emergency requests.

DOROTHY: Lillian. I really want you to stay, and I think what you've told me is absolutely accurate. I'll put through a request and the increase should be in your next paycheck. Be sure to let me know if it isn't, so I can walk it through bookkeeping for you.

LILLIAN: Thank you, Dorothy. I appreciate that.

Says "Thank you" and gets offstage without rehashing, overselling, or claiming "I told you so."

How many times should I ask for the same raise?

That depends upon the financial condition of your company and the economics of your industry. If you are being turned down because of difficult economic conditions, it is possible that you would have the same problems with any similar company. If times are good and your company is in sound financial shape, you should ask two or three times. If they keep turning you down for a raise that you are certain you deserve, you probably will never get any further than you are right now. You are in a dead-end job and should start looking elsewhere.

How else do you know if there's no future in your job?

When you see signs that the company is going downhill. Watch for these symptoms:

Tightened budgets
Slow deliveries
Noncompetitive pricing

Employee layoffs
Plummeting morale
Shady deals

When a company is in trouble for an extended length of time, their money problem will become yours. But remember to be realistic. It may be an industry swing and not just your company.

What if they promise a raise and don't come through?

Their promise may not have been sincere. Some people play on women's inclination to be compassionate and understanding. Tina, who is young and rather naïve, says she can't quite figure out what's behind the response to her requests for a raise:

> I had been doing some selling in addition to my secretarial work, and after seven months I was still getting my secretarial salary. The boss hadn't said one word about the raise he'd promised me. I finally got up the nerve to ask him about it again, and he said, "You've been doing good work, Tina. I'm sorry you didn't get the raise." I spoke right up: "I'm glad you really think I deserve the raise, but I can't believe you'd forget about me." He said that's just what happened; he'd try to put it through for me right away, and I should have it in a couple of months. I can understand how he'd forget, with so much else on his mind. We'll see what happens in a couple of months.

It is entirely possible that Tina's boss did forget and was glad when she reminded him. It is also possible that it was no oversight at all; her boss was just getting away with whatever he could get away with. As long as Tina continues to "understand," she will be giving him permission to take advantage of her.

Is it wrong to be compassionate?

No. The capacity for understanding is fine. It's a characteristic that makes us good listeners, gives us human insights, helps us read between the lines. But you have to learn to edit what people tell you, and not let compassion be a substitute for making things happen. Tina is the kind of woman who will "understand" when she asks for a raise again and the boss tells her, "Times are tough, business is slumping, my overhead is rocketing. I just can't afford to give you a raise right now."

A woman like this will stay on the short end of the stick until she takes it upon herself to make sure that other people understand her needs, and not let her compassion get in her way. You have to learn to understand the difference between a legitimate reason and phony excuses. It is selling yourself cheaply to bend over backward to accommodate cranky customers, accept suppliers' excuses, lie down like a doormat because you "understand" their problems. You have to respect your own needs and priorities; until you assert them, people will walk all over you.

Is it fair to accept a raise when you know you're going to quit?

Yes. It's fair to your employer if you've been giving the company its money's worth. It's fair to the people you'll work for next because it gives them a way to measure your ability and fit you into their organization accordingly. Certainly it is fair to yourself to be paid for what you have done. And you have to consider your future: The raise you get before you quit will show up on your résumé when you apply for your next job. Don't be short-sighted, like the woman who said:

> I'm depressed because I'm getting the same salary I've been getting for a year and a half. But I don't press for a raise because I know that I'm moving to Colorado in three months and I'll be getting a new job anyway. So what's the difference?

The difference is, if you get a raise and a better title before you move, you'll be in a position to command more in your new job:

Present Job		New Job
$16,000	=	$16,000 base
With 15% raise: $18,400	=	$18,400 base

Why do companies offer expense accounts instead of raises?

Expense accounts enable you to do your job efficiently, entertaining and traveling to get new business or to keep current business. An expense account is not taxable; it is regarded as reimbursement for money you put out for the travel, meals, and entertainment that are necessary to your job. If you had to pay for these things out of a raise instead of an expense account, you'd be spending your own pre-taxed income.

Expense accounts can be an advantage for employers, too. They are tax-deductible. The company does not have to kick in matching funds to the Social Security system or pay unemployment and pay-roll taxes.

This does not mean you should try to collect as much of your pay as you can in expense account form. Or, if you are the boss, that you should pay your staff in expenses rather than salaries. There are legal limits to how much non-taxable money the federal government will let you play with.

How do expense accounts work?

Sometimes you are given a sum of money in advance, and sometimes you spend your own money and the company reimburses you afterward. In either case, it is important that you keep clear, thorough records. You will have to itemize and justify your expenses to the people who are paying for them, so you need to present the following:

Receipts
Dates
Activity
Purpose
Names of people you took to lunch, telephoned, or spent other money on

You will need duplicate records for your federal income tax return, in cases where you are not reimbursed for expenses. (Reimbursements are not taxable because they are not earned income.)

What expenses are deductible from my federal income tax?

Expenses that you can prove are directly related to your or your company's business. For proof of travel or business meetings, for example, you need itemized bills, receipts for amounts twenty-five dollars and over, and diary entries that show the following:

Time, place, and length of meeting
Business purpose
Business relationship with the other person

Use this checklist and consult with your accountant or Internal Revenue Service office, to learn what other business expenses you can deduct.

TAX-DEDUCTIBLE BUSINESS EXPENSES

Accounting, including the cost of preparing your tax return
Advertising and publicity
Books, periodicals, supplies
Charitable donations for business purposes
Club and association dues
Commissions paid for business purposes
Entertainment: restaurants, clubs, theaters, trips, sports events, home
    parties
Gifts to customers, prospects, employees, colleagues
Insurance related to business
Interest on business loans
License fees
Meals and lodging connected with work for a part-time employer
Postage
Rent for business space
Taxes: sales, city, state (You cannot deduct federal taxes)
Telephone
Transportation connected with your job other than regular commuting
    to and from work
Travel, transportation, meals, lodging, tips, telephones, laundry and
    cleaning, entertainment for business purposes
Uniforms

Should I accept money from suppliers?

No. There is plenty of precedent for kickbacks in business, which is what money from a supplier is, but you will get further in the long run if you make it a rule to deal ethically and ignore under-the-table income.

A kickback, also known as padding the bill, is when you arrange to bill somebody for more than the supplier's actual charge and then split the overshare with the supplier.

A kickback arrangement has these disadvantages. It puts you in a position of having a vested interest in that particular supplier and limits your ability to shop around. It allows the supplier to stint on what they will do for you. Knowing they'll get the job anyway, they don't need to kill themselves working up imaginative proposals, to meet deadlines, or to turn in superior work. Finally, it can earn you an unfavorable reputation that will follow you around for years.

Will my husband be upset if I earn more than he does?

Possibly. Statistics say that three out of five couples wind up in divorce when the wife earns more than the husband. This may not be 100 percent cause-and-effect, but it does take a secure ego for a man to be able to accept the fact that you are the dominant breadwinner. It also takes a woman of independent strength to refrain from lording it over somebody because she makes a lot of money. Sandy, the director of development for a New England college, says that she sees herself and her husband as two individuals who pool their financial resources, and it doesn't matter to her whose resources are larger. Her husband agrees in theory, but when she began to earn more than he, theory went out the window:

> When I got this big job, he told everyone how proud he was of me. He used to brag to our friends to the point where I was embarrassed. At home alone, though, he wasn't that chatty. He was more tense. Tight-lipped. He didn't want to discuss my job at all. And he wouldn't even sit down with me to figure out how we'd handle our new financial situation. He kept ducking, finding other things to do. Finally I just pulled out our financial records one night and nailed him down. I said, "Darling, this situation is completely new to us and we have to decide now how to handle it so we won't have arguments about who pays for what. There are a lot of details to think about. Don't you agree that if we map them out now, that will help keep us from being steamrollered as events come up?" He was reluctant but I persisted: "We could take care of our living expenses by pooling our two salaries

in a joint kitty. Or you can keep your earnings and I'll keep mine. I'll pay for my own clothing, our vacations, and the household help. And you can pay for your clothes and car, the mortgage on the house, and major repairs. Does that sound fair?" He said that sounded fine. He'd leave everything up to me. Whatever I wanted to do was OK. It wasn't necessary to talk about it anymore.

There was a lot more detail to talk about; all I'd mentioned were the broad strokes. But it was obvious that he couldn't face the hard fact that I earned more than he. It was easier for him to gloss over our money situation than to dissect it. To him, that would be admitting that his male role was being usurped.

It's worked OK, so far. But just in case, I've checked with my attorney and our accountant and got their advice on whether to have individual or joint ownership of our property, bank accounts, insurance, and so on. People change, especially in a marriage. I think it's a good idea to be prepared for anything.

Amen. And remember that split-ups between unmarried people who live together are just as traumatic as marital divorces, and money is as certain to be an issue of contention. You can save a lot of grief if you set up the ground rules in advance, and perhaps even put them in writing.

Who pays for decorating my office?

The company supplies basic decor: paint, furniture, equipment, and sometimes wall and window hangings. The extras are up to you. Or your company may share in the cost of special decorating, and probably inherit the curtains and blinds when you leave.

In some places, there is no question about who pays for special decor because the personal touch is out altogether. There must be a uniform, corporate look for all offices. For juniors, it's one side chair and a print on the wall. Seniors move up to two couches, a credenza, and an oil painting.

When you invest in office decor, keep in mind that your work place is your home. It's where you will spend most of your waking hours. And it is the context in which other people will see you. How much you spend is secondary to how your office looks and functions. Here are some tips that will help you create an environment that is both attractive and professional:

- Living and dining room furniture is more distinctive and often more comfortable than standard office furniture. Think about how you work. You may not need a desk at all; just a round table for work space and conferences.
- Buy good quality organizers: letter trays, pencil containers, and so on. Cheap, junky accessories make you look cheap and junky. Besides, they are no economy: They become battered and fall apart quickly.
- Invest in the personal touches such as fresh flowers, a dish of mints, a bowl of fruit, or a beautiful crystal ashtray that stamp a room *yours*. They express both your hospitality and the fact that you are in charge.
- Hang good graphics and invest in decent frames. Tacked-up posters can make a room look like a teen-ager's. If you must bring snapshots of your family to work, keep the photo collection secondary.
- Rule out gags, gimmicks, and tacky souvenirs. I can remember being escorted into the office of a bank president who wanted me to do him a favor. He was supposed to be somebody important. I looked around and on the credenza, next to a plastic philodendron, was a statuette of The Finger. Immediately, I knew everything I needed to know about this man.
- Buy real plants, well groomed, and keep them in good health. If you can't keep real plants, don't keep any.
- Install lighting that is comfortable for your eyes.

How can I afford to dress like an executive on a secretary's salary?

You can't afford not to.

It is possible to dress rich on a limited budget if you know how. The first thing to do is forget quantity and go for quality instead. Three terrific outfits will take you everywhere for years; six junky things will never be right anyplace. What you need is wardrobe power: dresses, skirts, jackets, and coats that give you mileage as well as distinction.

Before you buy anything, check magazine and newspaper ads for expensive designer styles that would look well on you. News photos and personal observations around town will give you an idea of what the well-dressed professionals are wearing. A run through the better stores to check their displays will clue you to what is available. Then go shopping.

Shop discount stores and the sales racks in high-priced stores for designer labels. Buy basics and buy the best. Then you can go haywire and pick up frivolous, lower-priced accessories to give you variety and add fun, up-to-dateness, and individuality to your look. Fresh accessories brighten morale as well as your wardrobe; you would be bored out of your mind if you wore the same uniform season upon season. So would everyone else.

One way to get more mileage out of your basics is to buy with coordination in mind. Start with two colors that please you: wine and camel, or black and tan, for example. Then build an extended wardrobe by adding accessories in complementary tones: blouses, shoes, scarves, and sweaters in shades that go with both of your basic colors.

What is the executive look?

There's no single "executive" look that is good for everyone. One season's ads may insist, "A suit, pumps, and briefcase are the stamp of authority," but that's nonsense—true only when a suit, pumps, and briefcase are right for you. What looks well on one figure is awful on another. What's appropriate in one climate can be ludicrous elsewhere. You really don't have to worry about what to wear if you dress each morning as if you were going to meet the chairman of the board, or be interviewed for a very important position.

Will other women be jealous if I look stupendous?

The jealous other woman is apt to be somebody who doesn't work, possibly the wife or girl friend of somebody you work with. This woman is out of the day-to-day scene and, secretly or not, resents the fact that you spend more time with her man than she does. Furthermore, she is rightfully jealous of you because you have a career and she has been left out of the swim. You are the enemy, and if you look stupendous besides, that is the last straw.

Remember this as you dress for the party that includes her. Remind yourself that if you ruffle this woman's feathers, she can eventually find a way to shake up your life. She probably has enough problems of her own; do not add fuel to her fire. Dress nicely, professionally, smartly. But be discreet. Package yourself conservatively.

Look as if you are devoted to your job, not her husband or lover. Never try to outdo her in the looks department; you are sure to lose out in the end.

What should I do if I have a boss who is overly dependent on me?

You can do one of two things:

1. Go along with the system for the time being. Spend a year or two where you are, so you won't have a job-hopper's résumé, and learn everything from the job that you can. Then get out.

Set time goals for yourself: "I will learn four things from this job this month—the company's politics, who this boss really reports to, what the memos and letters I type are saying and why, and the history of this department within the corporate structure. Do not spend your time griping. Use it to learn, and advance.

2. Try to make the dependent boss your ally. Keep reassuring him or her that you are there to be completely supportive. Let this clinger know, unmistakably, that you are not going to upset any applecarts. Come right out with and say, "I really want to help you as much as I can. What additional things can I do for you?" This person needs all the reassurance you can give.

Is dependency a plot to keep us down?

No, it's just human nature. Some men don't even realize the effect their actions have on a woman's career. All they're trying to do is be protective. Take Scott, an appliance manufacturer. He's really a good man: innovative, outstanding in his field, not a middle manager type at all. He has a secretary he truly admires and wants to help. Yet he does everything in this power to keep her exactly where she is. Here's his side of the story:

> Joanne is the best secretary I've ever had. Just wonderful. She understands my priorities. Makes sure what should be done gets done without any fuss. I know that I can count on her to anticipate my needs and follow through beautifully. She's come to me a couple of times in the past year and said that she wanted to move on. I told her she didn't realize what would happen to her if she did. "Joanne," I said. "You'll never have it as good as you do here. You have my protection, don't you see? You can do anything you want to in the company; all

you have to do is use my name. I'm the senior vice-president; my title is your shelter. You just wouldn't make it on your own, no matter what they tell you in those books and articles about getting ahead. It's rough out there. So what if you get yourself a different title? It won't help you when the sharks start to snap." Both times I've given her a bonus, in addition to a raise. I couldn't stand to lose Joanne. Why, do you know how hard it would be to find somebody else as good as she is? And how long it would take to train a replacement? I don't even want to think about it!

How can I get a promotion when there isn't any job to move into?

Create one. Look for a need and then take steps to fill it. Florence, a designer for a very prestigious sportswear manufacturer, says if she hadn't taken the bull by the horns and invented a niche for herself, she might still be a designer's assistant instead of the head of her own accessories division:

I knew that the owners were planning to broaden their market by going into middle- as well as high-priced lines. That would mean expanding the company. It certainly wasn't my function as a design assistant to tell them how to do it, but I could take advantage of the opportunity. So, with the help of some experienced friends, I drew up a proposed organization chart. It showed how the new departments for design, purchasing, production, sales, and administration would relate to each other in terms of work flow. A second chart showed who would report to whom, and a third diagram illustrated how space for one line could be allocated to another during peak production seasons. On a separate sheet I itemized the new positions that would have to be created, to execute my expansion plan, and I appended a detailed description of the position I was suggesting for myself: the title, functions, salary, and the dollar-and-cents value my performance would bring to the reorganized corporation. I clipped a second sheet to that one, a résumé of a sort, listing my special skills, contributions, and training; how they had benefited the company to date; and how they would be utilized and expanded in my proposed position.

The packet was very professional: specific, clear, organized, and clean. I hand-carried it to the president, with whom I had made an appointment to discuss "something of great potential value to the company." He was very enthusiastic about the research and work I had done, liked my ideas, and said we'd talk again in a week, after

99

he'd had a chance to go over the plan with his partner, their lawyers, and accountant. I'd like to brag a little right here. They made very few changes in my original plan. And none at all in the new department I'd suggested that I head. Including my salary and other arrangements. I had a contract in my hands in a matter of weeks.

Should you always have a contract?

No. Support people rarely do. At middle management or above, you can have a formal contract, or you can have a letter of agreement or a memo. Anything so you get the facts in writing. Memories are short and details can get muddled, especially when money is involved. You may hear something one way and the person you're dealing with may hear it another. Or choose to remember it differently. I'm sure you have had that experience, getting estimates and then final bills from painters, dressmakers, the dentist. It's best to get possible disagreements out of the way before they become costly arguments.

Sometimes it's awkward to put things in writing. If you are in a small company, you may just have to trust that people will come through with whatever they've promised to give you. If they don't, you can always go to the bookkeeper and say, "I was expecting a raise. Maybe Mr./Ms. Jones forgot to tell you that there's to be a change in my paycheck. You're so good at figures; would you go in and get it straightened out for me?"

Is it fair for the person I trained to get the promotion instead of me?

I've no doubt you trained the person you're talking about very well in office procedures, but did you really teach them everything? Office procedure is important, but people who are promoted into management have a number of other qualifications as well. Check off the ones you trained your colleague in:

Planning	Motivational strategies
Problem-solving	Communications techniques
Decision-making	Interpersonal relationships
Organizing	Self-confidence
Delegating	Style
Controlling	Group leadership

The person you taught office procedure to probably learned these twelve skills elsewhere. You weren't in competition for the promotion at all, unless you had most of those qualities too.

How can I get more money if I'm already at the top of the pay scale?

- You can take on more responsibilities and move into a higher scale.
- You can expand your skills and get into another, higher-paying kind of work.
- You can go to a company that pays better.

You have to realize that a boost in pay and title can work against you financially. Suppose you move from clerk to supervisor of five or more people. You will become exempt from the hourly wage law and lose your right to time and a half for overtime. Also, you could be pushed into a tax bracket that chews up your added earnings before you see them, especially if you are married and file a joint tax return. You have to sit down with a sharp pencil and work out the arithmetic before you take that step up, and decide whether the move is worthwhile.

Will the new position be impressive on your résumé?
Will it add to your skills so you can make another leap up after a year or two?
Is there a chance for further advancement or is it a dead-end slot?

Sometimes it's better to move sideways, in terms of pay, to improve your long-range career prospects. Chris did this. As a matter of fact, after evaluating her position, she decided to take a drop in pay so she could acquire some marketable skills and be worth more on the job market later.

Chris is an extremely bright twenty-four-year-old who is blessed with the ability to learn quickly. She is ambitious, and she is realistic about her worth. She says that she never was worth the high salary she was pulling down, but left the job for other reasons:

I have a wonderful older friend, Alice, a real mover and shaker who I've known since I was in college. I used to do her filing for her then, as a part-time job. Two years ago Alice took a fifty-five-thousand-dollar-a-year job in San Francisco as head of the corporate communications department of a large research and development firm. The place was so big and so bureaucratically organized, and Alice was so strong in her position, she could do anything she wanted to and nobody ever questioned her. The first thing she did was get me a job as her assistant, at the outrageous salary of nineteen thousand dollars. I was thrilled. My first full-time job and I was earning as much as my father. I had fun, too, learning about office politics, chains of command, how to get things done. In six months I had the communications department organized and Alice got me promoted to office manager, with a two-thousand-dollar-a-year raise. Fantastic! In another six months, Alice put through another raise for me and I was was making $23,000. Even so, the job was getting dull. There's just so much challenge to learning office management and once you've licked that, the job becomes a daily routine. But how could I grouse? And where else could I earn that kind of money with so little experience or skill?

Then Alice got an offer from another company. They wanted to give her sixty-seven thousand five hundred dollars plus the costs of transferring to New York. Naturally, she grabbed it. This time she couldn't take me with her, so there I was—earning twenty-three thousand dollars, learning nothing, going nowhere, and bored out of my mind. But I'm lucky. I'm young and have no responsibility except for myself, so I can do whatever I choose. I chose to collect my paychecks for another six months, quit, and use my savings to go back to school. I am now earning no money at all. Instead, I am earning my master's in business administration and studying Russian on the side. When I go back into the job market next year, it will probably be for less than twenty-three thousand dollars. But I'll be equipped to rise as high as I want to in whatever I do.

When should I be paid for working overtime?

When you are classified as nonexempt personnel. This term refers to the federal wage and hour law that defines people as either exempt or nonexempt from such things as the minimum wage scale and overtime pay. To be nonexempt—that is, governed by laws about overtime pay—you have to earn $150 or less a week as an executive or administrator, and $170 or less as a professional. You also must fulfill certain duty requirements. You cannot be in a position where you supervise two or more people, make decisions, or do managerial work.

If you pass these salary and duty tests, you are entitled to time-and-a-half pay in weeks when you work more than forty hours.

Most likely if you are a secretary or perform other kinds of administrative, executive, or professional duties, you are exempt from these regulations. At that level your salary is supposed to compensate you sufficiently for whatever number of hours you work.

What if I'm entitled to time and a-half and don't get it?

First, check with the person you work for or the bookkeeping department to make sure that it wasn't just an oversight or clerical error. If you find that withholding your overtime pay was deliberate, tell them that you are aware of government regulations and that although you don't want to make trouble, you must get the pay you are entitled to. If they still refuse to pay you after that, contact the nearest Labor Department office in your state. Look in the phone book for the Wage and Hour Division and go there in person with your facts, figures, and time sheet records. If it is inconvenient to go there in person, you can write or telephone, and tell them your story.

Do you get paid for a leave of absence?

No. A leave of absence is an unpaid sabbatical. Time off to do something else, with the understanding that you can return to your job after a specified period of time. It's a privilege extended to key employees, a way of saying "We value you."

The most common reasons people take a leave of absence are:

- To go back to school and work toward a degree
- To travel
- To take care of a sick relative
- To stay home while the children are small.

Is exhaustion a reason to take a leave of absence?

Yes. Energy is crucial to success. It goes hand in hand with optimism and stamina, the fizz that keeps you eager to move forward. When you work at a whirlwind pace for a long time, you can get to the point where you are burned out. That's when it's a good idea to ask for a leave of absence: time out to let go, relax your mind, change your everyday schedule from frenzied to calm.

You also need to know how to cope with your return from a leave of absence. You may find that you can't get back into the swing. Your motor has slowed down. You've lost the rhythmic connection between work demands and your responses. Don't be alarmed if it takes a few weeks to catch up with job lag: If you're like most people, you can count on having an inner mechanism that automatically adjusts to work needs.

What about sick leave?

Company policy usually provides for ten days of sick leave per year. If you're in a union, the rules may differ. Or you may be paid for longer than ten days if you are covered by your company's key-person insurance policy. The number of paid sick days you are permitted is one of the details you should ask about when you are hired. You should also find out how many paid "personal days" you are permitted. The usual acceptable reasons for taking personal days off are to take care of obligations such as helping someone who is ill, attending a funeral, or moving.

Should I be paid extra for doing somebody else's work?

No. You are part of a team. Your responsibility is to help get the job done, whatever it takes. If that means you have to pitch in and carry somebody else's load, do it cheerfully and in the spirit of co-operation. Your extra efforts will be appreciated by the person you work for, especially if you make sure that they know you deserve extra credit. This is a delicate line to walk. You have to let them know that you have *willingly* assumed responsibilities besides your own. If you try to get credit for work that you obviously begrudge doing, you will sound like a complainer instead of an asset. Listen to the difference in these voices. Which of these women would you rather have working for you?

Gail, age twenty-eight. "I do my job and they should do theirs." The woman I work with is a tall, incredibly stunning model type. I do a lot of her work for her because we wouldn't make our department statistics if I didn't. You'd better believe I don't keep it a secret. Even so, she manages to get credit for herself. I suppose it's because she's always in the middle of things while I'm in the corner, slaving. I really hate this woman and I fight with her all the time. One of these days I'm going to tell my boss that either she goes or I do.

Sally, age twenty-nine. "You always get paid in one form or another." I started out as a secretary at a small PR firm. When I saw that nobody else would take on work in the financial area because they were afraid of figures, I stepped in and did it for them. I didn't get paid extra, but that didn't bother me. To me it was getting an education for free and making new contacts besides. Next I went to another company as an account assistant, so I could leave secretarial work behind me. But the man I reported to was one of those disorganized people who couldn't keep track of anything. So I wound up doing a lot of secretarial-type work anyway. Boy, did I work! My job, his job, and a few other jobs in between. But I learned to do everything myself, from typing captions to ordering the food and drink for press parties. It didn't do anything for my bank account, and I was absolutely exhausted, but it made me a valuable commodity. I am now the director of communications for a large appliance manufacturer, so I'd say that volunteering to do other people's work paid off, ultimately.

Ann, age forty. "You can make the extra work less difficult." My boss is a super guy and I often work weekends to help him out. I figure weekend work makes me look good; it's an investment in my future. But I balked when he asked me to chaperone a teen-age band for three weekends in a row, in three outlandish little towns. I thought, "Ann, you've got to find a way to trim this thing down." So I said to my boss, "Jim, I've been very fair about giving you my weekends, but this assignment is too much. Why, I wouldn't even have time to write up the reports on them. I have an idea. Let's divide the duties between us. I'll take the farthest trip to the worst of the tank towns, and you can cover the other two, easier weekends." He agreed that was fair, and I felt pleased that I'd stuck up for my rights. It's worked to my advantage. He hasn't asked anything outrageous of me since.

Leslie, age twenty-five. "If you do something that is not required of you, you can get to own the project." You're going to think I'm crazy, but I not only do work I'm not paid to do, I volunteer for work that's so grundgy other people just want to get rid of it. Like setting up the logistics of a sales meeting. Or rounding up speakers and prizes. I've been volunteering every since I found out what terrific visibility those nitty-gritty jobs can give you. Last sales meeting I really got involved, more than anyone else, and it's because of that that I've been asked to run the whole show next time. That's quite an honor for a twenty-five-year-old. And a lot of extra work, but I don't care. I'm on my way up and with this kind of exposure I'm going to get there faster.

Roberta, age thirty. "I have strict rules." If their secretaries are busy and they ask me to get coffee, I will do it—once. If we are on a rush project and they won't call in outside help, I will work nights to get the work done—but no more than two or three times in a year. If the typists are tied up on priority assignments, I'll get out my own correspondence. I will do other people's work for them at no extra pay if there's a good reason to do it, if I know they are not taking advantage of me, and if I can make sure that the right people know I am donating extra effort.

List four kinds of extra work where charges are optional.

Speculative Work.

People do not have to pay you to audition for a job. You may have to design a layout, write an ad or critique, or submit some kind of work at no charge to prove that you can provide what an employer needs. If your work is accepted and used, you may or may not be paid for it; that's an arrangement you should make clear before you do the work. If getting it accepted is what gets you the job or promotion you're looking for, consider the unpaid work an investment, not a loss.

However, you don't always have to audition. If you have an established track record, you can say that you no longer do speculative work, but will be happy to submit what they want at your regular fee. Usually at that stage, though, your samples or other evidence of success will be enough for an experienced interviewer to go on.

Proposals.

Do not expect to be paid for the time, research, brain power, supplies, and effort you expend on ordinary proposals. They are a form of competitive bidding, and your cost of acquiring new business. If you are an expert in your field, however, and somebody has asked you to present a complicated technical proposal, you have a right to ask for a fee. You can make an agreement with the people whose work you are bidding for that if the contract goes through, your fee will be deducted from the final price. If the contract does not go through, you will have been paid for your time and expertise.

Do not spend time and costs producing an elaborate proposal unless you are certain that you have a realistic chance to win the bid. Research it first. Confer with your prospective client or customer and ascertain what kind of expertise they are looking for, if your company meets their criteria, and exactly what it is they need to see in the porposal. Then you can decide whether it's worth your while to work up a proposal, or if you would just be spinning your wheels.

Speaking Engagements.

Speaker's fees range from fifty cents to two thousand five hundred dollars, but that doesn't mean everyone will offer to pay you for speaking. Many organizations try to get speakers free or for an honorarium. Women's groups are especially guilty; they are not used to paying out large sums for speakers. You can go along with them if you feel that the exposure will enhance your reputation, set you up as an authority, or lead to future business.

Free speaking engagements for legitimate nonprofit organizations are a way you can make donations to causes you believe in. But beware of the groups that call themselves nonprofit, that in reality can afford to pay speakers well. Before you accept a request, check it out. What is the organization's purpose? Who are its members (your audience)? How many people will attend the meeting? Have they paid for speakers in the past? What is their budget? Are they a prestigious platform for you?

Freebies for Friends.

We all help each other as much as we can, but there are times when you really can't afford to become embroiled in doing favors. You need to know how to get out of it gracefully. Ernestine runs into this situation all the time. She is a young and talented interior designer with a wide circle of acquaintances whom she categorizes as "dear friends, good friends, and just friends." She says it's the "just friends" who give her the most trouble. The others understand that she is in business to make a living.

> There's a woman named Norma whom I meet about once a month on social occasions. The last time we were at a dinner party together, she invited me to come to her home for lunch. She also mentioned that she'd love to have my opinions on redoing her daughter's room. I knew what would happen. She'd feed me a wonderful lobster salad and figure she'd bought me lock, stock, and tape measure. If I volunteered opinions, she'd follow up with, "Ernestine, you're in the decorator's building all the time. Would you mind picking out some samples for me?" Next it would be, "Furniture is so expensive. Could I get a few things at cost through your company?" So I thanked her for the invitation and said, "I'm sorry I can't come for lunch: I have a full week of client appointments. Anyway, giving opinions on your daughter's room sounds simple, but the fact is, it takes time to plan a room right. Much as I'd love to help you, I can't do a good job over lunch. Let's make a business appointment instead, so we can go over your daughter's needs and do justice to her room. I have next Wednesday open from five to seven, and my consulting fee is fifty dollars an hour." She was furious, but that's OK. I guarantee you if she'd made the appointment I'd have had a hard time collecting my fee, and it would have been my turn to be furious.

A lot of women don't think about money realistically. They don't like to talk about it. They're confused about the cost of professional advice and cost of products they buy off the shelf. They think their husbands should charge whatever they can get for the shoes or grommets or whatever they sell, but "friends" should give their products away. One way to get around the problem when it comes up with somebody you really want to help is to say that you want them to accept your service or product as a gift. If they find that hard to accept, tell them you've set a special price for them. Or else make a barter arrangement: "I'll do your room at cost, and you can pay for my services in dresses from your shop. That way, money won't become an issue between us." The thing you have to do is be clear about your arrangement.

How much time should I give away on career guidance?
Set practical bounds.

There comes a time, as you achieve success and your name becomes known, when it seems you are playing mentor to the world. Everybody wants you to give them advice, ideas, encouragement. It's all very flattering and gives you the feeling of superiority that goes with playing Lady Bountiful. Besides, you really do want to give others the benefit of your experience, just as people helped you on the way up.

At some point you must declare limits; otherwise you will wind up cheating yourself. People will pick your brains *ad infinitum* if you let them. They will use what you give them for their own profit and leave you with nothing but the warm glow of altruism. You have to remember that your time and ideas are worth cash, and find a way to shut off wasteful flow. A videotape producer, Mary, came up with a solution that works very well:

I set up my own business just a year ago, and as you can imagine, it's hectic. I'm understaffed, to keep the overhead down until I'm well into the black, so I have to chase around like an octopus with hives. I'm out on new business calls, on the phone getting estimates, auditioning talent, reading scripts. It'd take twenty minutes to list all the things I have to cram into each day. On top of all this, the telephone never stops ringing with people who want to find out how they can go into business for themselves, what it's like to be a woman on her own, where to buy this or that equipment. It's not my nature to turn anyone down; I feel it's my responsibility to help others when I can. But it was getting out of bounds. I finally hit on a solution that made me feel good and helped other people, too.

What I did was set up monthly help sessions. The last Friday of every month from three to five o'clock belongs to everybody who has asked for help. They are all invited to my office. If somebody says she or he has a special problem that simply must have my individual attention, I say, "Fine. We'll take five minutes out of the Friday session and just you and I will talk." It works beautifully. All these people are getting what they need. They're meeting one another and creating a network for themselves, which is what they really want. I'm not letting anybody down. And I'm giving two instead of twenty-two hours a month.

109

Another woman, Susan, the owner of a personnel firm, says she sets her limits this way: "If the person doesn't work for me and isn't a close friend, I make it a rule to charge for my time."

Should I pay somebody who steers business my way?

By all means. This kind of payment is called a finder's fee and is usually 10 percent of the contract you obtain because of their efforts.

If it is awkward, because of your relationship with the other person, to give a cash fee, find some other way to say thank you. Send a gift to his or her home or office, or take the person to lunch or dinner. At the very least, send a note of thanks.

What if I don't get the business people try to send me?

Send a gift and a thank-you note anyway, to express your appreciation for the fact that they have tried to help you. And to keep them willing to help you again.

THE NEW MANNERS

Are business manners different today?

Yes. They are in a state of flux, and nobody is sure of what they're expected to do.

It used to be that there was a set of rules for ladies and a set of rules for gentlemen: elegant little courtesies that obtained in social situations. When women crossed over from the social to the business arena, those rules became out of place. New guidelines had to be invented. Men didn't know what we expected of them, and we weren't sure what we wanted ourselves. We haven't completely caught up with each other yet—we are still establishing the ground rules.

Everything hasn't changed. Courtesy is still based on consideration for others, just as it always has been. The difference is, we are free to use good sense as our guide. Now we can be flexible and practical as well as considerate. That is probably the essential difference between yesterday's manners and today's.

I think that when problems arise it is for one of two reasons. Either the woman has misinterpreted ordinary courtesies as condescensions: "I don't need some jock to help me on with my coat or to take my elbow to get me across the street." Or the man, having heard or read that women are opposed to the traditional male courtesies, isn't sure what he's expected to do.

It may help to run down a list of accepted new practices for common old occurrences:

YESTERDAY	TODAY
Gentlemen held doors for ladies.	He opens doors for her if it's convenient; otherwise she opens the door. She holds doors for guests, male or female, and for people in higher positions. The position of power always goes first.
Ladies first.	
Men rise, ladies remain seated.	Women rise for visitors and when they are introduced. Rise again

YESTERDAY	TODAY
	when visitor leaves, and see him/ her to the door.
Men hail taxis.	The person in charge hails the taxi, or whomever it's easiest for.
Men open car doors for ladies.	She opens her own door unless it is inconvenient for her to do so.
Men pay all bills.	Whoever benefits from the transaction pays the bill.
Ladies are introduced first.	The name of the person in the higher position comes first.
Men carry women's packages.	There is no standing rule. The man usually offers, unless he is burdened with many packages himself.
Men shake hands; women do not.	Women shake hands with men and women.
Men help women on with their coats.	Men and women help each other.
Men light women's cigarettes.	Men and women light each other's cigarettes, if they choose. If there are no ashtrays in sight, ask permission—if you are sure smoking won't put you in a bad light. Otherwise, forget cigarettes altogether.

Does modern behavior mean being completely honest?

People are more open and direct than they used to be, but no truly courteous person can be completely honest. It is still important to master the diplomatic white lie that spares people's feelings. You don't turn down an invitation with, "I wouldn't lunch with a jerk like you for anything." You say, "Thank you, but I have another commitment." That's not honest, but it's kind. We do the lie of kindness every day: "I'm so pleased to meet you. . . . Do look me up when

114

you're in town again. . . . I'm sorry that we have nothing right now; do keep in touch."

Where today's honesty differs most from yesterday's mannered ritual is in the matter of coyness. It's gone and good riddance. People, women especially, used to pretend a lot. It wasn't *nice* to talk about money, discuss desires, express opinions, ask personal questions, accept an invitation without pawing the carpet to be sure Little Me was really wanted, or veer one iota from the rituals of protocol.

The new freedom to be forthright, within the bounds of courtesy, gives us a way to let people know what we want. You have to be able to communicate your needs if you want to get action in business.

Is off-color language part of the new straight talk?

No. Blue language is not only offensive, but passé; a relic of the anti-Establishment sixties when people thought four-letter expletives symbolized freedom. They didn't stop to think that it was just the sign of an uninformed mind. Unfortunately, some people have clung to the vulgarities, unaware that blue language has lost its shock value and merely detracts from ideas they want to convey.

Is there still form and symbolism in things like who answers the phone?

Yes and no. For some people having a go-between answer the phone is a symbol of power. For others, who answers the phone is a matter of convenience and practicality. These days when you dial the president of a company, you are apt as not to hear his or her voice say Hello at the other end. And when you do get a receptionist, or a receptionist and then a secretary first, they answer for the sake of convenience: to prepare the person you're calling for your query, to prevent his/her phone from ringing in the middle of a meeting, to screen out unwanted calls. Symbolism or one-upmanship is not always the point. Nowadays when you hear, "I'll have my girl call your girl" usually it's either a gag or "the girls" are conduits for information. "My conduit will call your conduit"?

Telephone intermediaries save time. I'm rushed. I need to speak to you. I ask my secretary to call yours and find out when it's convenient for me to place the call. Or, as a courtesy to you, I ask my secretary to phone you and say that I've received your proposal and will be back to you next week, when I've had a chance to review it.

Telephone buffers save nerves. I want to call somebody on the phone company's long-distance Wide Area Telephone Service (WATS) system. This entails punching twenty-two numbers. I always flub it by number eighteen. If I have to go through that again, I will lose my mind. So I ask my secretary to punch the WATS system numbers for me.

What to say when you call and a phone buffer answers

I'd like to speak to Ms. Green.
My name is Jane Jones, secretary   Your name. Your titles.
to Ms. Smith of the Brown Com-   Your affiliation.
pany.

What to say when the secretary asks why:

I'm with the White Company and   Mentioning your affiliation adds
I'm calling in reference to a job.   to your status.

Or

This is a personal call.   You are giving the information the secretary can pass along.

What to say when the secretary says he/she is in conference: ("Conference" may or may not be a code word for "He/she won't take your call.")

When would it be convenient for   Polite, considerate, practical.
me to call?

What to say when they put you off:

My number is 555-2323. When   You have left a way for the per-
may I expect Ms. Green to call   son to get back to you, and paved
back, or when will it be conven-   the way for your repeat call.
ient for me to call her again?

What to say when the phone rings in your office and nobody answers:

Hello. This is Jane Jones.	It would be absurd to let the phone go on ringing just because a secretary isn't around to answer.

What to say when a machine answers:

This is Jane Jones. It's eleven o'clock on Tuesday the twelfth. Please call me today, if possible. I'll be at 555-2323 until six.	Give your name, phone number, and a short message. Include the time when you called, as a convenience. Limit your message to twenty seconds; many machines click off after that.

What should I do when the boss asks me to pour coffee?

Pour coffee. It makes perfect sense for him or her to ask you to take care of the coffee detail when there are visitors. And there is nothing demeaning about your taking away the empty cups when they're finished. You are simply making it possible for them to conduct the business that generates your paycheck. You don't have to carry on about Lincoln and slavery when the boss is alone and asks you for coffee, either. If he or she is a good manager, he/she brings you a cup from time to time, too. You two are a team, and in a good relationship, you work together to make life simpler for one another. Today's secretary, male or female, values willingness and cooperation; class distinctions went out of style with upstairs and downstairs maids.

How often should I get the coffee?

It doesn't matter. Your purpose is to get ahead, not to get into fights. If getting coffee for people helps make you a valuable team member, go ahead and get it. It's not a big deal. The big deal is to make points for yourself by being a cheerful, cooperative person, the kind people like to have around.

What do the new manners say about asking the boss to lunch?

They say, not a great idea. First of all, your boss has a thousand other things scheduled and would be irritated by your presumption upon his/her scarce time. Second, you would create an awkward situation about who pays for lunch. It's silly for you as an employee to expect to pick up the tab, and an imposition to force your boss to play host. Find some other way to make friends.

By all means, accept the invitation any time the boss asks you to lunch. It's your opportunity to cement a good personal rapport.

I can think of two nonsocial situations when it would be a good idea for you to do the inviting. When you have something very important to talk about and simply cannot get your boss to make time for you during office hours. And when you can make yourself look important by trotting out an interesting friend for a lunch threesome. "Interesting," in this case, means somebody who could benefit your boss: a journalist or prospective customer, for example.

Incidentally, the same answers about socializing at lunch pertain to the question of whether to ask the boss to have a drink with you after work. It's one thing if the occasion comes up naturally—if you're both on your way to the 8:02 and have a few minutes to kill, or you've been working on a project and have reason to celebrate. It's quite another to try to make a social appointment with a harried executive who has many other demands on his or her time.

Is Dutch treat the rule these days?
It's not the rule, but it is acceptable practice. The situation dictates whether you pay, he pays, or you split the bill. If it's a casual get-together, you should both expect to go Dutch, the same as if you were another man or as if you were with another woman. If you are out with a supplier or a business acquaintance who's on an expense account, let him pick up the tab. If you are the host—that is, if you are the one who has something to sell and will gain from the meeting—you should pick up the check. Or at least give it an earnest try.

What should I do when there's an argument over who treats?
Don't argue. Get used to being in charge. Have two or three personal or company credit cards in your wallet, to simplify the transaction. It's psychologically easier on both of you if you just sign, implying that this is a business expense, instead of fiddling with bills and coins and the right amount for a tip.

118

There will be times when your guest will object, even though you are the one who will benefit from the meeting, and even though you have gone to elaborate lengths to set it up so the waiter presents you with the bill. Some men cannot get comfortable with the idea of letting a woman pay. It's against their upbringing, it makes them feel like a gigolo, it just isn't *right*. Don't force the issue. You've made the point that you would like lunch or dinner to be your treat; that's enough. You don't have to belabor it and prolong his agony. Just accede graciously, say Thank you, and accept his need to play the game of who pays according to the rules he's been taught. If your need is always to win, stifle it this time. You can win later, at something more important.

Is it enough to say "Thank you"?

It's an added grace note to follow lunch or dinner with a thank-you note. So many people have forgotten this courtesy, your note—typed or handwritten—will underscore the favorable impression you've made. It will also give you a second chance to remind your host of the purpose of your meeting, and perhaps toss in some extra ammunition:

June 20, 1980

Mr. Robert Smith
The Vanguard Bank
23 Mountain Avenue
Denver, Colorado 80000

Dear Bob,

Thank you so much for the wonderful lunch yesterday. You are indeed a generous host, and I do enjoy the occasions when we can get together and talk.

I hope you'll give my suggestion about taking on our fashion consulting service some thought. It's occurred to me that by being the first in your industry in this part of the country to add this benefit for your employees, your company could gain a great deal of favorable publicity in the local and national press. The Helix Company in New England had that experience last year; I'm enclosing reprints of some of their clippings so you can see the results that are possible.

119

I'll phone you next week, Bob, so we can nail down some of the details. Meantime, thank you again for lunch.

> Cordially,
> Susan Johnson

To whom should I address a thank-you when a businessman entertains me at home?

To both the host and the hostess—at their home, since that is where you were entertained. A gift is in order, as well. If your gift is flowers, send them before or after the dinner. *Before* gives the hostess a chance to arrange and place your cut flowers or plant for the party. *After* gives her something to enjoy and remember you by. *On the spot* can be disturbing for a hostess who suddenly has to interrupt what she is doing and hunt for a vase or rearrange her decor.

What do you think about having drinks with the married men in the office?

It is perfectly acceptable to ask them to lunch or to have a drink with you. Just be clear in your own mind about why you are socializing. Do you want to keep the relationship strictly business, or do you have something more intimate in the back of your mind? If you want to stay on a professional level, you will have to be careful not to let your talk or actions spill over into flirtatious or provocative behavior. For this reason, it is also not a great idea to have dinner or drinks alone at home with them. The very setting is a come-on, the scene of movie and real-life seductions.

Will men think I'm putting them down if I refuse an invitation?

You can always evade an invitation gracefully with a social white lie: "Gee, thanks. I'd love to. But I have another appointment, and I'm already running fifteen minutes late."

It's just as easy to handle situations that seem awkward. You may be having a business meeting in a social environment—your home office, for instance—when the Let's-have-a-drink prospect looms. All you have to do is guide him to the door as you say, "We had an excellent meeting, don't you think? I'll see you next Wednesday at the same hour. Bye."

You should, however, accept invitations or invite yourself along to after-work drinks at the local watering hole. A lot of business is conducted over bent elbows at these places, and it's crazy to subtract yourself from the scene simply because tradition says a lady always goes to a bar with an escort. But when you drink with the boys, drink with care. Know your limits and stay within them, so you will have your wits about you and be in control. The safest way to drink is to drink little and drink light. And if you can't handle alcohol, don't drink at all. There's nothing wrong with a spritzer, mineral water, or a Virgin Mary. Repeat: You are in business to do business. You can't do it well if you fall into the alcoholic traps of the loosened tongue, the erased inhibitions, or a personality change to silly, bellicose, amorous, or worse. Nowhere is it written that a sober person cannot be good company, or is automatically a prig.

What if one of the men is attractive to me?

Whatever you do about it, be discreet. Don't babble about him to your co-workers. They will babble to others, and the word will get around. Keep your distance during office hours. Refrain from the urge to hang around his office, manufacture excuses to be near him, touch, gaze, and otherwise give the impression that you are emotionally out of control.

How do I handle a lesbian overture?

The same way you handle any sexual situation. If you're not interested in having an affair, just say so, politely and kindly, and get on with your business. If you *are* interested, respond as you see fit. But remember that you are taking a risk: The enchantment may wear off and turn to bitterness. A lesbian affair is no more fatal than if your boss were heterosexual. But it is just as loaded.

Claire's affair was with another manager, Sally, who worked in a different department of their company. Claire says:

> I'd recently ended a twenty-three-year marriage and was free to explore new relationships. I met Sally at a mutual friend's dinner party, and it wasn't long before we became lovers. After two months, we knew that we wanted to live together, and I'm afraid the whole office knew it, too. You can't hide anything in an office. They'd see Sally

come in day after day to pick me up for lunch, and the two of us leave work together. We were an item, and the troops had a field day buzzing about it. What worried us wasn't the troops; it was our customers. Sally and I talked long and seriously about the impact our personal life could have on the company. We decided that if this were a bank, a brokerage, an insurance company, or some other conservative firm with a conservative clientele, we'd have seen to it that our affair was kept secret. But since it's a more liberal company, we felt we could take the risk. So far things have worked out OK.

What should I do when they offer marijuana (pot, weed, joints, grass, hash)?

Proceed with caution. While marijuana-smoking, according to the statistics, is quite common and is no longer a shocking thing to do, it is still illegal in many places. And there are still some people who disapprove, even though at some business parties rooms are set aside for smoking. If in doubt about how your smoking pot will be received, you'd be wise to say "No thank you." Nobody will fault you for that. If you do smoke, just be sure that you are not the one to make the first offer. Let somebody else take on that responsibility.

Is there a way to criticize a staff member's appearance and not hurt her feelings?

There are two ways, depending on how readily the other person accepts constructive criticism.

You can be subtle. Give this person a gift certificate for one of those Saturday "Day of Beauty" routines. Or tell her about this marvelous shop you've found where the clothes are just right for her.

If that doesn't take, be candid. Tell her in a firm and friendly way that some important people are coming in and although she is a wonderful worker, her appearance does not reflect well on your company. What you have to get through to her is that if she looks bad, so does your office. The truth is, if you have a messy assistant, she can repel the people you need to do business with.

"No Nipples in Denver"

That's what Thelma calls her tale of an innocently provocative assistant who could have cost her a big account:

I run a company that makes television commercials, from concept through production. We're a loose, creative outfit and so is the atmosphere. One of my top writers, Wendy, is a twenty-four-year-old with a terrific body—a great bust and just the right amount of hips—usually encased in nothing but a snug bodysuit and jeans. I had a new client in Denver who wanted me to come out there to shoot on location, and I was to bring Wendy with me so we could make copy changes on the spot. Before we left, I told Wendy to please go out and buy a bra. She didn't catch on so I had to tell her why: "Because your nipples stick out." She still didn't get it, so I explained: "This client we are seeing is from the conservative, corporate Midwest. He would consider your appearance freaky and be totally unnerved. He would also consider my company freaky. The reason I want you to get a bra is, I want to keep this man as my client."

The story got around our office and when we got back from the trip, there was a gag storyboard waiting on my desk. The title card was, "No Nipples in Denver."

What should I do if I'm visibly pregnant?

Wear maternity clothes.

It is standard procedure nowadays for women to work as long as possible during pregnancy. The populace is no longer shocked by "business as usual"—full term.

You will probably be in for some special treatment—a little pampering, expressions of concern. If you like being pampered, relax and enjoy it. If it annoys you, just say, "I'm perfectly fine. Thank you for being considerate, but I really am able to handle my job, or I wouldn't be here." And if you don't feel terrific some days, stay home. Better to moan alone than to become the office invalid and give everyone else a pain.

Should I ask the people who work for me to my home?

Most people who have done so have pulled back.

Virginia, twenty-eight, president of a PR firm: I never socialize with my staff outside of the office. It makes it too hard for me to give orders. You have to maintain the division between friend and employees. I try to keep a personal touch with them, but in the office only. I'll bring them birthday gifts, give them baby showers, take them out for lunch or a drink to celebrate. I want them to like me and I work at keeping them happy. But not in my home.

Sunny, twenty-nine, videotape company president: I invite the staff to my home every year for the office Christmas party, but that's all. I find it very difficult to be chummy and then ask them to do something, especially if I've become dependent on their friendship. There was a time I was having rough going with my daughter and Jill, my office manager, was very supportive of me. She saw me through the worst parts, gave me advice, listened to my woes. Then she started to let down on the job—she just wasn't getting her work done. I couldn't bring myself to call her on it.

Harriet, thirty-six, partner in jewelry manufacturing firm: I was very close with my partner for years. We'd been through each other's divorces, played tennis together, had dinner three or four times a week. Then Debbie fell in love with a man who, it happened, was very demanding. He wanted her to travel with him, to meet him at airports, to be wherever he was whenever he beckoned. She was so intent on having this man, her priorities changed. Instead of concentrating on business, she was concentrating on him and did whatever he asked. She was in the office less and less and business began to suffer. I covered for her as much as possible, but finally, when we lost two major accounts and our profit margin was visibly anemic, the board of directors called me on the carpet. The chairman said, "Harriet, I'm aware of what's been going on and I realize it isn't your fault. I am also aware that you are physically exhausted and cannot continue to shoulder Debbie's load along with your own. You are either going to have to get her back on line or bring in another partner to take up the slack." My friendship with Debbie was so strong that even with the chairman of the board snapping at my heels, I wasn't able to ask her to let up with her lover and get back to work. I am still trying to carry her load, but I can see that something is going to have to give.

Frances, fifty, owner, data processing company: When we were a small company and there were only about ten of us, we were all very palsy. We'd socialize after hours, visit around at each other's houses. But now that we've grown to sixty people and I've gotten older as well, I find it takes too much energy to keep my position as boss separate from being their friend. I have to be able to say "Do it!" and not schmooze around. Also, I find that with sixty people there are cliques, and where there are cliques, there are jealousies. You can't keep the same level of friendship with everybody; noses are bound to get out of joint and the business suffers. I very carefully distance myself from them now, and leave emotional involvements to family and friends.

How can I entertain at home when I don't have help?

Hire help. It's a worthwhile (and deductible) investment in your career. I can think of at least a half-dozen reasons to hire help rather than have a do-it-yourself party:

1. Your time is worth more at work than it is running around to grocery stores, cooking, arranging and cleaning up afterward.

2. Your time at the party should be spent talking and listening to your guests, not heating and serving food, pouring drinks, and emptying ashtrays.

3. Your party will probably be more effective and pleasing with professionals in charge of the details.

4. Your appearance will be as the gracious hostess and executive in charge, rather than as the harried domestic with potholder and steaming brow.

5. The help will pay for itself, eventually, when the party's purpose is realized: to bring in new business, to build favors with suppliers, to repay favors you owe.

6. You don't have to spend a fortune to have an impressive party.

What do I do about socializing with the boss's wife?

Build a rapport but don't go for intimacy.

That's a by-and-large answer. When you get down to cases, there are as many answers as there are individuals, and what is death in some instances can work out beautifully in others. By and large, however, a boss's wife who doesn't understand the nature of a working relationship is apt to see you as a rival. She may resent you, fear you, not understand what you do or how you got where you are. You are not only different, but possibly better in some mysterious way. Given all this, the wisest thing you can do is to get her to trust you. This may be hard for you if you are one of those women who automatically view the wives or lovers of the men they work with as adversaries. Try to cast aside that response and become friends instead.

Basically, you have to remove the possibility that you are a threat. Let her know that you are not on the make for her husband.

When you are together—at her home, at your place with other friends
—talk about things you have in common: your children and the educational system, the joys of Oriental cuisine, your mutual devotion to
Bette Davis films. In this way she will see you as a warm, friendly
person who is interesting to talk with, and who is tuned in to the same
things she is. The mistake is to exclude her and confine your conversation to the exclusive world that you share with her husband.

Your relationship should be cordial and your manner professional: Be friendly but don't go overboard. It's usually not a good idea
to mix private and office lives; one or the other is bound to suffer.
You can be helpful to the boss's wife, but don't let her use you. If
she needs airline reservations to visit her aunt Sally, you might help
her out once. But guide her away from making a habit of imposing
on your—and your boss's—time. You are his secretary, not hers. Be
courteous but firm. Tell her, "I'd be happy to track down the reservations and make them for you, but there are so many things I must do
in the office that I'm afraid I can't get to your request for some time."

What do you do about using first names in the office?

Go with the flow. In service and creative businesses such as advertising, publicity, and research, informality usually prevails. Everyone from the president down is on a first-name basis. Conservative
companies in conservative industries or in conservative parts of the
country usually go the Mr. or Mrs. route. In some places you hear,
"Smith called. Jones is out." Listen, and ye shall learn what to do.
Especially when you are new to a situation, listen to what other people do and take your cue from them. If you were brought up to
believe that titles and surnames should always be used, try to forget
it. When "Mr. or Ms. Whosis" is not standard practice in the office,
you will just make yourself an outsider if you insist on clinging to
what Mother taught you.

Should I call the boss by first name in front of strangers?

It depends on what you call him or her in the office, and how
strangers should view your position.

The scene: a trade association dinner.

The characters: You. Your boss, whom you always call Jack when
                you're in the office. Other association members.

You say:

Mr. Jones, I'd like you to meet the president of our company, Jack Smith.	Introducing two peers.

Or

Jack, may I present my friend, Mary Green. Mary, this is my boss, Jack Smith.	Casual introduction. Now Mary has to choose—Jack or Mr. Smith. If he is an older man or if she is in a position several rungs lower than his, she will probably choose "Mr. Smith."

Or

Mr. Smith, I'll take your briefcase to your table for you.	Personal remark in front of a stranger. Restraint lets others know that you are Smith's assistant and that he is a man to be respected.

Or

I am very pleased to meet you, Mrs. Smith. Your husband has so much respect for your ideas.	"Jack" might sound too intimate.

How should I introduce myself?

Same scene: a trade association dinner. You rise, shake hands, and say:

I'm Jane Jones of the White Company. And this is my husband, Dick Brown, with the Black Company.	Your first and last name, and company affiliation. You identify him as your husband without going into song and dance about using different surnames. If they ask, just tell them.

Or

127

I'm Jane Jones . . . Mrs. Dick White in private life.	"Jane Jones is my professional name." Or, "I use my maiden name." Actresses have done this for years, to nobody's great consternation. I don't know why civilians get upset.

Or

And this is my friend, Dick White.	You live together but are not officially married. This is your business. There is no reason to begin a discussion of the pros and cons of having a roommate.

Note that the question of whether you should introduce yourself to strangers has been relegated to folklore. The question now is, to whom should you introduce yourself. The answer is, to the right people. If you are a person who is on the move up, the right people for you are the people at high levels. They are why you are attending this function: to make contacts. You have to remember that you are not there to party; you are there to *use* the party. Your job is to work the room.

The way a politician works a room?

Exactly. Move around. Shop. Keep your eyes and ears open to spot the interesting people, the ones who attract the groupies. Otherwise, you could waste the short time you are there talking and listening to wallflowers—people you may never see or hear of again. Spend your time with the leaders. Circulate. You want to get into conversation with the key players, the ones it's important to get to know. The ones whom you want to know you. If it's up to you to get the ball rolling, go ahead and do it: Invite the right people to sit with you, or ask if you may join their table, so you can further the association you are trying to make.

Toni used to think that working a room was a terribly manipulative thing to do. I told her not to let the word "manipulative" get in her way. To manipulate means to work, to manage, to direct. It's the way successful people get to where they want to be. Now that Toni has been in business for herself for a year or so, she agrees:

I used to absolutely cower in the shade of my husband, although at the time I didn't see it that way. We entertained at home a great deal and I, of course, was his hostess. Looking back, I realize that for years the most important people in town were constantly at my dinner table, in my living room, at my fingertips. And all I ever did about it was make nice—talk perfect-hostess talk—discuss the weather, the Mideast, the guest's relationship to my husband. It never occurred to me, until I lost my job as a bookkeeper and decided to go for my real-estate license, that these people could help me. That it was OK to ask them for help. That I was a person too, not just a hostesslike figurine. Now that I'm in sales for myself, those parties are key to my making it. I use them. I use our guests. The parties are no less gracious than they ever were; they are just more interesting—and productive.

Nor do they end when the last guest says good night. They extend into lunchtimes. Every day of the week I make it a point to invite someone to lunch with me, to strengthen the contact, to build a base I can work from. It's no one-way street: I always come up with a tip I can give them, a favor I can do, an idea we can bounce off each other. We're both piling up IOU's. I'll give them information they can use: "I hear the Steele Building is for sale." "Did you know that the city is talking about taking over that plot on the west side for a park?" I'll test ideas: "How do you think the California land auction idea would go over here?" I'll catch up on history, maybe find out where some bodies are buried: "I hear Henry Steele was a genius. How did he wind up in Chapter Eleven? And who has charge of the company now that he's dead?"

By the way, this kind of table conversation does something else. It gives the other person something to latch onto, so we're not sitting there listening to ourselves run out of things to say. As a formerly shy person, let me tell you, that is the most panicky feeling in the world: when you can't come up with anything decent to say.

What can I say to break the ice?

Something personal: I love your necklace. Is it an antique?
Current events: The traffic is simply wild today! Did you have trouble getting here, too?

Feelings:	I am so excited. I just got word that we're getting a huge new order. Have you ever had one of those terrific weeks when everything's golden?
Old reliable:	This morning's paper says my horoscope for the day is fantastic. I wonder what yours is. What's your sign?

Please notice that all of these icebreakers are open-ended. You make a comment, and then add on a question. Something the other person can respond to, so the conversational ball can be lobbed back and forth over the net.

There is one more trick you need to know:

How to remember people's names

1. When you are introduced to somebody, look at the person carefully and repeat his or her name: "How do you do, Sally." (Think: Sally. Short black hair. Horn-rimmed glasses. Very short. Fat.) Observing the person and repeating the name at the same time will help to engrave that person's identity in your memory.

2. Make a connection you can latch onto. "Hello, Sally. My best friend at college was named Sally, though her real name was Sarah. Is that yours, too?" Now you have associated the name "Sally" with someone you know, and can visualize them together in your mind's eye. Next time you meet the new Sally, you'll have the association to remind you of her name.

If you don't catch the name, ask. "Sally? I'm pleased to meet you. I didn't hear your last name. You're Sally . . . ?" Sally will fill in the blank, and you will have another deposit for your memory bank.

Should I bring an escort to a party or convention?

It depends. There is no reason for an unescorted woman to be uncomfortable in a roomful of couples. As a matter of fact, going alone to conventions may be the best option of all: It forces you to get acquainted with new people instead of huddling in a corner with your date or worrying about his welfare.

However, when the other business people are mostly men and they've brought their wives along, the fact that you have a male in evidence might take the heat off your appearing to be the femme fatale, stag and on the prowl. Besides making you less of a threat to the wives, the presence of an escort will help to get rid of any ideas the men might have.

If you are married, the natural person to ask as your escort is your husband—if he can get away and if he is willing to go. Otherwise, you can choose a professional colleague. If you are single, you will probably do better to ask somebody other than the man you are seeing, so you won't have to baby-sit and will be free to circulate.

Do husbands like going along to business functions?

Some do. Others, like Gary, loathe the whole thing but won't say No because they think you'll be angry if they refuse to accompany you. Gary and his wife, Gretchen, are both fairly well-known chemists. Now in their early forties, they grew up in a small Missouri town, were married there, and moved to the West Coast to develop their professional careers. They have retained their cultural ethic of family togetherness—in public. Privately, their marriage is stressed, in large part because of their backgrounds. Neither has the emotional ability to handle what has become a nontraditional marital role for Gretchen. If you could eavesdrop on their minds when they are at one another's conventions, you would hear something like this:

GARY: I wonder if she knows how I feel when I hear her being presented on the podium, or when she is introduced at the Noted Doctors Convention? They treat me like a nonentity, one of the admiring throng. Don't they know she'd never have got where she is today if it weren't for me?

GRETCHEN: I hate going to his conventions and just being an appendage. He gets the limelight and I stand there ignored. I wonder if he knows what it's like to feel jealous?

131

Other times, their feelings often run along these lines:

GARY: She works late every night, and every weekend, too. And she travels too much. If I complain, I will sound petty. As if my male ego is wounded. It is. I worry that she is escaping into work to get away from me.

GRETCHEN: I'm so overworked. These awful hours, and running around the country on speaking engagements. I'm losing weight . . . and gaining recognition. The truth is, I love every minute of it. At home, I'm so—well, old shoe.

Both Gretchen and Gary are having some very unpleasant private thoughts as a result of Gretchen's career success. One way she could relieve his discomfort is to involve him in her activities: seek his advice, listen to his opinions, ask him to coach her in public speaking. Incidentally, Gary could do the same. If he asked Gretchen to handle their joint extraconvention activities such as dinner and entertainment plans, she would feel part of a team and less competitive.

How do you handle being on your own at a convention?

Thelma is in the printing business, and because she is an especially pretty woman in her early thirties, she usually has to face the man question:

It can be tricky. A lot of the men are more interested in looking for a one-night stand than they are in doing business for their company. When you talk to them, the trick is to be charming but thoroughly professional at the same time. One way I do this is to dress tailored, to help get my message across. You have to laugh with them and be sociable, and you have to know where to draw the line. If you go to too many of the hospitality suites, you begin to look like a party girl. But if you skip all the cocktail parties, you miss out on a lot of good contacts and useful discussions. One thing I do that I'd recommend for anybody is, I make a note on all the business cards I collect—or jot down a name if I don't have the card—so I'll remember when we met and what we talked about. Some reminder so I can pick up on this person again. Then I transfer the names—with the company, address, phone, and reminder note—into one of those wallet-size address books. I have a different book for each city. That way, if I'm going to be making a trip to Chicago, say, I just whip out my Chicago book before I go, and I have a whole directory of people I can contact. While I'm passing on advice, I might as well tell you what else I do about contacts. I keep them cross-filed in an index box in my office. Say I meet a textbook production manager named John Doe in Chicago. I cross-file him four ways: under Doe, John; Production Managers; Chicago; and Schoolex, Inc.

I'd hate to have to rely on my memory for something I might need four years from now. Or even a month. You meet so many people at these affairs, and they're usually in groups. It's impossible to keep them sorted out unless you're systematic about it

What do you do at night?

The usual convention routine is to have a drink and dinner, or attend a convention function. You can go it alone at these things, invite somebody to join you or join a group. What I like to do is find out which hospitality suite has the poker game. I find that's one of the best places of all to build contacts and do business. If it's a late-night game, I'll stay with it in favor of making the eight o'clock seminar next morning, because I want to be where the action is. I'm careful not to be an intruder, of course, and to stay with the crowds. Lingering with the last person in the room is a signal that you're looking for an affair, and that is not why I am there.

Usually I buy a few chips and sit in. It's an excellent business investment. It's also an excellent lesson in one of the differences between men and women when confronted with money. When one of the men at the poker game rakes in a kitty, the others congratulate him, or joke, "Hah! You bandit. I'll get you the next time." When women win at cards, they can't wait to give their money away: "Oh, it's too much. Here, take some. Are you sure you have enough money to get home?" Meaning: I don't deserve it. . . . You might not want to play with me again. . . . There's something dirty about my taking money from you.

What do you do when you travel alone to strange cities?

Whatever pleases you. You can be busy during off-duty hours, or you can catch up on your reading and sleep. The choice is yours, and there is no reason to make a problem of the fact that you are alone. Sometimes it happens, though, that you are stuck with time and

133

energy on your hands, and no good ideas about what to do. Here are three practical ways to get going:

1. Before you leave home, try to get the names and numbers of people to call. Bring a letter or message from your mutual friend, to provide an opening wedge. Phone and say, "Lila thought you and I would have a great deal in common, and wants to be remembered to you. I'd love to meet you, if it's convenient. Would a drink or dinner be good for you, or I could stop by your office?" If the contact is busy and can't see you, or doesn't want to—well, you tried. And the turndown couldn't have been anything personal. Move on and do something else.

2. Phone or stop in at the local office of your professional or trade association, and talk to the executive director or the president. Ask if there are any events scheduled for the next couple of days that you could attend. Or ask if there are some people you could meet who are in your business so you can talk with them, get advice, see new equipment.

3. Ride your hobbyhorse. I collect art and like to keep up with new regional talent. So I go to art galleries around town. Other hobbies and interests that are easy to pursue when you are on the road lead to other things to do:

> Go antiquing
> Catch up on movies
> Ogle architecture
> Visit a bridge club
> Do advance Christmas shopping
> Take a guided bus tour
> Play golf

What can I do to stop feeling grim about hotel rooms?

Put some personal cheer into your room. Whisk the hotel tent cards and Bible into a drawer, then group your cosmetics and toiletries where you can get at them. Make the room your own, with a photo of your children or dearest friend on a tabletop, some hard candies in one of the ashtrays. If nobody's sent you a hospitality gift, buy yourself a fresh flower and pop it into a cheap vase from a nearby variety store. In other words, create an environment for yourself that will make going to bed, dressing, and nibbling at your room-service breakfast a pleasant experience.

Just remember this: The world is light-fingered. Never leave anything valuable around. Keep your jewelry with you in your purse at all times. Lock your suitcase when you leave the room. Double-lock the door when you're in it.

Who are you supposed to tip when you travel?

This is one of the most vexing questions for women who have not traveled alone often. The answer is, practically everybody, and in varying amounts. Therefore, the first thing to do before you set off on a trip is to arm yourself with five or ten dollars' worth of dollar bills and quarters. Keep some of this in your pocket and some in your change purse, so you can dip in quickly and easily. That will remove some of the nuisance. Now the details:

Sky cap and train porter	50¢ per bag. More if you want to get his attention.
Taxi driver	15% of the fare in most cities, 20% in New York. 20% or more if the fare is small (give the driver $2 for a $1.50 ride, for example). Add 25¢ per bag if he handles them.
Private limousine	15% to 20%
Car valet	$1
Hotel bellboy	50¢ per bag plus 50¢ for showing you to your room; $1 if you think you will want additional service during your stay.
Hotel maid	$1 per night
Room-service waiter	20%
Ladies room attendant	25¢–50¢. 75¢ if she provides service.
Coat room attendant	50¢. $1 in a fancy place.
Waiter	15%–20%, before the sales tax
Bartender	20%

Wine steward	10% of the wine cost
Maître d'hôtel	$3–$5 depending on the restaurant.
Hotel doorman	25¢ for hailing a cab. Up to $1 if it is difficult. No tip if cab is in line. 25¢ per bag for handling luggage.

DO NOT TIP:

Airport limousine driver
Rental-car company shuttle bus
Doorman
Desk clerk
Concierge (in U.S.)
Flight attendant

WHAT TO DO ABOUT CHAUVINISM AND QUESTIONS OF SEX

What is a male chauvinist in the office?

A man who, through his cultural background, brings prejudices about women to work with him. He believes that women are emotionally, physically, and mentally weaker than men. That they are best qualified to look nice, bear children, tend to the home, and take care of him. His attitude is, "She takes care of the inside—I do the outside work. It's all very simple."

Some office male chauvinists are tricky. They spout equality all over the place and mouth all the reasons in the book why you should get to the top. They make grand claims about how proud they are of your performance. Deep down, they think that you have a nerve trying to make a career for yourself. You'd be better off if you stuck to female-role things like typing, keeping their appointment books, and choosing gifts for their women. Their deepest convictions concern money and authority, the areas people at the top deal with. They believe that women cannot be trusted to handle either successfully, and therefore they do not belong in top management.

What are women's chances of getting into top management?

Not terrific. A recent survey shows that 78 percent of all managerial jobs are held by men. The reasons are that we are new to the territory. We lack training. And there are enough male chauvinists around whose visions are blurred by stereotypes that keep them from helping us get ahead.

What are some of the male-minded stereotypes that hold us back?

A male chauvinist thinks it is natural for all women to place home and personal life above career. Therefore, he reasons, if there should ever be a conflict between your family and work obligations, you'd quit your job or give it short shrift. So, since you probably won't be around very long, he thinks he'd better keep the big responsibilities away from you and give them to a man. Men, after all, can be counted on to assign top priority to their careers.

Another belief chauvinists have is that any man has more business sense that a woman. If there's a choice between you and a man for a managerial job, or if he has to pick one of you for managerial training, he is bound to select the man and leave you behind.

A third chauvinist point of view that can hurt you is that it's OK for a man to play around, but taboo for a woman. It's not so much that he wants to protect your virtue; it's his belief that men are more valuable than women and when push comes to shove, he will favor the man. For instance, if you get involved in an affair that upsets the office and one of you has to be let go, you can be sure that the male chauvinist will hang onto your lover and get rid of expendable you.

Is male chauvinism disappearing?

It's beginning to. The Victorian gentlemen who were reared to believe that a woman's function is to make a home are dying off of old age or retirement. Some of them are being replaced, however, by the kind of young man who is determined to hang onto the *status quo*. To him, you are a threat to the established system. You get in his way. You may even take over his territory. This is why women today have to work extra hard to prove their worth, and must be extra cooperative to keep resentment from growing. You have to bear with the fact that it is hard for people to overcome longtime prejudices.

The good news is that we are on the threshold of real integration. It is my feeling that within the next very few years the most diehard, conservative, all-male company is going to open up for us. All it will take is a few hard-working women who are smart enough to take advantage of the fact that they can still be bought cheaper than men, at first. They will get their foot in the door and then work their way up to top management, opening the door wider for the rest of us. It is a bottom-line fact of life that in today's market you pay less for a woman to do an executive job. There is nothing the president of any company likes better than a bargain that makes his bottom-line figures look better.

Should I take a job as a token woman?

As I've said, sometimes it's a good way to get your foot in the door. Dorothy's story is a good illustration. She is now the vice-president of a data processing firm, but she got there by rising from a token sales job that she got because the company "needed a woman." She says she knew that she started out being paid slightly less than a man would have been. But she didn't take umbrage: Her ultimate goal was what was important. She could see that there was a mutual advantage to be gained: They had an employee at bargain rates, and she had her stepping-stone job. Her greatest problem, Dorothy felt, was that she had to work for Carl, a man who feared women to the point where he all but isolated her from the business. He wouldn't give her important accounts, wouldn't listen to her ideas, never shared information with her. It was frustrating, but Dorothy made it plain that she could pull her own weight. She did whatever she was permitted to do as well as possible, and she never cast blame on anyone for not letting her do more. She figured, if she failed it would be nobody's fault but her own.

At a certain point, though, things got too bumpy even for Dorothy. She couldn't get ahead no matter how hard she worked. What she did was confront the problem directly instead of letting it fester. She went to Carl and said to him, "I have a problem and I need your help. I am the only woman in this office. I can see that there are no women in executive positions, and I wonder if there is a future for me with the company. I am delighted that I am working for you, and I really admire the company. My concern has nothing to do with you personally, it's just that I'm feeling frustrated. What do you think I should do?"

She made a friend. Even people who are none too happy about having a woman on their turf love to feel they can pass along the wisdom of their experience.

Describe how the president of a Fortune 500 company is chauvinistic.

His name is Jim. Age, fifty-eight. A former professional ball player, he is the president of his own and a director of six other corporations: a force in American life. Jim came from downstate Illinois, where he learned very early what is right, what is wrong, and what are the basic values. A man of great probity, he has never cheated on his income tax or used the company plane or limousine for anything but strictly business purposes. He would be shocked to hear of anyone charging a meal to business if the occasion was even

141

slightly social. He is not only honorable, but extremely courteous, considerate and charming. His secretary, whom he addresses as Miss Smith, has been with him for thirty years. To this day Jim leaps to open doors for her and never fails to say "Thank you, Miss Smith" when she serves his coffee. He would be as respectful to any woman.

Jim worries a lot about what he sees and hears nowadays, especially the part about women who work. It confuses him, even though his wife, his neighbor's wife, and his younger colleagues have all told him that it is perfectly acceptable for women to drop their dustpans and come into the office. And even though he has dealt personally with two or three women who have serious executive careers, to him they are the exceptions. As a whole, the idea of career women knocks Jim off balance: It is different from the catechism he learned as Truth. He cannot change.

There is a woman on one of my boards and several others with whom I work from time to time. I am uncomfortable with them because, for one thing, I have to keep worrying about what I say. They glare if I forget and do as I have always done: refer to Miss Smith as "my girl," or my family as "the gals." I have to be conscious all the time of steering the conversation away from the things I have talked about for decades: golf, fishing, hunting. I am most uneasy with those women who are overly assertive, who always want to make it clear that they are equal. Equal to what?

I would like to be able to attract more women into executive positions in my company; I know it's the right thing to do. But I do not want to have to keep thinking about whether I am offending them with my vocabulary or my manners. Here's a recent example of what I mean. I was interviewing a woman attorney, a very competent woman I thought would do well on our staff. I had seen her résumé, and it was quite remarkable for someone only twenty-eight years old. She'd done a lot of complicated behind-the-scenes work for the firm she was leaving, and one of the partners there had assured me that she could be trusted utterly to follow through on any assignment given her. She came into my office, and I held out a chair for her and said something complimentary. At least, I thought it was a compliment. I said, "A young lady as pretty as you are would be a great addition to this office." To my astonishment and enormous discomfort, she became enraged and told me off in very direct terms: "My physical appearance has nothing to do with why I am here, and I resent your flirtatious approach." Maybe she's right. But I never thought of myself as a chauvinist before.

Describe six types of male chauvinist who may be in charge of the office.

1. The Victorian who, like Jim, means well but is confused by the women's movement. He knows the rules have changed and he can't keep up. Should he open doors for you or not? Should he promote you into "man's work," or will that upset the rest of the office? He's not sure what he wants of you, or what you are capable of giving. So he plays it safe by praising you from time to time, and making sure that you don't get to take on too much authority.

2. The adversary who is afraid he will lose a piece of the turf that has always been his, and who resents you for being bright enough to threaten his territory. At least, he sees your brightness and professionalism as a threat. Nobody else, except another man, has ever challenged his right to run things before; he is not about to let anybody from the weaker race challenge him now.

3. The jock who thinks that the only real people are the boys in the locker room. They are the real team players. Women, in his view, are too emotional and excitable to play the game well. They are apt to blow up or flood the room with tears at the slightest provocation. So he gives you the cold shoulder rather than risk fireworks. Besides, everybody knows that the brute male is intellectually as well as emotionally superior to women.

4. The secret dreamer who feels guilty about working closely with a woman. There are men who have been trained to think that it's sinful to enjoy spending time with a woman out of wedlock. They fear the undercurrent of sexuality. They keep their distance from you and won't admit you into their masculine circle because they're afraid there'll be trouble. They are fighting themselves, not you, but the problem of working with them is yours nonetheless. There is probably very little you can do about it except to try to break down their resistance by gaining their trust over a period of time.

5. The lord of the manor who sees all women as helpless slaves. If they weren't, they'd fight back the way men do when he lays down the law. Probably this attitude is related to his own family upbringing. As a kid, if he got sassy his father would punish him. His mother

would feel hurt or be momentarily angry, but she'd never reject him. He doesn't understand that you are not his mother; you are an independent, responsible, capable woman with a life of your own to consider. You are a co-worker and not his inferior.

6. The man who had A Mother and has spent his whole life being afraid that other women will dominate him, too. He may seem meek and agreeable, but if you come on too strong or try to take charge, watch out. The worst thing you can say to him is what he grew up hearing: "I know what is best for you" and "I'm here to take charge." He hates a woman like that and will do anything to get rid of her. Listen to what happened to Dorothy when she first went to work as assistant to the director of a commercial real estate firm:

> I didn't know it at the time, but I had a number of strikes against me. For one thing, I was forty-six years old and a little stout. Right away, I looked like somebody's mother. Further, I'd spent the past eighteen years more or less in the driver's seat. I'd run a household, directed three children, issued instructions to the volunteers on various charity committees. That was the extent of my work experience. I hadn't been paid for any of it, but it was a form of leadership, and quite possibly a major reason why I was hired. I had proved that I could take over and had every confidence that I could transfer that ability to business.
>
> It didn't take me long to learn my job and understand where the company stood in its field. At that time we were concentrating on developing office and shopping malls in several small cities where any outsider was looked upon as a carpetbagger. We were having trouble getting building clearances and zoning ordinances, and my boss was worried that there would be resistance when it came to leasing out the space. Having absorbed all this information, I came up with a terrific idea for solving the problem.
>
> My first instinct was to take the idea in to my boss and, if need be, shove it down his throat. That's how sure I was that the idea was right. I squelched the urge; it would have got me nowhere. This was the kind of man who could never let anything happen that might result in a woman's getting the credit. He'd be scared she would take over. Instead, I pulled out the old psychiatrist's technique and sold him my idea by making him think it was his. What you do is just keep playing back words, repeating and repeating, in a way that keeps your own opinions and criticisms out of the conversation. That way there is no way he can feel threatened. Our conversation went something like this:

ME: I'd like to suggest that we begin a massive program of community relations.

HIM: I don't like your suggestion.

ME: You don't like my suggestions?

HIM: I most certainly do not.

ME: What in particular is it that you don't like?

HIM: It's stupid. We can't just go into the community with a massive program. The only way your idea would work is if you selected the bankers in the community and did a public relations job on them.

ME: The bankers. I see. Can you tell me anything else that would make the program work better?

HIM: You don't have much experience, do you? It's obvious that you would also have to hit the rest of the financial community: the accountants, the attorneys, the investment advisers. And the investors themselves.

ME: Yes, of course. We should go for the financial community. As you said, we should be selective. Who else do you think would be a good target?

HIM: Selectivity is the key to any good marketing program. You have to realize that what we are really doing here is marketing.

ME. Marketing, yes. Do you think we should market to business owners?

HIM: Not business owners—*large* business owners.

By the time we got through, I had elicited his ideas without frightening him off and knit them together with mine. He had his input, I had the program I'd envisioned, and he thought the whole thing had come from him. We both won.

In general, what is the best way to deal with a male chauvinist?

Be professional. Keep business and your personal feelings separate. Work with, not against them. And keep your touch light. Personally, I find that a little gentle kidding of the subject helps. You can acknowledge what is going on that way without being hurtful if you say something like, "I understand your point of view because I grew up with people who thought the same way you do." In other words, you get further by expressing yourself sympathetically than by being antagonistic. If you are obstructive or make them wrong, they will resent you and nobody will win. The best thing you can do is to gain their confidence, and the way to do that is to let them know you understand their difficulty in seeing women climb to influential positions.

Just be sure that you really do understand. Women in high places is still a new concept, and hard for many men to accept. They feel it is unnatural and that it places a burden on them. Most likely they mean you no harm personally; it's just that they fear change. Most people do.

How can I be sure that male chauvinism is my problem?

Test it. Remove the element of male chauvinism from your thinking and ask yourself if a female boss might treat you the same way.

- Do you know your field?
- Do you harmonize with the other people with whom you work?
- Are you willing to learn from criticism?
- Do you take responsibility for your own mistakes or do you try to blame others?

Some women, especially younger ones, make it a habit to focus on a scapegoat so they can displace blame from themselves. Their problem is that they won't assume full responsibility for their own behavior. They use whatever alibi is handy. For them, an excuse of male chauvinism is the easy way out. They haven't learned that excuses can only hold you back.

You have to assess yourself and your situation very honestly before you can claim that "they" are discriminating against you.

What if they won't promote me because it's always been a man's job?

Make them question their thinking. Ask them what it is about the job that they believe you can't handle. If it entails selling, directing other people, or administering a budget, and you have already shown that you do these things well, ask what it is that's exclusively masculine about the job. If you approach them reasonably and not contentiously, your probing can help make them realize that they were just taking tradition for granted.

You have to conduct your discussion the way a good salesperson does. Find out what it is they really need, then point out how you can help them get it. Be persuasive. Get them to agree with you. Don't

146

make them wrong. If you argue or complain, they are certain to argue and complain back.

Cindy's experience is a perfect illustration of the right way to tackle a situation like this. She is a production assistant who wants a $26,000 job as associate producer. When she applied for the job, they told her they couldn't pay that much. What they meant was, they really wanted a man for the job. But they couldn't come out and say it that way because there are too many government regulations about job discrimination based on sex. So they made up excuses like, "The job's not for you, Cindy. You can't lift heavy things." What heavy things? There are union people who do that and everyone knows it. Cindy realized that something else was going on: They already had their quota of female associate producers. She decided to confront the issue head on, but in a way that would get their willing agreement to give her the job. She spoke to the producer, the person who had the authority to hire her and a man who also had a good track record in hiring women. Cindy said:

"Bob, I know there is a slot open for an associate producer. I would like to have the job. I've got superlative ratings in every performance evaluation and have proved that I am a well-qualified professional with a good feeling for the work. Do you agree that's correct?"

Bob agreed and Cindy continued:

"I have counted up the associate producers you have now, and I see that there are four women and four men. I realize that if I came on as your ninth person, I would upset the balance and create a situation that's unusual for this company. But I feel that I can do the work for you very well, and I want the chance to prove it. Do you agree that I can do the job as well or better than any other candidate you may be considering?"

She had him. Bob had to agree that Cindy was an excellent worker. She hadn't been kidding herself; she could do the job at least as well as anyone else. And the way she'd presented her case gave him no grounds for argument or resentment. He agreed to let her go into the job and prove herself to the company.

What do you think of a boss who gives me raises but won't promote me?

Your boss sounds like one of two types. (1) He or she may be a perpetual middle manager—somebody who is holding a job, not doing it. (2) Your boss may be a clinger, a person who is overly dependent on you. Or he/she may be a combination of the two.

Typically, perpetual middle managers are order-takers with no decisive power or ability. They worry more about the pension plan than about brilliant performance. Whatever has to be done, they get you to do it, and then claim the credit. What happens if you are good at your work is, you become so valuable as an aide that you are trapped. They won't let you move up because they need you to make them look good. Furthermore, if this type is a man, the chances are he sees all females in business as stereotypes. He thinks, "You are a woman, therefore you are a secretary." If you submit to this thinking, you will in fact always be his underling.

Do most women earn less than men?

Yes, and the inequality is staggering. Look at the statistics compiled as recently as 1976, and bear in mind that all indications point to an even greater disparity for the eighties:

- Forty percent of American men earned $15,000 or more. Only 7½ percent of the women earned that much.
- Women in sales earned 55 percent less than men in sales.
- Women in clerical work earned 36 percent less than their male counterparts.
- The national median income for women was 27 percent less than men's.

In New York, where women are paid more than in other cities, the difference was nearly 20 percent.

There are three reasons for this income disparity: Women are in careers that don't pay as well; substantial numbers of women are not in middle or upper management and are, by definition, younger in their careers; discrimination against women still exists.

148

What are the laws that protect me against discrimination?

Two important federal laws are on your side: the Equal Employment Opportunity Act, which says that people in companies with fifteen or more employees cannot be discriminated against because of sex, race, color, religion, or national origin. Your other protection is the Equal Pay Act, which says that employees in most but not all companies who perform equal work must be paid equal wages regardless of sex. "Equal" refers to skill, effort, and responsibility that are substantially the same.

The Equal Pay Act is helpful, but it contains gray areas that are still being worked out. One is the issue of comparable worth. There is no assurance as yet that female nurses, secretaries, and other "pink ghetto" workers will be paid as well as male laborers. Proponents of the women's movement are trying to find some way to measure the value of different, gender-oriented jobs so that unequal pay can be eliminated across the board.

What is the Equal Rights Amendment?

The Equal Rights Amendment (ERA) consists of just 24 words: "Equality of rights under the law shall not be denied or abridged by the United States or by any state on account of sex." What this will mean when the amendment is added to the Constitution is that women who work will be granted legal rights as full and equal citizens in such essential matters as employment, credit, and Social Security benefits.

ERA will become the law of the land when at least 38 states have ratified it. To date, a majority but not 38 of the 50 states have approved. Detractors claim that under the amendment, women will be drafted, state divorce laws will be abridged, and women will lose their property and Social Security rights. Those of us who feel strongly pro-ERA believe that these abuses, many of which take place at the present time, will be ameliorated when we have Constitutional assurance of fair and equal treatment.

What are some national organizations that are working for equal rights for women?

• The National Organization for Women (NOW). Lobbies for passage of ERA. Gives specific legal advice on discrimination cases.

Raises male and female consciousness. An independent arm of NOW, the Legal Defense and Education Fund, raises funds for its work on equal opportunity through education, legal actions and public awareness programs.

- Catalyst. Has education and training centers. Conducts research, funded by government and private grants. Books and pamphlets available in libraries and at Catalyst offices. Catalyst is headquartered in New York City.
- Grey Panthers.
- Displaced Homemakers Alliance.
- Women's trade and professional organizations.
- Small Business Administration (SBA). Strong interest in providing loans, advice, education for women. Conducts seminars and conferences.
- Other government agencies:

U.S. or State Equal Employment Opportunity Commission
Department of Labor, U.S. Wage and Hour Division
U.S. Department of Justice, Civil Rights Division
State Department of Law, Civil Rights Division
State or City Human Rights Commission
State or City Department of Consumer Affairs
U.S. Federal Communications Commission (radio or television)
U.S. Office of Personnel Management (federal employees)
U.S. Labor Management Relations Board, National Labor
Relations Board, State Labor Relations Board (unions)

What is your opinion of women's groups within companies?
I think it's an excellent idea to band together with others who are fighting the same battles you are. It's a way to use common resources for strength and credibility. I'll tell you about a group of middle management women at the United Nations who did this not long ago. Each of them had been trying to attack the problem of gaining recognition on her own, and none of them was getting anywhere. People thought they were oddballs, trying to force their way into positions where they weren't welcome. They got together and agreed that in spite of their varied cultural backgrounds, they would all go

150

further if they cut out the backbiting and aimed at a single goal as a unit. They got the ball rolling by giving themselves an identity, The Information Network. Whenever one of the women had a request for information from her boss, she would say, "I don't know the answer, but I'll put it through the Network." They did this repeatedly, and eventually the group became known as *the* resource by everyone in their arm of the U.N. As a group they achieved the recognition none of them had been able to get individually.

Women in other organizations use the group concept in other ways. Some appoint a spokesperson, so when sex discrimination problems come up, one voice speaks for them all and it is apparent that there is determination and muscle behind her.

How do you start a woman's group?

Get together with two or more other career-oriented women and discuss your common problems. Does management give you a hard time? Is the company not paying or promoting you as you think they should? Are you having difficulty penetrating the male network? Be specific, and then formulate concrete goals. Make a marketing plan you will follow, step by step, target by target. Then meet once a week, or as often as you feel necessary, to exchange information, check up on each other's progress, and air helpful ideas.

Select your group members wisely. A marketing plan is only as good as the people who will act on it. Look for women who are at least as earnest, purposeful, and creditable as you are; career women whose support will help all of you.

Federal law says that employees are entitled to organize in order to better their working conditions. Under Title VII, bosses may not take retaliatory action if women band together so they can confront illegal sex discrimination; and the National Labor Relations Act guarantees harassment-free organizing for purposes of bargaining, petitioning, meeting after work, and so on.

Most companies, especially large ones, have come to accept women's groups as something they can no longer fight. They have no need to if you act in the spirit of common good rather than militancy. One way to get management's approval is to hold your meetings outside of work time, so they won't feel you are robbing them of their due. You may find, if you present your plans in a way that says we are not trying to make you wrong, that they are willing to have you meet on company grounds and on company time.

Should you join mixed groups as well?

Definitely. It's a mistake to isolate yourself in a sexist, we/they position. You need all the advantages career men can give you: skills, viewpoint, and the benefit of their experience. You need their acceptance and cooperation, and you need to be where the action is, on the mostly male decision-making team.

What do you do when somebody calls you sweetheart?

Ignore him. He's not going to change because you lecture or tell him off. He probably thinks it is his birthright as a male to call women Sweetheart, Honey, or Doll. Or snap his fingers at you for coffee. Maybe he has a need to let you know you are his hireling: an inferior being who should stay in her place.

Audrey, a twenty-two-year-old college graduate, drew a "Sweetheart" as her first boss. He is the ultimate jock, a man who goes crazy if he does not have women's complete subservience. Audrey says she can tolerate the fact that he orders her around. It's her trade-off for learning everything she can from him about the organization so she can move up to a better position:

> He insists that I serve coffee and sandwiches even when logic and efficiency dictate that he pass the plates himself. I have no objection. I feel it's a gracious, hostessy thing to do; something I was taught to do well and with pleasure. I have never felt that serving the coffee is a symbol of subservience; to me food is a symbol of power. Whoever controls the food controls who gets what. You can be sure that when I am the boss or own my own company, I will always be the one in control—of the food, the power, the people with whom I meet. Meantime, I can live with this domineering person I work for without feeling put down. He has a brilliant mind and has risen to a position of great influence. I am going to use those qualities of his to the hilt, and learn everything I can from him about this job and this company. I see him as my opportunity to move up the ladder and reach my goal. My plan is to serve unstintingly as his secretary for the next two years, and then to move up onto the next rung. It is true that he sometimes

upsets me. When that happens, I just go into my office to recover, or else I'll walk around the block until I shake things back into perspective. It's worth it to me. If I didn't believe that, or didn't have the kind of personality that could put up with him, I would quit the job and go someplace else where I could learn all the things I need to get ahead.

Audrey knows that she has something else going for her. She is the only one who is willing to put up with this jock's rudeness, so she has an exclusive opportunity to observe at close range how a brilliant executive strategizes and operates. What is more, he is so blatant about calling her Doll and treating her like something stuck on the bottom of his shoe, everybody in the office sympathizes with Audrey. He is a roughneck, but she uses his style to her advantage.

Is there a law against sexual harassment?

Yes and no. The Supreme Court hasn't decided yet whether sexual harassment comes under the heading of sex discrimination, which is covered under Title VII of the Civil Rights Act. Decisions have come down pro and con in different states. Private suits have been filed, through attorneys and through city and state Human Rights Commissions. These bodies have the power to arbitrate cases and sometimes to prosecute the violators. While no state has a law that provides recourse for sexual harassment *per se,* some states have taken on a number of cases, with varying decisions. Complaints, but not lawsuits, go to women's organizations, women's committees, personnel offices, and presidents of companies, and sometimes these complaints bring relief from the problem simply because the companies "don't want any trouble" or else because the heads of the company have a conscience.

Sexual harassment is very difficult to prove. You need complete documentation, witnesses, and a referee without male bias. At that you run a risk. One of the worst things about accusing a hard-core harasser is that he can punish you in a hundred different ways. He can smear your reputation, claim it's your imagination, fill your personnel file with bad performance reports, pick at your work, get his buddies to hound you, see that you're transferred to the boondocks at reduced pay, threaten you with a libel suit, fire you, and make you unemployable by anyone else. It's a tough problem to handle, and you have to be very sure of your ground. And be prepared to walk over a lot of land mines, too.

How can I get out from under sexual pressure?

Here are some of the typical questions and answers that may help solve your problem:

AMY: He's a married man, and he's been after me the whole two years I've worked here. I was very strictly brought up and the whole idea shocks me. I've turned down his invitations for dates. I've said No thanks when he asks me to lunch. I've squirmed my way out of corners when he tries to kiss me or, you know, touch. Six months ago he started to make my life miserable. He won't let me take phone calls anymore from my little girl when she gets home from school. He's made me take on responsibilities that involve math, which is something I can't handle and hate. He moved my desk from a regular office to an open space in the middle of the typing pool. I need the job so badly because I need the money, and I'm afraid to make a move. What can I do?

ANSWER: Make the move. Start looking for another job right away. You could confront this man and ask him to stop bullying you, but he would only deny that he has done anything out of the way. He obviously has a more dominant style than you have, and is in a position of greater power besides. Your best bet is to get away from him as far and as fast as you can. Don't feel that you have no place to go; even the smallest town has more than one company that can use good help.

CATHY: I'm not the first one he's harassed, and I can prove it. This guy has a record at Personnel a yard long. Do you know what he does? He makes remarks about my bust. "Are you built!" he says, staring all the time. He's always putting his hand on my leg or making sexual cracks. I'd like to give him the knee. That'd take care of his problem.

154

ANSWER: For about two minutes. After that you'd have an angry sexpot on your hands. It would be better for you to tell him, very calmly and courteously, that his behavior bothers you and you'd like him to keep his remarks and his hands to himself. Rehearse what you're going to say ahead of time so you won't get carried away by emotion and not handle it well. He'll probably reply, "There's no harm in trying." Then you have to decide whether to make a federal case of it. If you feel that the situation really is out of control, you can report him to Personnel. If it's true that Personnel has already received similar complaints, yours could be the one that will cause them to take action.

There are recourses other than Personnel, since all companies don't have such departments. You can make your report to the National Organization for Women and let them take charge of the situation. You're in a good position for them to help you, since other women in your office have been bothered by this man. My advice is to band together and make your report as a body, so there'll be enough complaints against him to stand up.

LINDA: What I have to put up with! He calls me Sweetheart. Puts his arm around my shoulder. Touches my knee. Talks about my appearance more than he does about my work. If that isn't sexual harassment, I don't know what is. He'll probably fire me if I keep giving him the cold shoulder. What am I supposed to do?

ANSWER: Keep things in realistic proportion. It's likely that calling people Sweetheart and putting an arm on their shoulder is nothing more than this man's style. He probably acts that way with everyone. Do you really dislike it, or are you translating light banter into heavy advances? You have to consider the possibility that you may be feeling a little needy, putting out signals to which he's responding. All the sexual byplay that goes on in this world does not come under the heading of harassment. Often as not it's just ordinary, well-intentioned, human-to-human communication; the harassment aspect is in the eye of the beholder.

Are men the only ones who go in for sexual harassment?

Women can indulge in the sport, too. Take the story an insurance executive in Denver told me. Brad is a tall, outdoorsy, Levis and boots type. He says that he loves women, especially charming ones, but he hates to feel that he's been seduced. I can see why:

I hired a secretary who was twenty-one, smart as a whip, cute as a button, and ambitious as all get-out. She came to me after a month or two and said she had to make more money and would I promote her to sales. All you have to do is be pretty to get to me—I'm a pushover for girls like her—so I said, "Sure. I'll get you into the training program and you can start right away." She did everything she was supposed to do, or so she told me, and I agreed to take her on some sales calls with me so she could learn faster. Well, we wheeled around the countryside all day calling on clients, and when it got past office hours, she said why don't we stop at this roadside place for dinner and drinks. By golly, we had a lot of drinks and before you could say Jack Robinson, I had my arm around her, and we were kissing. Not a bad way to end a busy day, I said to myself, right? Wrong. The whole thing was a setup. After that performance, the little . . . excuse me, the girl let it be known around the office that she and I had a special relationship. Somebody'd ask her to do something and she'd say, "Oh, Bradley and I have discussed that, and he says I don't have to do it." A lie, of course. Or she'd not bother to come back from lunch, or not show up at work at all. And then mince around dropping my name all over the place as if I'd given her permission—or as if she'd been off rendezvousing with me. Naturally, everybody resented the hell out of what they thought was going on. There she was, goofing off, being teacher's pet, while they had to work their tails off. Morale around the office got so bad that I called her in and said, "You've got to quit doing this," and I even told her why. She just sailed on, cocky as could be, and kept right on doing what she'd been doing. I'll bet she felt sure she could keep on being promoted for years to come by using me, and then the guy after me, and then the guy after him. Maybe she has, I don't know. I fired her for nonperformance and haven't kept track of what's happened to her since.

How do you handle ordinary sexual advances?

With a firm but light touch.

There is no point insulting anybody you do business with. The best way to turn aside an advance is calmly and with kindness.

"You are a very attractive man and under other circumstances it would be fun. But mixing business with pleasure just doesn't work for me."

"That sounds exciting, but I am very loyal to my husband."

"Thank you, but you know how hard it is to get a baby-sitter."

Whether you want to accept a pass or not is entirely up to you. If your aim is to keep your business relationships on a business basis, it is best not to become sexually involved. Entanglements backfire too readily. You can become emotionally snared and lose sight of your career priorities. You can unwittingly step on somebody's toes and lose your job: An uptight client, a jealous colleague, or a wife nobody told you about can easily slice you off at the knees.

You can become a love object for a while, but when the affair is ended, it could be difficult resuming a professional footing with the man who has known your bedroom personality.

When should I file a complaint?

After you are certain that you are being discriminated against because of your sex, and after you have tried many other options.

Before you start to think about lawsuits, you had better realize that you will have a tough time winning a discrimination case. And you might lose more in ill will and energy than it is worth. What you have to do first is build a strong, factual case: what your specific duties are, how long you have performed them, what they are worth on the market, what your male counterparts earn. You would have to back all of this with evidence: newspaper ads showing job descriptions and salaries, affidavits from accredited experts. Then, armed with the results of your in-depth research, you might have a case you could win. It is also possible that you would win your case and lose the war. It has happened to other women before you. A legal judgment is made in their favor, but then they find themselves stuck in the job and salary they've defended, unable to move on because nobody else will hire them. Many have been right, and unfortunately for them, some have had to be our martyrs.

What are my other options?

Speak to the person you work for and try to iron out the problem without resorting to legal action. Marshal your facts and state them calmly and objectively. Do not even mention the word "prejudice"; it will only raise hackles. Assure them of your competence and your desire to fit in. Tell them why you believe you should earn more than you are being paid. State your case firmly and without emotion, the way Nancy did to Paul:

> I'd been offered a promotion to associate director of the trade association I work for, and I was so thrilled about the twenty-thousand-dollar salary and the impressive new title, I grabbed at it without a moment's hesitation. I was to start in three weeks, when the guy who'd been associate director left. Meantime, I was telling all my friends about my good luck and that's how I heard that my predecessor had been getting twenty-five thousand dollars. You'd better believe I was upset. Well, I'd got myself into this pickle; I'd just have to get myself out of it. So I went to the director, Paul, and had a talk with him.

Here's how that talk went:

NANCY: I'd like to talk to you about the promotion you've offered me, Paul. You know how pleased I am about it, and with the confidence that you're placing in me.

Opens the subject on an upbeat.

PAUL: I'm glad you feel that way. I'm sure you will do a topnotch job for us.

NANCY: I've been thinking about it a lot this past week or two, making plans and whatnot, and there is one thing that bothers me. The salary is a problem.

Broaches the money differential without relating it to sexism.

PAUL: What's the problem, Nancy?

NANCY: You're asking me to take on substantially more work than I've been doing and to assume a great deal more authority, but the increase in salary doesn't quite match. It's only a 10 percent

Saves the male/female issue as her trump card.

raise over what I've been getting, and I'm taking on 25 percent more in responsibilities, hours, planning, work. Do you agree with me that being associate director is 25 percent more work for me?

Asks for Paul's agreement.

PAUL: I hadn't really looked at it that way. Maybe it does seem like 25 percent more work to you, but I think after you've got into the job, you'll find it's a lot less than that. It'll balance out to 10 percent.

NANCY: I've really sat down and analyzed it. Let me show you where the additional work comes in. I'll be responsible for four people instead of just one. I'll be working weekends and attending conventions, versus the nine-to-five job I've been doing. I must maintain contact with our association members, and that will require travel. I'm told that my predecessor spent 30 percent of his time traveling. Is that true?

Presents hard facts.

Starts to lead Paul down a logical path.

PAUL: Yes, it is. You will certainly need to meet with our people constantly.

NANCY: And there are systems I want to put in that will require additional work. For instance, I feel that the newsletter doesn't give our members enough detail, and I want to revamp it. Do you think that would be a good idea?

Shows she has given the job thought and has valuable ideas. Asks for more agreement.

PAUL: It's a wonderful idea and I hope you can get on it in the very near future.

NANCY: You see what I mean, don't you? All of what I've been saying adds up to substantially more work without appropriate recompense. As much as I'd love to take on the job, I'm afraid I can't be very enthusiastic about it unless I'm paid for what I do.

Hinges her willingness on enthusiasm.

PAUL: I do see what you mean, Nancy, and I agree with you. I think we can bring your salary up 20 percent instead of 10.

Paul is still getting a bargain.

NANCY: Thank you, Paul. I know that my predecessor was earning twenty-five thousand dollars for doing the same thing, and I anticipate equal pay soon.

Finally uses her trump. but avoids saying "sex prejudice" except by implication. Knows Paul would only have balked and thought up ways to say how Nancy's job was different from her predecessor's.

PAUL: But you have to remember that he's been in the job three years. He's proved himself.

NANCY: That's true. Let's have a review of my work in three months, and talk about the 25 percent then. I guarantee you I'll have proved myself to you by then.

You have to remember that there is no law that will change ingrained attitudes. If you have tried speaking with your "Paul" and that doesn't work, and you don't feel intensely enough to start legal action, you have three other options to choose from:

1. Live with the situation.
2. Resign your job and take a different one.
3. Ask for a transfer out of your department or region.

What do I do about getting them to let me travel?

Ask. Mickey, a statistician for a midwestern food processor, told me that she'd been ignored time after time whenever there was a convention or seminar in another city. Finally it dawned on her that people assumed she couldn't travel because she had a young child.

I'd never discussed with them whether I could or could not travel. In my head, it was "Why don't they ask me?" In theirs it was, "She's not free to go because she has to take care of her child." It took me a while to add two and two, and realize that they were afraid to ask me to travel. But as soon as that light bulb went on, I went in to my manager and told him I'd like to go to San Diego and attend the seminar that was coming up. I told him that I had a wonderful *au pair* at home whom I trusted implicitly, and that I was very pleased about having such excellent child care because it allowed me the freedom to travel. I also wanted to let him know that I was committed and would be around for a while, and that I realized I am an investment to them. So I added, "This seminar would be valuable to us both. There's a lot on the program that I can learn from and apply to our operation. And I feel that I'd fit in very well with the others who are attending and could represent this office in a favorable light."

Sometimes other people are more afraid than you are. You have to take steps to remove that fear if you expect to move ahead.

Why do the men in my office keep me out of their talk sessions?

Because they see you as an intruder trying to invade their historically male turf. And because a lot of their talk sessions are on stamping grounds beyond your reach. Golf courses, health clubs, steam rooms, and corner saloons do not exactly encourage co-ed memberships.

The fact is, a lot of decisions are made in men's talk sessions and one of the big problems career women face is how to break into these informal decision-making groups.

How can I get men to accept me in their groups?

Approach them as individuals, not as a group. Diane, a thirty-two-year-old financial analyst, succeeded in becoming part of a decision-makers' network in gradual stages. Although she is not particularly attractive, has always been too quick to blame herself, and is the kind of woman who worries that other people won't like her, Diane has a good head on her shoulders. She is capable of detaching herself from a situation and analyzing it objectively. More important, she is the kind of person who acts on her analyses. Diane is determined to make

161

good things happen for herself. Here is how she describes her experience with a men's group in the office:

> I'd come into this brokerage firm as a computer technician, worked very hard, and in eighteen months was promoted to product developer. I was pleased with the way I was advancing, but I knew my future was limited unless I could break into the male network. That's where the action was. But it was a closed society—closed to me, at any rate. They would pass me by every time the list went out to attend planning meetings. I was never included on the memo route. Never asked to join the daily lunch groups. That kind of thing. I was isolated from the natural ways one gathers information and contributes ideas, and it was deliberate. I may sound paranoid, but believe me, that's the way it was. Those men saw me as somebody from Mars—a stranger who was just a little too bright, too eager, too much of a change for them to cope with. They figured, if they gave me an inch I might take a yard, and wind up in a position where I'd be telling them what to do. As a matter of fact, they were right: My long-range goal is to become a partner in the firm. But I could see that the only way to reach my goal was to become part of the system, and that I wouldn't become part of it if I just walked over the bodies that were in my way. Or hunkered down like a hurt, sulky child. I decided that if I was going to be a mature, professional woman, I'd better start acting like one and do some intelligent strategizing.
>
> The first thing I did was take a good look at the group I wanted to get into. Not as a group but as a collection of individuals I could cultivate, one by one. To start, I selected Tom as a man who was not only knowledgeable and influential, but who could also handle a male-female friendship without fear of sexual involvement, or feeling he would be smothered and used. I began to stop into his office from time to time, just to chat. I learned that we had some common interests. We both dote on Astaire-Rogers films and love Chinese food. This provided grist other than shop talk for the conversational mill, and gave me a reason—which at that point I felt I needed—to suggest that we lunch at a Chinese restaurant neither of us had tried.
>
> Once I'd made up my mind that it's better to be direct, to relax and be myself and not be self-conscious because I was a woman, I found it easy to build Tom as my confidant. I told him that I was upset about being left out of meetings, and that I believed I was being purposely omitted from the memos that went around. The one thing I never did was to blame "them." It was just a question of "What should

I do?" I asked his opinions and advice, and he gave them to me freely. We had a good rapport, Tom and I—we still do—and he became my adviser, and my champion as well. For instance, he suggested that at the next staff meeting I mention that I'd been accidentally left off a memo and inquire if there was something I should know. He also began to include one or two other men in our lunches together. Gradually, one by one, the men began to accept and include me in their conversations and groups as someone who was just another human being—somebody agreeable and cooperative who could help them get their jobs done without the ranting and screaming and carrying on that they thought was part and parcel of being a female. I won't say it was an easy, overnight trip. It took time and patience and a switch in my own attitude to one of self-confidence. But I recommend the technique to any woman who wants to get ahead.

CAREER POWER AND HOW TO GET IT

How do you know which people have the power in your office?

You can't always tell by their titles; it's how they act and how other people act toward them. They're the ones who get cooperation without argument. The ones other people come to for information. The ones who are at the center of the action and in on all the important meetings. They are innovative in their thinking, unbound by rule books. They know how to lead people and have no need to domineer or pick at details. They treat everyone fairly, but in accordance with their relationships to them. They reward top people for excellence and aren't threatened by somebody outstanding. They have been variously described by the people who work for them:

"A power person has turf and status. Somebody who's in charge of a lot of people and directs more than one kind of work."

"A take-charge person who's used to having people do things for them. You can tell by the way they carry themselves: They have this air of 'I'm entitled.'"

"Someone who makes things happen."

"Someone who controls other people's actions and has sole control over his own."

"Whoever makes the decisions."

"The one who doesn't have to say 'May I?'"

"Whoever controls the money."

How do you get power?

In broad strokes: by originating activity, and by using strengths that other people have originated.

Power Through Innovation.

By going beyond the job manual and devising fresh ways to achieve company goals: Set up a new office, develop new procedures, hire outstanding personnel, create an improved system, plan an additional department, sell to people who haven't been sold to before. Successful innovators create their own power: Whoever invents a job makes the rules. He or she is the expert other people have to check with and consult before they can move.

Power Through Association.

Seek out the top people in your field and attach yourself to them. People you trust and respect, people with different skills, people you can make your sponsors. When you ally yourself with power, you develop a pipeline to information about what's going on in the company: what's being planned that you could get in on. And you develop support: people who will fight for you when you need help, serve as sounding boards for your ideas, teach you how to move up.

Should you associate with a power person you don't really like?

Of course. The closer your association with a strong, influential person, the better your chance to move up the ladder along with them, and improve your title and salary as you go. This does not mean you should become personal buddies with somebody you don't like. Keep the association within the framework of business. Friendship must be based on genuine rapport or it won't work. At least not for long. People with different interests wind up boring each other. Contrived drinking buddies become tiresome. Artificial male/female attachments almost inevitably crash of their own weight.

Are office romances a route to power?

Sometimes. An office affair can succeed so well that the "protégé" marries the boss, if that is what she wants. Sometimes the sexual ploy results in a job promotion. If that is your goal, you'd better be able to handle the job you've moved up to. A man in Los Angeles describes what can happen otherwise:

> A friend of mine, Naomi, is an ambitious but fair-to-middling theatrical agent. She works for a man named Ken, with whom she has had an affair for the past couple of years. It started back when they were both at a company that went under. Ken, being a valuable property, was offered another job immediately, and the first thing he did was hire Naomi as his senior agent. She doesn't know beans about negotiating, and she's way over her head. Ken is doing everything in his power to keep her in his job, but she knows she's in trouble and comes to me

for advice. I tell her she'd better do a lot of listening to other people and not run around pulling rank. And that she has to watch her step extra carefully because if she makes too many errors, it's going to reflect on Ken. Not only will she lose her job, she'll put his in jeopardy. And when that happens, love or whatever it is will fly out the window fast. I should know. I fooled around with my secretary for nearly a year. Then my boss found out, became resentful of the favoritism that was going on, and put the lid on the moves I was making to help her get ahead. She dumped me in a hurry, let me tell you. What the hell, my wife would have rained on the parade sooner or later.

What are the chances of a woman making it to the top?

Better than before but not fantastic, as we've seen by the statistics. The reasons behind the figures are, for one thing, there are very few people at the top of the pyramid, men or women, and the competition is strong. For another, power tends to be shared with like kind, and most of the people at the top still are men, which cuts down your chances of being drawn into the executive circle. The odds are improving, though. More and more women move into line jobs each year. You see women lawyers in action in the courtroom, not just looking up briefs backstage. We are TV producers now, not merely keepers of the log. More of us are becoming the people with hands-on authority: the ones who plan, decide, and control results. It is no longer true that the front row seats are reserved exclusively for men. Depending on the field you are in, your chance of sitting there is as good as anybody else's.

Still, there are difficulties. All corporations are not tuned in to the changing times. Saleswomen still have to convince people to let them travel with men. Reporters have to argue their way into dangerous assignments. We still have to work extra hard at the outset, to prove ourselves worthy newcomers to traditionally male executive ranks. It is not easy: Women are only now beginning to learn the career games that men have known for generations. It takes all the skills we can muster.

There is also the danger of backlash. As the newness of women in business wears off, women can no longer count on preferential treatment because of their gender. We have to really earn the keys to the inner sanctum. It still takes a lot of doing to get to the top.

Here is one male executive's advice to women entering business:

Theoretically there is no difference between a man's and a woman's making it. The reality is that we are all products of our history. We have come from aeons of conditioning that the sexes have different roles to fulfill. No matter how much you're exposed to consciousness-raising and intellectual exploration, it's very hard to escape the assumptions you were raised on. There's a lot for a woman to surmount. I think she needs to be genuinely and thoroughly grounded.

She must take her work seriously, and not be in it just for the glamour or the title.

She must concentrate on the job itself, and not be paranoid about the facts of life.

Enthusiasm and a high energy level are imperative. I've actually created openings when I had no job or budget available, because somebody has come to me so interested in the job—in a substantive, intelligent, positive way—so adaptable and eager to do anything and do it well, so bubbling with zest that I couldn't have stood *not* to have her around.

And intelligence. Take the person I just mentioned. I love somebody who's a bundle of energy and enthusiasm, but if she hadn't been a smart, competent woman, what would I have done with her?

You have to show that you have initiative, that you'll go beyond the limits of your assignments. Take off and do extra things that will enhance what I'm trying to accomplish. By "initiative," I mean a self-starter. Somebody with imagination, creativity, and enough judgment and confidence so she doesn't have to rely totally on other people's ideas.

I think any woman who wants to make it must have all of these things, not just some of them. What I'm not sure of—speaking in generalities—is why it's harder for a woman than it is for a man to let people know that she has these qualities. Do you think it goes back to conditioning? That women are afraid they'll look like climbers if they show that they want to get ahead?

Will I be a threat if I let people know I'm on the climb?

The trick is to tell your ambitions to the right people. Certainly you should let your boss know you are eager to get ahead. But first you have to assess whether he or she is the kind of person who will help you or hinder you.

A Helpful Boss:

Includes you in some of his or her projects.
Encourages you to learn new skills.
Recognizes and praises your success.
Defends you when you make mistakes.
Does not put you down.
Realizes that the street to success is two way: You will help each
other reach your goals by being mutually supportive.

A Hindering Boss:

Is self-defensive.
Is scared powerless.
Protects his/her own turf and nobody else's.
Never takes risks.
Won't share credit.
Is scared that you are going to walk in and take over.

If you tell your ambitions to an insecure boss, you will be perceived as the superbright person who's out to rake their brains and then take over. They will think of you as a competitor who must be squelched. They would be much more comfortable with somebody who is mediocre and willing to stay that way.

Is competitiveness a big problem for women?

Apparently. One of the drawbacks many of us have is that we don't understand that competition is the element that makes business gears click. That it's a stimulating challenge, a game of wits and skill. People tell us that competition means "cutthroat," so we back off, intimidated. One reason we shy away goes back to the theory that boys learn to compete in team sports, and girls play alone with their dolls. Another, more immediate reason is that most of us have been educated in the arts rather than in business management and administration. We've been schooled in the niceties of creativity, and not the bottom-line thinking that men learn from logical sciences. Given this kind of education, it's no wonder it is hard for women to see that competition is not just for killers; it's an intellectual, pragmatic means to an end.

171

Will other women compete against me?

Of course. They are after the same jobs you are.

One way to shift the balance in a you-against-me situation is to join together with the other woman and make it "you and me versus the competition." I'll give you an example. Two actresses, Moira and Ann, were in constant competition for the same roles, and neither was getting very many of them until they worked out a strategy. They agreed that when either one heard about an audition call, she'd let the other actress know about it. That way, if Moira didn't get the casting, her buddy Ann might. And the next time around, if Ann lost out at an audition, she could tell Moira to hustle right over to the call. In other words, they'd be feeding each other jobs instead of starving separately. What they did, when they got rid of seeing each other purely as rivals, was double their chances to win.

What are some power techniques men use that will help me get ahead?

By "men," you probably mean people who have had years of business experience and understand the tools of self-advancement. These tools are often a mystery for women because, as newcomers, they tend to concentrate on immediate tasks and overlook long-term career goals. A recent phone company survey illustrates this with the fact that women use the telephone, mails, and memos far less often than men. The statistic is revealing. What it means is that women as a whole have not learned to use the power of keeping in touch. Test yourself and see if you agree: Do you count the cost more than the career value of making long-distance phone calls? Do you feel it's an imposition to call somebody when you have nothing urgent to say because it might interrupt their day? Power people don't think that way. They communicate constantly, whether they have anything important to say or not. It's their tool for building relationships, for keeping their presence in other people's minds. Listen to how the effective men in your office carry on:

"Hello, Joe. This is Tom. . . . Everything's great. And you? . . . You'll get a kick out of this, Joe. I was in a meeting yesterday and your name came up. . . ."

"Morning, Bill. How's it going? Just thought I'd check in and see what's new. Say, did you watch the ball game last night? . . ."

Do you see what they're doing? They are staying tuned in, making sure they are part of the game, keeping up contacts that will lead them to where they want to be.

What's another way lack of communication can hold you back?

Women miss out on power when they are secretive. Actually, their behavior stems from being afraid to share information. They're not sure if they should disclose budget figures, so they're evasive or curt. They hear industry news that might be helpful to another person, and keep it to themselves because they're afraid they'll be accused of gossiping. They haven't learned yet that it's OK to be open; that it's to their own benefit to become a source of valuable facts; that there is power in making people want to be on their grapevine. It's all in the newness: Once you learn how business really works, you can relax, be cordial and cooperative, become a key player on the team.

Is there a drawback to being in an all-female office?

Yes. In terms of power, an all-female office can be downright dangerous to its occupants because it can encourage isolation and perpetuate feelings of us versus them. This can happen when the head of the office makes the place a convent. She's afraid to hold her sales meetings and seminars at resorts, the way male or mixed offices do, because "they" will think she's just there to play. She clings to her all-female image, in the office and outside, because she thinks that the men out there won't take her or her business seriously. She is avoiding the mainstream, limiting her chances to learn from it and grow. She may be the boss and she may have power within her enclave, but she is restricting her own horizons.

Can women hold you back?

Yes. Women can be as chauvinistic as any prejudiced, competitive male. Take the Queen Bee. This is a woman, usually forty years old or more, who made it to the executive suite when things were tougher for women than they are now. She may have made it on brains or personality, and she probably had to claw and scratch some as she struggled up the ladder. Nobody cheered her on. The chances are she gave up her personal life for her career: In those days you often had to choose one or the other. Now, having suffered through all this, she sees you come along: younger, fresher, and possibly brighter than she. You may have a full-time husband and children if you want them. You have society's permission to pursue a career or not, as you choose. What is more, you are not just her file clerk or secretary. You are her peer, and ambitious. Of course she is not going to make it easy for you. She thinks, "Nobody helped me get where I am. Why should I help this upstart?" The Queen Bee will clip your wings if she can. You will have to work very hard, show her that you are conscientious, and be considerate of her feelings if you expect to get ahead while she is your boss.

Is it true that Queen Bees used men to get to the top?

Some did. In any era, there is always a man who keeps a casting couch in his office. And there is always a woman who will respond to him.

It's smart to be gentle when somebody gives you the invitation; a little flattery goes a long way in almost any kind of situation. It's smarter still, if you know that you are in a male chauvinist environment, to stop short of the casting couch. You have to remember that if the affair gets sticky and management has to choose between letting him go or you, they will probably fire you. Chauvinists are nervous enough about having emotional, fluffy women around. When the chips are down, it's their buddies they trust, not you.

Why do some younger women give me a hard time?

They are running so fast they can't take the time to sit down and be pleasant. They see you as the competition, after the same pot of gold as they are, and they're determined to grab it before you do. They don't understand that destination isn't everything. It's good to have goals, but getting there is half the fun.

There is a paradox about women like this. Even though they were brought up with consciousness-raising and are all for equal rights, some behave like out-and-out chauvinists themselves. They really think that men are better, smarter, more powerful. You may have heard this come through on the phone. When a man calls them to ask for information, it's "Yes, Mr. Smith. I'll get the answer for you right away." But when a woman is on the other end of the line, they say,

"Oh, Mary. I haven't got time to look up all that stuff. Try the library." To them, men are still the voice of authority. Women are first-name people you treat with less respect.

Probably when they have had another ten years' business experience under their belts, they will catch up with the fact that female executives command the same respect as males and can be excellent and willing mentors.

Is it wrong not to want power?

No. Everybody doesn't have to be an executive. Good assistants are what make business tick. If a support position is what you find most rewarding, you should do your job well and be proud of the contributions you make. Just remember that it takes skill, experience, a good mind, and a lot of common sense to be an effective subordinate. You need to understand business as much as the people who control it.

When should you turn down a promotion?

When It's Not What You Really Want

Connie's story: I'm a writer and never had any ambitions to be in management. But the publisher of my magazine asked me to take over an editor's slot, and I found it hard to say No to him. Besides, it was a very flattering offer, and my ego said, "Grab it!" So I did, and I was wretched. All of my time was spent either trying to keep up with the waterfall of paper that deluged my desk or fending off people who came to me one after another with managerial concerns I wasn't mildly interested in. The publisher of the company saw before I did that the job was all wrong for me. Luckily, he viewed the mistaken promotion as his failure, not mine, and opened up a spot for me back on the writing staff. We both realized that creativity is my thing, not managing people, and you never saw anybody as glad as I to get back into harness.

When the Cost Is Too Great

Irene's story: Adele and I were bench workers at a small, fine-quality doll manufacturing company. The assembly line chief and his first assistant got fired for not keeping the work up to standards, and the owner promoted us into their places. We were the only females who had ever gone higher than bench work in the whole eighty years the company had been in business, so you can imagine what happened. Four of the old-time guys quit right away, and the rest of the men began grumbling and threatened to quit. It was really hard on Adele and me, feeling like turncoats and outcasts besides having to work longer hours than we'd ever had to before. We were scared to death we wouldn't be good enough for the job and, it's funny, we were scared that we'd be too good and get promoted higher. See, I'd got a raise that brought me up to a higher salary than my father's, and that made him nervous and hard to live with. Adele's pay was bigger than her boyfriend's, and he quite dating her because he said he "couldn't keep up." We should have stayed in our place as women. In fact, we went to the company's owner and said so. We said we thought maybe the promotions weren't such a good idea and we'd just as soon go back to our old jobs on the bench. He told us, "Once you get into management, you cannot go back. Stop worrying. I wouldn't have put you there if I didn't think you could make it. Look, good people are impossible to find and you have the ability I need. Your jobs have nothing to do with your gender. I will help you in every way I can: send you to school, buy you books, whatever you want. But you have got to stick it out and do your best for me."

Adele and I are exhausted, and anxious all the time. The boss says that eventually we'll adjust and so will the men. It's a good thing we have each other to talk to, and I hope we stay together for a long time. Everything else in our lives has changed completely, and I don't think things will ever be the same for either of us again.

Should my boss take me along when he or she is promoted?

If you've been a very good secretary or manager, the person you work for may request that you move along as a team so they can eliminate the nuisance and gamble of finding another good team member. Or your boss may wait before asking that you come along, so he or she can use the secretary or manager who's already there, to find out who's who and how to get things done quickly.

Think carefully if your boss wants you to come along in a higher position. You may not be ready for more responsibilities or the challenge of a new office. Talk it over thoroughly, in realistic detail, and don't let them snow you with persuasive sales talk. Some of the unhappiest women I've met are women who have been propagandized into thinking that a job and title is everything. The concept may hold up in magazine articles or on television shows, but that doesn't mean it applies to you. It could be that what will satisfy you most is a forty-hour week that gives you enough money for your daughter's tennis lessons, enough time to take in your son's track meets, and the energy for what your husband needs.

It's easy to become confused when opportunity comes along and pushes you up in the office network. If you find that you're afraid to say No but are not fully prepared to say Yes, you had better do some hard, clear thinking about your true goals. List the pros and cons:

Do you want more responsibility?
Do you know how to handle it, or do you think you can learn the job quickly?
Can you manage if your boss's new job isolates him or her from you?
Will there be more work than you have time for?
Will you have assistance?
Will your lifestyle be damaged?

How can I get people to treat me with more respect for my new title?

This is a common question. I hear it from advertising copywriters who've been promoted to account executive, publisher's readers who have moved up to editor, secretaries who have gone on to line jobs. What happens is, people are so used to seeing you in one context, they need time to adapt to your new position. You can help them along. When the salesmen shout, "Sally, would you bring me a box of paper clips?" answer them with a reminder: "I'll send Ellen right in. She's my replacement as secretary, you know." Be clear about it, but be gentle. People aren't trying to put you down when they treat you the way they always have; it's just hard for them to break old habits and take you more seriously than they're accustomed to.

There are other things you can do to speed up the reintroduction process:

- Move to a different office. The physical and slightly dramatic change will emphasize your new, elevated status.
- Dress for your new role. If you're out of the creative department and into sales and service, shed your jeans and T-shirt as a snake sheds its skin. If you're up from secretary and into management, get rid of those dowdy high-school cardigans and squashy old loafers. You have to package yourself as an executive if you want people to see you as one.
- Learn the language of your new territory. There's a business or professional jargon peculiar to every field. Advertising has one vocabulary, computerdom has another; you'll hear buzzwords among sociologists that would baffle a banker and vice versa. Superficial though it may seem, you do build communications and recognition more quickly when you can leap into conversations without missing a beat. To learn the lingo, listen hard and ask a lot. Not only will this help you understand what's going on, but it will give the impression that you are already a knowledgeable member of the gang.
- Make sure you go in knowing what your responsibilities are, how much authority you have, and where you stand in the hierarchy. Ask the person who is promoting you exactly what your new duties will and will not be; in what instances you are supposed to make final decisions; who you report to, and who reports to you.

Describe eight of the kinds of bosses you meet in an office.

Dictator.

Distant, tough, unfeeling. Motivated by his/her need for control and a tunnel vision that sees only the goal and not the people who can help reach it. Obsessively righteous, rules by fear: You will obey or be punished. Variations from the Dictator's decrees are not permitted, which is why bright, innovative people usually quit and find other jobs. Dictators have a problem in that they breed resentment. You will notice that when they are deposed, they are rarely forgiven.

Eccentric Genius.

Paper-ripping, table-pounding, off-the-wall social misfit. Screams, shouts, even curses you. It's not that he/she hates you personally; it's just a matter of style. Try to ignore the eccentric part and learn as much as you can from the genius.

Plodder.

Competent, agreeable, undemanding. Settles for OK-to-mediocre results. Never makes waves, won't confront issues, can't say No, whatever the cost. The Plodder is such a nice person, you never really know where you stand. It's like running in quicksand. A Plodder can't call a halt to bad or half-baked ideas, is a nonleader, and a frustrating boss.

Parent.

Confers wisdom and care. Knows what's good for you and says so. Encourages you to leave everything in his/her hands. Behind the façade is either a Dictator whose orders you'd better not stray from or a Plodder who is just trying to have a good old family time.

Hipshooter.

Rattles off decisions with machine-gun speed. "Yes. No. Just give me the four basic facts and I'll tell you what to do." Never has time to listen to your carefully structured rationale. Doesn't need to; the quicksilver intellect is backed by experienced, professional judgment. Reaches good decisions by rapidly eliminating unnecessary factors.

Tortoise.

Drives you crazy by going over well-trod ground again and again, probing the pros, the cons, and all of the options. Sometimes reaches a better decision than the Hipshooter because he/she has explored false premises and elicited fresh ideas.

Technician.

Believes you can get anybody to work hard by the reward system. Encourages people to assume added responsibility by offering pots of gold at the end of each rainbow. Very good at setting goals and commitments; not so good at deviating from the rules to meet individual needs. Does not understand that one set of rules cannot apply to all people.

Ideal Boss.

Enthusiastic, stimulating. Makes every job sound like the greatest opportunity in the world. Lets people see their accomplishments, however small, so they feel there is progress. Imparts pride and a desire to stretch for high standards. Is respected and liked, in that order. Maintains control but doesn't make a production of the fact. Understands what makes each of his/her people tick psychologically, and how to bring out their best. Flexible. Interesting. Realistic. Occasionally throws a fit or fires someone on the spot, but they always know why and it is never for a trivial reason.

Are there other kinds of bosses?

Certainly. There's the Grinch, the Grouch, and the Grind. The Wheedler, the Preacher, and the Hail-Fellow-Well-Met. You'll meet Legends and Frauds, great people and small: Overlords, Underdogs, and crossbreeds of all types. One thing to remember is this: They are not refugees from Central Casting. They are real people with real problems, the same as you and I. Another thing to remember is that real people are in transition all of their lives, so watch out when you typecast. Just when you think you have somebody pigeonholed and there are no more surprises coming your way—surprise. They will move to another plateau, and unless you are open enough to see that change, you will be left trying to deal with a person who no longer exists.

What do I do if I have a boss I don't like?

First, figure out why it is you don't like him or her. Then you will be able to analyze realistically what you should do. Something like that happened to Donna, a computer analyst, who faced an unhappy situation with a new boss. Donna, in her mid-twenties, is a prototypical middle management technician, anxious to be an asset to her company and to improve her standing there. Like so many other young women in her position, she often feels thwarted by circumstances she doesn't quite understand. Donna tells how a revelation relieved one bewilderment and enabled her to move ahead:

The director I reported to was promoted and an outsider, Keith, replaced him. I found Keith very hard to deal with. He'd give me instructions that were different from the way I'd been doing things, never explained why he wanted me to do such and such or precisely what results he expected. I felt as if the guidelines I'd been used to had been rubbed out and nothing had taken their place. As a result, because there were no clear objectives, I began to feel that I was backpeddling. I mean, I'd done a good job for my previous boss and had had a good, open relationship with him. Lots of give-and-take. Keith was an enigma, and he frustrated me. So, I suppose in some kind of unconscious retaliation, I developed a dislike for him. A disrespect, really—and that's a feeling I just can't bear. It's degrading.

I was well on the road to "Life is too short to spend working for somebody I don't like," when I ran into my former boss and he said, "How about lunch?" That lunch maybe was the most important meal of my career so far. We talked about his new position and then he asked how I liked his successor. I practically burst into tears, I was so pent up. I blurted out everything that had been going on in my head, and in one short paragraph that dear soul succeeded in straightening out my whole mess. I can't believe how simple it was. All he did was point out that Keith had come into the job without anybody's explaining to him exactly what it is that I do in the public relations department, and that it was too much to expect him to understand the details and complexities on his own. He had no way of knowing if I was doing a good job. If I would take the trouble to explain my job and show him the mechanics of it; teach him what is effective PR and what is not, he'd have a way to judge and direct me. Then, if I would keep Keith informed of all my actions, I could open up the two-way communication that was missing. Otherwise, I would always be blocked, and so would the new director. What great advice! I only wish someone had given it to me earlier in the game, so I wouldn't have had to go through that rough stretch. But it's OK. Once Keith got plugged in, he turned out to be a really good boss, a great sounding board for the ideas I'd bring in, and somebody that I can honestly say I've learned to like and respect.

181

What should I do if I have a boss who slows me down?

If you like your job and the company and see a good future for yourself there, you had better adjust to your boss's way of doing things. Before you rattle your cage, you have to remember that it's the boss who will win the fight. He or she has the upper hand, with the power to fire you or get you out of the picture some other way. If you try to go over his or her head, it's your head that will roll.

All bosses are not superachievers. Some settle for mediocrity, others are plain inane. Just the same, your boss is your boss, and is in that position for a reason. Maybe by default: some people get there just because they outlasted everyone else, they climbed rung by rung without making waves, they shine at one important function such as sales, they are related to a major stockholder, or they play tennis with the chairman of the board. In other words, somebody up there is protecting them, and you are not going to get anywhere but out the door if you call them on their bad decisions.

You, on the other hand, are a part of the team they're in charge of. Try to break their link in the chain of command and you will find that you have just broken your connection to the next link up. Even in a small company where the chain is more loosely linked and where most of the power rests in the president's hands, with very little of it in your boss's, you will be breaking the rules of the game if you cast blame on your superior.

It is never a good idea to step on anyone's toes or make them wrong by calling them on bad decisions. If you want to try to change what is going on, approach the matter constructively. Present your suggestions in terms of helping the other person reach your common goal:

INSTEAD OF SAYING:	SAY:
It is a stupid waste of time to have me sitting here addressing envelopes.	It would save the company a great deal of money if we use someone who is lower paid than I am, or an office temp, to address these envelopes. Then my time would be at your disposal to help you get out your weekly reports and answer your correspondence.

If you'd just open your eyes you'd see that Jennifer is so lazy she just sits around half the time and I have to do all her work. I think it's a dumb use of help to have me doing everything.

I'd be very happy to address all the envelopes for you, but I think Jennifer is feeling neglected. Would you like me to ask her to do it, or would you rather deputize her yourself? I'm sure she'd be flattered by your attention.

You're being very arbitrary and just not thinking clearly. Anybody can see that it's unfair and senseless, the way you distribute the work load. Either there'll be some changes made, or I'll go to your superior and get him to straighten things out.

I'd like to talk with you about an idea I have that I think would make our group perform better. May I have a few minutes with you at the end of the day?

Should I let anybody know that the person I work with is a heavy drinker?

The question of what to do about heavy drinkers comes up again and again. Alice, an insurance broker, tells it this way:

> I came into this company two years ago, straight out of college with everything to learn. It's a large, well-organized firm, very departmentalized. The man I was assigned to team up with on sales baffled me for a long time. He's one of those people who talks a great game, charms everyone, and turns in enough sales—though he often loses customers after a while. Somehow there's no follow-through. You can't pin him down. If you ask the details of a sale, he starts to talk about fishing. If you're looking for a report or a confirming letter, it's never there. He's elusive: He'll go out of town for three days in a row and not call in once. But nobody ever calls him on it, and he's held his job for twelve years.
>
> I know this sounds dumb but I never put it all together until recently. Then suddenly it struck me: The man is an alcoholic. Somebody has to do something about it, and I guess since I'm the one who works with him and recognizes the problem, that somebody is me.

Alice is in a very common situation. According to the National Council on Alcoholism, one out of every ten to sixteen workers loses time and money on the job because of alcoholism, and the numbers are growing by the gulp. Neither she nor you can turn off the tap, nor can you change the person you are working with. However, there are ways you can cope.

First you have to realize that the drinker is holding down his or her job for a reason. He/she makes money for the company. He/she is related to someone at the top. Somebody important has been covering for him/her for a long time. You have to understand that you are not going to change the corporate setup. Your colleague may be a drunk, but he/she is "our drunk." Therefore, you had better learn to work with and around this person.

How do you work with a drinker?

Be very realistic and very practical. Here are five keys:

1. Get all your business done with him or her before noon. That is when the sun goes over the yardarm for an alcoholic. Only a fool or an innocent tries to talk sense with a drinker once the liquor starts to splash.

2. Whatever answers or agreements you get, before and especially after noon, put them in writing. Cover your every conversation with a memo. Otherwise you'll never be able to pin anything down.

3. Repeat whatever was said the next morning. It's most likely that he or she will have forgotten arrangements that were made, or will have them completely confused. Never trust a drinker's memory.

4. If the drinker is in a position above yours and you need something important from him or her, make your approach when his or her mood is agreeable, not truculent. If you can't get what you want no matter what, work around him or her. Go to somebody else who has the authority to say Yes or No.

5. If the alcoholic is in a position below you and you are in charge, try to discuss the situation with him or her, privately and in the context of business. If the person is unwilling to listen, or won't attempt to solve the problem, you will just have to get rid of him or her. You have a loser on your hands and so does the company. You will do everybody a favor by keeping a drinker out of their hair.

184

Should I try to help an alcoholic?

Only if you're very careful. You may feel a moral obligation to help, but that probably comes from the old business of women being the caretakers of the world. There is nothing wrong with being humane in business, but you have to remember that you're probably not going to get anywhere with a drunk, and that saving him or her from the bottle is not your primary goal. The first things to focus on are your company and your career objectives. Your colleague's personal problems are his or her personal problems; you are not responsible unless they interfere with your work. Then you should cope in work terms, not personal terms. The furthest I'd suggest you go is to let him or her know that you understand there is a problem and that you will help if you can. At that, be sure of whom you are dealing with. Most drinkers turn very surly when they're called on it.

How do you solve personality conflicts?

Elaine is a whiz at this kind of thing. I will let her tell you the answer:

> There was a minority complaint at the university where I work in Personnel. Four people came to me and claimed racial discrimination against a certain department head. My method, when something combustible like that comes up, is to cast myself as an objective reporter in search of the facts. I think you don't get anywhere if you personalize or get embroiled in the emotions of a situation. So I listen to what each person has to say, and then scan it through my mental operation to discover the implications: who would be affected by this action or that, what would be the long-run outcome, what are the ramifications. All functions are interrelated, is my theory. In this case, I listened to the four complainants one by one, and got the specific details of what had happened to them. Their complaints weren't major; just the sparks of discontent. But there were enough of them to possibly add up to a valid charge. I thought through what would happen if I took formal action against the department head they said was a racist, and who would be involved: our board, the other department heads, the student council, our public affairs officer, and so on. I then spent several days telephoning each of these people to sound them out, to find out what their past experiences had been and, without mentioning any names, to ask how a complaint about

racism would affect their area. I learned that it would cause a lot of trouble and alienate about fifty different people. So instead, I went to the department head in question and had a discussion with him. I suggested that he may have spent too little time getting to know his people, and that perhaps his work expectations were unrealistic. I also gave him some ideas as to how he could run his department a little differently. I could see that his abrupt manner with people may have had a lot to do with the complaints, so I did some discreet coaching as well, to help him handle his job more successfully. Fortunately, he was open to suggestion and cooperative. If he hadn't been, if he'd balked, I'd have said, "Well, I think we do have a real problem." But I still wouldn't have made an issue of the racism complaint if I could help it. I'd have tried to solve the problem first by asking some of the people I'd talked to on the phone to bring in their ideas for a workable solution.

What do you do if your job is threatened?

Maneuver so whoever is threatening you will dig his or her own grave. Leslie, the public relations director of a manufacturing conglomerate, had an experience you should know about. Her corporation had hired a public relations consultant who was so uncooperative and inept, she came close to handing in her resignation out of frustration and anger. But when she realized that what was really going on was a power struggle, she dug in her heels, determined not to let them lick her.

To understand Leslie's approach, you have to know her style. She is deliberately low key. Dresses quietly. Speaks in a low voice you have to strain to hear. Operates in a steady, calm, even rhythm. Yet she is an opinionated woman who feels strongly that her decisions are right. She wants no opposition, and her style is calculated to make people respect her so she can get her points across without argument. Leslie learned something about herself long ago: If she speaks forcefully, people resent her and try to fight back. She says, "It's better for a person like me to take the low road, even though it may seem like the long way home. Somebody else who's a jollier type, more 'one of the gang,' can get away with being direct." You'll see how that self-knowledge helped Leslie:

We're a fairly young company, and a couple of months ago we found ourselves in the position of having too much too soon. We'd been acquiring companies so fast and of such disparate nature, we couldn't keep up with ourselves. Our corporate name was obsolete. The business and financial press weren't sure what we represented. The public, meaning our potential stockholders, was mystified. We lacked definition, an identity, and I'd been doing everything to create one. In fact, I'd done a very good job, and I am certain that there were ulterior reasons why the chief executive officer brought in Ben as public relations consultant. To this day I don't know what those reasons were, but it's no longer important. What matters is the mess he caused.

I was told by the CEO that Ben would be with us on a nine-month contract, to apply his expertise to our image problem. And that he was to confer with each of our twelve company presidents, analyze our corporate position, and then submit written recommendations to the CEO and to me. I was to continue to perform my PR functions as I saw fit, in cooperation with Ben. I interpreted this to mean that my authority was undisturbed. Ben chose to read it otherwise: He thought he could make whatever changes he wanted to on his own. As far as I'm concerned, the CEO was foolish in defining Ben's position so loosely, and that was the root of most of the trouble.

Here's a list, which I've compiled for my files, of the things Ben did in his first two months:

1. Called for the financial statements of each of our companies, but failed to confer with any of their presidents.
2. Positioned the corporation as a consumer-oriented entity, when in fact all of our companies sell direct to manufacturers, not to the public.
3. Revised all twelve of our company logos at enormous expense and discarded our overall corporate trademark.
4. Failed, after my repeated requests, to submit any written recommendations.
5. Gave directions to my staff that conflicted with mine.

You can see what a tangle it was. What Ben did was negate all of my good work, countermand what I directed, and weaken the corporation's image considerably. Clearly, I had to protect myself. If he weakened the corporation further, my job would be in jeopardy: A PR department is always one of the first to go when there's financial difficulty. Or else he'd undermine my authority to the point where I'd be reduced to a small cog in the coporate machinery. Let me tell you, I spent plenty of sleepless nights plotting my strategy:

I could go to the CEO and tell him that Ben had fouled up. But that would make me look like a tattletale and a meddler, and would also have the effect of telling the chief executive officer he'd been wrong to hire Ben.

I could ask for a three-way meeting of Ben, myself and the CEO, state the facts of my case in an objective, unemotional manner, and ask each of them to suggest different ways we could handle the situation so we could reach our common goal successfully. But again, the cards were stacked against me. Ben was the CEO's boy, and I'd come off looking like nothing but a troublemaker.

I could start talking to people in the organization and let them know that Ben is inept. In this way, I could create allies, so that when we get into a him-or-me situation, I'll have a little army on my side who'll agree that I know what I'm doing, and he was a mistake. The trouble with that is, Ben already has considerable strength on his side, and it would wind up a battle of factions in a divided, unhappy office.

I could keep a flow of memos going to the CEO, with copies to Ben and the company presidents, so they'd know exactly what was going on from my point of view at all times. I decided this was a good move, with two provisos: I must remember that the CEO is not a memo-reader and back up the memos with phone calls. And I had better let my memos cool off for a day before I sent them. I tend to write heatedly when I'm mad, and these memos would be in the records. They had better lead off by saying something positive, and than very carefully and nonlibelously, make my points. Something like this:

> I am delighted with our new consultant and appreciate all the time and effort Ben has devoted to our corporate image problem. I am particularly pleased by his excellent suggestion that we standardize all internal forms. This will save the corporation several thousand dollars a year.
>
> A conflict has arisen that I would like to discuss with you informally, before our next staff meeting. It is a misunderstanding that I have temporarily resolved by putting out a memo to all staff that they are to report directly to me. A copy of the memo is attached, for your files.

Reviewing the options, I've decided to do the memos and to tell people my side of things. That will at least keep the record straight. And if the struggle gets nasty, it will shore up my standing with management. Ben is the kind who is sure to defend himself by calling me names or rewriting history. By the time he gets to that point, it will be too late. Everybody will already know that I have done my job and done it well. It won't even look as if I've been battling for supremacy, because I'll have kept personalities out of it.

What do you do when you get two sets of instructions and don't know which boss to report to?

If your boss and your boss's boss are telling you two different things, you should listen to your immediate boss. Then if his or her orders were wrong, you can leave it to superboss to take care of things. You will be out of the line of fire.

What if it keeps happening?

Go to your immediate boss and tell him/her the position you're in. Say you're not sure what you should do, since it's superboss who pays your salary. If your boss gets sticky about it . . .

Should I tell superboss?

Yes, but don't do it behind your boss's back. Let him or her know that you're having a problem and this is how you're trying to solve it.

Can you do it more informally in a small company?

Yes. Ask for a quick three-way meeting, explain the situation, and let them work it out between them.

What if my two bosses are partners in the company, and they don't speak?

Go to each of them individually, tell them you're being asked to do two different things, that it's impossible and you'd like them to straighten out who you should report to. If you can, offer them solutions they can choose from: A part-time worker to take on some of your load may be the answer that they haven't thought of.

What if the two bosses I'm caught between are the president of my company and our client?

Do what you have to do to keep all lines of communication open so that you do not become a pawn shoved back and forth by the people you work for, the way Abbie did:

189

I was to produce a videotape that would introduce a new product in department stores. The client wanted two sets of dialogue that would fit into six vignettes. I listened very carefully, went back to the office, and wrote the script. When I showed it to my boss, he said, "They don't know what they're talking about. They don't know how to market anything. Do it this way." So, since I worked for this man, I changed the scripts and took them back to the client. For this I got screamed at. "This isn't what I asked for," the client yelled. Of course I knew it wasn't, but I was caught in the middle and didn't know who to listen to. How do you resolve that kind of thing? I had to go back to my boss and say, "He wants six vignettes and two sets of dialogue, period. We bombed with what I brought him and now I'm over budget." He answered, "You're the clever producer, you resolve it." So I figured out a compromise, and then went out of my way to deliver it to the client's house on a Saturday so he'd feel I'd given him special attention. It wasn't a very good solution because it wasn't what he really wanted. If it happens again, what I'll do is ask my boss to put in a three-way conference call so he, the client, and I can discuss the project directly, and I won't be caught in the middle.

How do you handle people who yell at you?

Unemotionally. The minute you start to take a business scream personally and react on an emotional level, you lose your ability to control the situation. You wind up in a yelling match, with the focus on passion and not on the facts. You have to be objective about people who criticize or call you names, and realize that most likely they are giving vent to their own frustrations. People yell when they feel thwarted, or guilty, or unsure of themselves. It's their way of letting off steam when they don't know how to take care of a problem. What you have to do is cool off that steam. Let's suppose that you've submitted a design, a report, whatever you were assigned to do, and your boss hurls it on the table and yells, "That's absolutely the worst job I've ever seen. It's unacceptable and I don't know how anybody could turn out such rubbish." If you react emotionally, you could produce a scene like this:

YOU: That is not rubbish and you have no right to yell at me that way.

BOSS: I have a right to yell at you any way I want to. Don't tell me what to do. I'm the boss around here and if you can't do your work right and insist on challenging me besides, I'll just have to make some changes.

Now consider the same situation with you handling it factually, detached from emotion or personality:

YOU: I'm sorry you feel that way. If you'll let me, I'd like to explain the thinking behind this report so you can see if I understood your instructions correctly. I think that basically it does the job, and I'd like your suggestions as to how I can improve it.

BOSS: You want me to patch it up for you? OK, but I just wish I didn't have to do everybody else's work for them.

At least you have roped your boss into listening to you. If he or she still doesn't like the job after you've tried to sell it, do not feel hurt. It's the job that's been rejected, not you. Just throw it away and start over again. You may be the target of more yelling on your second submission, but hang in there. As long as you can take this boss's style and not be upset by it, you can make use of the opportunity to learn how to do things so they're satisfactory. Of course, if you're the target of repeated irrational abuse, you'll probably start looking around for another job or a transfer. And you'll be right: If your boss consistently refuses to listen to reasonable explanations and is nasty about it, you are in a no-win situation and you should get out.

Lorraine, a saleswoman for a cosmetics concern, says she'd been the butt of a surly employer for so long that she was on the brink of tears every time he stepped into her office. As a matter of fact, she has always been hypersensitive to criticism, and about a year ago went into therapy to try to overcome this handicap. She says she has gained a great understanding of herself and what makes other people tick, as well. Her awareness has enabled her to cope with her boss, although he is no less surly than he's ever been. Lorraine gave me a very specific instance of what she means:

I worked for Neal, who is the vice-president in charge of sales, for four years, and it seemed whatever I did was either wrong, stupid, or not good enough. My feelings were so battered that if Neal said, "Good morning," I'd hear it as "Here comes that dimwit Lorraine. What's she going to screw up today?" I was so uncomfortable that my tension made other people uncomfortable, too. One day I had a heart-to-heart about it with a good friend. She pointed out that I was frequently punished as a kid, and I grew up believing that everything I did was wrong. My friend said, "Conditioning like that is very hard to disbelieve, and I don't think you can overcome it all by yourself. I'd like to suggest a therapist who might help you. If it works, you'll feel a lot better about yourself, and other people will find you easier to deal with. If it doesn't, well, what have you got to lose?"

I took her advice and concentrated hard on the therapist's suggestions. She'd ask me questions like, "This boss you have, Neal, does he attack you personally when he yells about your work? Do you think he could have another reason for yelling?" I'd have to think it through and come up with alternatives, which she'd play back to me— making me continue the thought process. What she did was remove my emotional responses and allow me to see people as individuals who are responding to their own problems. The turning point came when Neal blew up over the way I'd handled a customer order. Instead of taking it as a personal attack, I realized that Neal didn't have all the information on the order that he needed, and was frustrated because he couldn't find a solution. So I said, "Neal, I'll take care of the problem for you. Let me get back to you in an hour and I'll fill in the details that are missing." As if on cue, he quieted down and went back to what he'd been doing. When I brought in the answer, he took it, said, "Thanks," and that was that. He could relax once he knew that somebody had the solution to his problem. He didn't need to think about it or be angry anymore. That proved to me that Neal's "attacks" were all in my mind. What they really were was problems he'd been stuck on. Just give him the solutions and he's happy as a clam.

How can I get my boss to stop using me as a scapegoat?

Are you really a scapegoat, or are you being assigned a legitimate role? Sometimes a higher-up can get more done by staying out of the line of fire and sending in a subordinate to do the dirty work. That doesn't mean the subordinate is a scapegoat; he or she is the effective tool without whom the boss could not function. To see how the method works, imagine that you are a boss who wants the board of directors to increase his budget for executive salaries. If he issues a letter to that effect to the board, they will read it as an attempt to increase his own pay. So he asks you, his deputy budget director, to send the letter over your signature. The board can then assess the request on its objective merits and make its decision in terms of money and not personality. And if they're wise to the method your boss is using, they still can't accuse him of trying to jack up his own salary. Everybody comes out clean. Were you used? Certainly. Is that terrible? No, it's your job. Have you lost anything by signing that letter? No, you have helped your boss reach his objective and, incidentally, got your name before the very influential board members.

Of course, some people really are scapegoats. They invite the treatment because they would rather be used than a user. They are willing to do their own job and everyone else's besides, without credit or pay. They are always willing to do the dirty work, and they seem so happy about it that people never think of asking them to do anything else.

How can I stop being a scapegoat?

Practice what they teach in assertiveness-training courses. In the examples that follow, the assertive statements communicate your needs clearly and without anger. The passive, apologetic statements obscure your needs and will help keep you in the position of a scapegoat.

ASSERTIVE	PASSIVE
My time is booked full today. Would you like me to ask Laurie to go to the post office for you?	Of course I don't mind your asking. Sure I'll go to the post office on my lunch hour.
I feel frustrated when you make general complaints about my work. I think we'd have more success if you could tell me exactly what it is you are looking for.	I'm sorry that I always seem to mess things up.
I can't respond to that right now. Give me an hour or two to think about it.	Yes. No. I don't know. I haven't had any experience. I shouldn't say this but the question is over my head.

I feel this is an urgent matter and I'd like to have your decision on it this week. Can we meet Thursday afternoon, to wrap it up?	This is the third time I've asked for a decision. I'm sorry to keep nagging you. Would you mind if I ask you again next week?

The point of assertiveness is to let people understand your needs and to reapportion the balance of power so you have a say in what happens to you. It is a problem-solving technique, with communication as the tool.

Do older executives sometimes become disinterested in their work?

Yes. They may have done the same thing so long that they are bored by repetition, or they may have personal problems that sap their vitality. They may have no initiative, and no boss to keep their enthusiasm lively. They are apt to become what's known as deadwood: somebody who is taking up space and a salary, and not earning his or her keep. Or these people may have let down because they are nearing retirement: their minds are on the gold watch and fishing for trout. People like this come to work, do their jobs, and go home without making a ripple. They're disinterested, disengaged. They'll say: "Sure, that sounds good" when you present an idea that could benefit the company. But they have no intention of becoming involved. They did all that when they were hotshot youngsters; now it's time to relax and forget it. You have to forgive them for feeling that way, especially if they really did contribute to the company in their time.

Can you take over a deadwood's job?

You may have the opportunity, but you had better think carefully before you make your move. Be very realistic about yourself, and about your position in the company. Really think it through. And get feedback. I'd suggest you do what Bonnie, a nutritionist, did. She was all set to go after her boss's job, until she sat down with her mentor, Lenore, and talked out all the possible consequences:

LENORE: As I understand it, Bonnie, you've been turning in a very solid performance for the past nine years.

BONNIE: That's about right. Of course, I still don't have my doctoral degree, and haven't built a national reputation for myself.

LENORE: Which your boss Scott has. Let's start to build a list of pros and cons about the decision you're trying to reach. It always helps me to have things in writing.

BONNIE: That's a good idea. You can write on the balance sheet that Scott has both of those things, and has certainly been around a lot longer than I. He's sixty-one years old, you know, and will retire from the company in three years.

LENORE: Now, Bonnie, would you sum up for me what has happened to you to date?

BONNIE: Scott was out sick for four months. During that time I took over his responsibilities and reported directly to the head of the company. By the time Scott came back to work, I had everything completely under control. He really had nothing to do, so he made busywork that is taking up too much of my time and is driving me up the wall.

LENORE: Exactly what kind of busywork?

BONNIE: Oh, Lenore! He goes over and over and over all of my written reports quibbling with me about whether they should be in the past tense or the present, if there should be a colon or a semi-colon, if all caps mightn't be better than underscoring phrases for emphasis.

LENORE: Let's write that down. What do you think you should do about it?

BONNIE: I'm going to the president and tell him that this is absurd. Scott's wasting my time and effort and the work would go better without him.

LENORE: Let's look back at our balance sheet and see if we can predict what will happen. Scott's a sixty-one-year-old man with a national reputation, has served the company well for many years, and will retire in a short time. In my

195

opinion, the president's hands are tied: He can't fire Scott at this point. But he can learn to think of you as a trouble-maker. You'd be a sitting duck in a losing battle.

BONNIE: Do you mean I should just go along listening to Scott discourse on semi-colons? I've got better things to do than that!

LENORE: I agree. And here's how you can do them. Use the time while Scott is picking over your reports to figure out your other problems in your head. Go over outlines of the other projects you have in mind. Make concrete plans for what you will do when Scott retires and they bring in his replacement . . .

BONNIE: But I want to be his replacement!

LENORE: Will your name be as valuable to the company as his has been? That's one of the criteria they'll be judging you on. They want a nationally known expert, and you're going to have to work very hard to catch up in three years on what Scott's built in forty.

BONNIE: How do you think I could do it?

LENORE: Get your doctorate. See that you're published. Sit on important committees. Build up a national reputation. In other words, use your energies constructively for your future, rather than giving in to the daily trivial irritations and, in fact, getting so crotchety that Scott may decide to fire you.

BONNIE: Whew! That's a tall order, but I think you are absolutely right. If I do all that, what do you think my chances are of stepping into Scott's shoes three years from now?

LENORE: Fifty-fifty. The company is quite likely to find somebody else with a Scott-size reputation, one that's bigger than yours. But try it, because that way at least you will have a chance. And if you don't get Scott's job you will be in a better position to go to another company at a high level.

Does it mean that I'm doing something wrong if I have problems all the time?

Absolutely not. The one time you won't have problems is when you are dead. Or have decided not to move ahead. As long as you are alive and doing well, you will always have problems on your hands. That's life. You face one set of challenges, solve them, move on, and *wham*—there's a fresh set to figure out. Of course, you are free to choose *which* set you want to solve. Or whether you want any new challenges at all. But having new problems all the time does not mean you are doing something wrong. It means you are progressing, and must be doing something right.

Let me stress the word "new." If you find that you are dealing with the same old difficulties over and over, that's your clue that you are at a standstill. At that point you are in trouble, and you had better start to make changes.

What can I do about the pileup of jobs on my desk?

• Stay organized. Handle each piece of paper that comes to your desk only once. Instead of riffling through the IN box clutter again and again, deal with each memo, letter, or clipping the first time you pick it up. Read, process, then file or destroy it. Otherwise you will waste hours rereading each paper, rummaging through the pile, wondering if it's too late to respond to this or that communiqué.

• Have a written plan of action on your desk each day: a calendar marked off in hours, or a schedule your assistant types up for you.

• Try to keep up with trade publications as they come in, instead of letting them pile up and go out of date. Your secretary can preread and underscore magazines and papers for you, so you don't need to wade through every line yourself.

How do I know what to do first?

Learn to set priorities. You have to recognize what tasks are urgent, which calls are important, and what jobs can wait for a while. What you do is key your priorities to your boss's objectives, then organize the work load and make sure you take care of first things first. You also have to learn to anticipate your boss's needs, so problems don't swell into crises. Experience will teach you to set priorities.

Intelligence will hone your judgment. Pride will make you a valuable assistant to the executive who is too busy to do what you're hired for.

Can you teach somebody to set priorities?

You can, if the person you are in charge of is bright and willing. Bring them into your thinking. Keep explaining the reasons why each task must be done. Set guidelines: "In this office, our reports to clients take priority over everything else excepting emergencies. Any emergency jobs must be cleared with me first." You have to be patient, and allow leeway for practice and error—up to a point. If you have an assistant who keeps on muffing the job and you cannot refine their sense of priorities, you will have to find a replacement. You cannot afford to let somebody stand in the way of getting your job done efficiently.

How much work should a manager delegate?

As much as possible. The idea is to get other people to execute details and leave you free for the big picture. Your job as the person in charge is to plan and make major decisions, not to spend time carrying out what you have planned. You have to learn to hand over the actual doing to somebody else.

There is an art to delegating, and at the same time controlling the people you assign tasks to. It is important that you learn the art well: An axiom of business is that the best leaders are those who delegate most effectively. Yet, many women find delegating one of the most difficult business skills to master. We are unaccustomed to letting somebody else do our work; often we're afraid they will not do it as well, so we can't let go of the reins. It is hard to learn not to nurture, hover, handle every detail. We tell ourselves: "It's easier to do the job myself than to explain how to do it. Anyway, they won't do it the way I would."

So what? It's true that nobody else can read your mind. But they can learn to know what you want. Teach them. Take your support people to meetings with you. Have them monitor selected phone calls. Train them to be your clipping service; your reservations agent; your customer follow-up person; your eyes, ears, and extra set of brains. The more they know about your job the easier it will be for you. While you are at it, kill two birds with one stone: Have your assistant set up a book of procedures. Then if he or she is out sick or leaves the job, the next person can pick up the pieces and you won't have to go through the training process all over again.

Failure to delegate is self-defeating. If you don't give your staff enough responsibility, they will become bored, frustrated, rebellious, and disrespectful. You have to give people work to do and then let them execute it in their own style. Otherwise you will stifle their potential, and limit your productivity.

What are the techniques of delegating?

First you must identify what has to be done. Then you have to organize a plan for its execution and establish the priorities. Then you are ready to delegate. There are two major steps in the process: (1) Decide who is best suited to carry out the details. (2) Stay on top of the job until it is successfully completed.

1. Who Is Best Suited?

• Somebody who knows the subject and is close to the matter on a day-to-day basis.
• A person who is eager, and able to be taught.
• Somebody able to make basic, day-by-day decisions.
• A person you can depend on to complete assigned tasks, independently or with supervision.

Which candidate you select depends on how important the task is. To test your choice, ask yourself these questions:

• Are the stakes so high that you cannot risk mistakes?
• Is it worth your while to spend time grooming this person?

2. Stay on Top of the Job Throughout.

Assign the Job. It is not enough to say, "Michael, will you please go to the library and get me a list of electronics companies within a fifty-mile radius?" You must say, "I want only the companies that manufacture components for small appliances, and that do a volume of five hundred thousand dollars or more." You have to give specific, complete instructions.

Set a Timetable. The list must be on my desk no later than March 10.

Give Guidelines. Your research is to be done between the hours of 1:00 and 4:00 only, so that you will be in the office during our busy morning hours. You may take as many afternoons as you need to do the job thoroughly by March 10. You are to return to the office every day from the library, so you can keep up with your daily routine.

Set a Budget. You will be reimbursed up to fifty dollars by bookkeeping for transportation and photocopies. Submit vouchers for all taxi and copy-shop expenses.

Establish Authority. You are the only person assigned to this task. Contact me if you find that you need assistance.

Request Confirmation. Please tell me now if this assignment creates any conflicts for you. Tell me before you begin the work whether you are completely clear about the instructions. Check back with me as you progress if you have any questions.

Here are some general guidelines to help you delegate effectively:

Give Reporting Instructions. There are six ways to instruct people you delegate work to:

1. Take action and report to me on completion.
2. Take action and keep me informed of your progress.
3. Investigate the problem, give me your recommendation, and then take action.
4. Investigate, recommend, and then wait until I approve action.
5. Investigate the problem and give me as many alternative recommendations as possible. Include the advantages and disadvantages of each, and tell me which of the alternatives you think is best.
6. Investigate the problem and give me all the facts. I will then decide what to do.

Stay in Control. It is your function as leader to see that everything goes as it should. Therefore, you must be in constant control of whatever you delegate. Set checkpoints: a system of early warning signals that will avert May Day disasters.

Practice Cost Control. Before you do any delegating, stop and figure out whether the results will be worth the time and money invested, and if they will enable you to take useful or valuable action.

Establish a Timetable. Set a deadline for when the task is to be completed, and set checkpoints along the way so you can measure progress and make changes if the work-rate is lagging.

Request Progress Reports. Get verbal or written feedback at set intervals so you can iron out snags, be sure your delegatee stays on goal, and evaluate situational changes that may dictate a fresh course of action.

Suppose the person to whom you've delegated work is messing up?

Take corrective action. If the job is not going well, do not hesitate to alter your plan, reassign personnel, or provide them with different resources or equipment. Before you make changes, find out why there is a problem. You can waste a great deal of time treating symptoms, when you should perform surgery on the cause.

What shouldn't you delegate to other people?

Direct reports to your client, customer, or boss.

Always remember that the person who has direct access to the top is the person who has the power, especially if he or she is convincing and can sell ideas. Once you give away your client or boss contact and they find they can get what they want from somebody else, you give up your power and territory.

Sometimes it's a temptation to delegate power contact. You may have a bright assistant who is more knowledgeable than you about bothersome details. You'd like to get rid of the nitty-gritty and tell him or her to deal with management directly. Stop. Think it through. Is your assistant good at dealing with personalities? Does he or she know how to read warning signals? Or have a thorough knowledge of the industry? If your assistant doesn't meet these criteria and you surrender your turf, you will lose your control, your client, and your importance in the situation.

You have to set priorities in the number of relationships you can control effectively. If you have a minor client or customer, delegating contact with them can let you make better use of your time. But keep on top of the person to whom you delegate, and do not let them feel alone. Go over their conference reports with them. Discuss the decisions they are making. Don't let go the reins altogether. If you are having an office party, extend an invitation to the customer personally. Call them from time to time and let them know you are interested in their problems. Let them think that you are supervising your surrogate every step of the way. And be prepared for the fact that your assistant may win the client's confidence and take them from you when he or she moves on to another company. If you have made sure that it's only a minor client you gave away, the loss will not hurt you.

HOW TO RUN A MEETING:

Strategies for Group Control

Why is my boss always in meetings?

It's part of the job. To be effective, managers have to keep abreast of what's going on in the company as well as in their department. They go to meetings to get in on corporate decisions. To express their needs and opinions. Get other people's agreement on their plans. Stay informed, exert control, and keep in touch with the big picture.

Meetings are the crossroads of management. Smart career people take advantage of them to gain visibility and add to their power.

Why so many meetings?

The higher you are in management, the more areas you are responsible for and the more decisions you have to get in on. That means more meetings.

When you are in a support position, a weekly staff meeting may be all you're expected to attend. As you go up the ladder and add to your duties, you have to cover departmental as well as staff meetings. and don't forget special committee meetings. Subcommittee meetings. Executive meetings. By the time you become a key executive, all of these bodies will require your input and decision-making ability. The question at that point is, which of the myriad meetings you're invited to are effective and which are a waste of time.

What makes an effective meeting?

A skilled leader. A person with conference-room skills who knows how to cover the six basic requirements of a production meeting:

1. Set clear objectives.
2. Prepare all details thoroughly.
3. Stick to a timetable.
4. Keep everyone interested.
5. Get your ideas across.
6. Get action.

How do you get your ideas across in a meeting?

With practice and skill. Let's watch how Louise learned to do it. She is a tall, lanky, well-educated woman of thirty-five or so; reserved in manner and very goal-oriented. At present she is the district manager of a group of suburban banks, a position she won only after she put in time as a secretary. Louise says she has no regrets about the eight years she spent on the lower rungs: "It led to a line job because I was persistent. I firmly believe that any intelligent secretary can learn almost everything she needs to know about top-level management if she keeps her eyes, ears, and mind open. And then does something about it." Louise did plenty: She took business administration courses, joined trade associations, and cultivated a network of people who could help her get ahead. She had to put out a lot of effort because, as you know, although banking is loaded with women at the teller and middle management level, as an industry it still resists women who want to occupy chairs at the top. Nonetheless, that is where Louise plans to be inside of six years. You can be sure that whatever she does now as district manager is well calculated to move her toward her goal:

I had been told by top management to increase my banks' sales by 10 percent. Meaning, attract more large depositors, make bigger loans, persuade customers to put their money in our hands. Management gave me no plan, no guidance, no offers of support. Just the directive. I had to start from scratch: meet with my people and map a campaign.

First, I went through the four initial steps of problem-solving that I'd learned at business school: Refine the problem, think up all the conceivable solutions, assess the various solutions' feasibility, and select the best of the lot. The reasoning that led me to choose a particular solution went like this: "My objective is to increase our sales 10 percent. To do this, we have to halt the erosion of our business caused by all the new competitive foreign banks. We have to sell against them. At present my banks are structured according to banking functions, and I am the only person designated as sales. To get more business we need more salespeople. We could have them without adding to staff if our tellers and bank managers also act as sales representatives in an active campaign to sell services and get new accounts.

To complete the problem-solving process, I had to put it into action. I decided to present my sales plan at our next staff meeting, where everyone would be able to receive the information at one time, air any doubts or complaints, add suggestions and techniques, and become part of an enthusiastic team. I wanted that meeting to be effective, so I took the trouble to do preliminary spadework. First I went to the head teller and each manager individually, told them the plan, and asked for their ideas as to how we could best achieve our goal. My purpose was to have nine people come to the meeting already mentally adjusted to their new function. I wanted them to come with additional ideas, a feeling of involvement, and an eagerness to follow through on my plan because parts of it would be their own suggestion. I was lobbying, to gain acceptance.

Next, recognizing that I still had to sell my idea to the staff, I wrote an outline of what I would say to them and rehearsed it from beginning to end until I felt completely sure of myself. I even rehearsed the obligatory gestures, nods, smiles, and return to my seat, so I wouldn't have to cope with details that could distract or unsettle me.

At the meeting, the staff voiced many objections, as I had anticipated they would. Several were valid. The head teller pointed out that her staff would require sales training and would not relish the additional meetings that would mean. With some—shall we say guidance?—from me, we worked out a schedule where the training sessions would be limited to short periods, and the trainees would be rewarded for their efforts.

I would call this meeting successful. It put me in a strong position of leadership. It led to achieving the goal management had set. And it defused the resentment my staff might have felt toward me if I had just handed out dictatorial instructions. I think the results were worth the effort I put in. I'd had an idea, I'd sold it, and I'd set it up so I would stay in control of the follow-up.

Tell me how to run a meeting, start to finish.

Skillfully, the way Louise ran her staff meeting:

Start on time.	Begin promptly, even if there are only one or two people in the room. The others will learn quickly to be punctual for the next meeting.
State your objective.	Louise defined the problem in positive terms, clearly, so that everyone would focus on the same goal: "The purpose of

this meeting is to work out the process by which we will increase our sales 10 percent."

Decide how the group is to discuss the problem and make decisions.

If Louise wanted to railroad the group and get them to agree with her preconceived conclusions, she would have adopted an *autocratic* style. But she had done enough spadework to know that she would have to overcome resistance.

Optional participatory style.

So she chose a *participatory* style: She opened up the discussion so others could inject their ideas.

Keep the discussion relevant.

When somebody strayed from the subject, she forced them back on track by saying, "How would that relate to our objective?"

Redefine, clarify, and summarize throughout.

Louise summarized frequently to keep the basic problem plainly in sight, reestablish her point, and add new dimensions. For example, when the talk turned to their need to attract small-business customers, she made the point clear: "We're agreed, then, that in order to increase our sales 10 percent, one of the things we must work out is how to attract small-business owners to our banks."

Involve the groups in problem-solving. Give them credit.

To open up avenues for problem-solving, Louise said, "Meg has suggested that we do a direct mail campaign to small-business owners, their accountants and attorneys. Does anyone else have additional suggestions?" To encourage a flow of fresh ideas, she made the group feel free to explore alternatives: "Let's play a game where the only skill you need is imagination, and there are no wrong an-

Look for options.

Keep an open climate.

Keep enthusiasm high.

Keep the discussion open until you get plenty of ideas. Summarize and evaluate the alternatives.

Reassess the options and select the best.

Decide how to implement the plan. Conclude the discussion firmly, so it does not straggle on.

swers. The object is to come up with as many ways as you can think of to bring more traffic into our banks. Anything goes and all things are possible. Let's see how many different solutions you can give me to write down on the blackboard." Louise got the ball rolling with a practical strategy, to give them ideas, and a blue-sky idea to give them zest for the game. "What if we gave away a pocket calculator to every customer, old or new, on their birthday? Or suppose we hire a mime troupe as our spokespeople on TV, to attract attention?

Without comment, she wrote down every idea they offered. When she felt the flow of good ideas was exhausted, she said, "Now let's see what we have." Then she evaluated each idea in terms of its feasibility and potential value. When she was through, Louise had agreement from the room on five viable options:

1. Newspaper and radio advertising campaign.
2. Direct mail campaign to small-business owners, their accountants and attorneys.
3. Gifts for new depositors.
4. Financial seminars for the public.
5. Sales training sessions.

Number two, the direct mail campaign, was the option Louise liked best, so she sold it to the group by presenting it in a way that would benefit them: "A direct mail campaign will help us increase traffic and won't burden you with extra work. We can have an outside PR group handle

209

Keep summarizing.

Use deadlines to get action.

Delegate tasks to ensure support of your project.

Leave room for subcommittee questions without taking the entire group's time.

Conclude the meeting firmly.

the details for us, and report to me on their progress." Louise explained additional details and then wrapped it up: "We have decided to attract more small-business accounts by a six-month direct mail campaign, starting March first. I will contact an agency and ask for a proposal management can approve in advance. Second, Jeff and Meg are to look into gifts for new depositors. They will give us a report two weeks from today. Our third project is to explore sales training methods. Charlotte, will you please ask four other people in this room to comprise a task force with you, and report your findings and recommendations at our next meeting? If any of you on committees have questions, please check with me before you leave.

"The meeting is now adjourned. Thank you."

What are some other reasons to call a meeting?

Louise doesn't always have an urgent need for her meetings. She calls them every six weeks anyway so that she can touch base with all of the people who work for her. That way, nobody feels ignored, and everybody can communicate. She is building a team where cooperation and common goals are the overriding considerations. If she directed her people separately all the time, they would lose that feeling of unity and understanding.

Louise also makes it a point to connect informally with each member of her team as often as she can: several times a week when that's possible, once a week when she is snowed under with work. She doesn't want to lose the personal touch. Whenever she can't manage the once-a-week visits, she buzzes each of her people by phone, and says, "I'm just checking in to see how things are going. Did you straighten out that customer-loan problem you had last week? Is there some way I can help you?" The effect of all this connecting is that Louise's people get the feeling that she cares about their progress. They also get the feeling that she knows everything they are doing. A little Big Sisterism doesn't hurt.

Is social conversation acceptable at a formal meeting?

Yes, at the opening stages, when people are settling down. Once the meeting gets going and the agenda is in swing, extended small talk is out of place.

The purpose of meetings is to get something done. You will make points if you have something valuable to say when you speak. Be substantial. Know what you're talking about. Remember that you are on full display, and avoid irrelevancies and nonsense like the plague. Your role is to be a useful addition to the meeting: one of the people they'll want to invite to future meetings where important things happen.

How do you get people to come to a meeting?

There are three ways to call a conference: by memo, phone, or in person.

1. To announce a meeting by memo:

Send a notice like this one to the participants.

	MEETING NOTICE	Title calls attention to purpose of memo.
From:	Jane Jones	Your name.
To:	F. Archer, N. Bates. L. Brown, C. Little, J. Stewart, C. Wise	Alphabetically, so noses won't be out of joint.
Time:	Thurs., June 6, 3:00	The details for their calenders.
Place:	Conference Room 401	Neutral territory.

Subject: Status Reports, Dept. Activities

Announced purpose. (You may have another unannounced reason such as putting through a departmental change.)

AGENDA

You want each participant to come to the meeting prepared to contribute to the proceedings. You also want a strict outline of subjects to be discussed, so you can control the meeting and not waste time on digressions.

1. JONES: Announcements

You plan to tell the group that you have hired a new staff member. You want to present the news personally so you can field any dissent and disarm the rumor mill.

2. ARCHER: Report on Project Y, development of new product
3. BROWN: Search results, outside consultant
4. LITTLE: Product Y, packaging sources
5. STEWART: Feasibility study
6. WISE: Market research analysis
7. NEW BUSINESS

You will control this portion of the meeting tightly and not let people use it to gripe or air inconsequential matters.

You don't have to distribute an agenda for every meeting. Sometimes you want to keep the agenda open so that you can encourage fresh ideas from the group. You may want to create curiousity about why you are calling them in. Or you may be calling a fast meeting with no time or real need for a formal agenda.

2. To call a meeting by phone:

Just call and invite people. State the purpose of your meeting, the time, date and place, and tell them what you would like them to think about or prepare. Make sure your meeting is actually on their calendar.

- Follow up with a memo restating the time, place, and purpose of your meeting.
- Ask their secretary to be sure your meeting is posted on their boss's calendar.
- Ask the person you are calling to check their calendar while you hold the phone, and to write down the time, place, and purpose.

3. To invite people in person:

Go to their office, stop them in the hall, speak to them at lunch, or wherever you see them. But again, do something to make sure your meeting is on their calendar. Memories are short, schedules are heavy, and excuses for not going to meetings are easy to come by.

When do you call a fast meeting?

In an emergency. When a situation comes up that you must deal with quickly. Keep track of how many fast meetings you call. If you find they've become a steady routine, watch out. It means you're putting out too many fires, and something is wrong.

Where is the best place to hold meetings?

In your own office or in a conference room. When you hold a meeting in your office, you are the host and you are in control. A conference room is good because it seats more people than an office, can be set up more formally, and is impersonal. In neutral territory as well as in your office, make sure that everyone knows you are the host. Stay in control. Do not let anyone preempt your authority.

The one place not to hold your meeting if you can help it is in somebody else's office. The other person automatically owns the territory, and you will have to work harder to stay in charge.

Should you call meetings when they appoint you to head up a task force?

Yes. A task force is a working subcommittee. To do your job, you will have to meet with the people you've been appointed to head. Here are some pointers on heading a task force:

1. Keep your task force small. More than nine people usually is an unwieldly group.

2. Appoint an even number to your committee, to avoid deadlocks on votes. As chairman, you will cast the last vote when the others are tied.

3. Do not load your committee with other women. Choose your workers on the basis of effectiveness, not gender. Remember that you have two goals: to accomplish the project and to make yourself look good.

4. You can extend the main chairperson's style or use your own. Directive or participatory, whatever works and is comfortable for you is right.

5. Use other authorities to strengthen your leadership. When you think your committee will resist you, tell them management is concerned about your project and anxious that it be completed in time for the next board meeting. Offer to help, if any of them has a problem. In this way you will:

Retain leadership
Link your authority with management's
Get rid of excuses for inaction
Establish a firm deadline.

What is the purpose of lunch meetings?

Not to eat. When somebody asks you to a lunch meeting, it's to conduct business. Their purpose is to set up an informal situation where they can play host, and make their points when you are relaxed. Go along with them. You can often learn more in restaurant conversation than you can in a conference room.

You have to understand the protocol of a lunch meeting. Although the purpose is to conduct business, it is considered poor form to discuss nothing but. You want them to feel relaxed and open. You can wait until dessert to get down to business. If time is short and you have a lot to discuss, it is all right to focus on your subject sooner.

With whom do I set up lunch meetings?

Whomever you're trying to sell an idea, or whoever's ideas you want to hear. Whether you're a manager or an assistant, it's a good idea to meet with your co-workers at lunch. You can learn a lot about what's going on in other departments. If you are a secretary, you can help your boss by taking another boss's secretary to lunch. Use the meeting to strengthen your working relationship. When you suggest the idea to your boss, be sure to explain that the purpose of your lunch is business. If he or she doesn't tell you to put the bill on an expense account, bring the subject up yourself. Say, "I'm glad you think it's a good idea for me to take Mr. X's secretary to lunch, so we can build up a liaison with his office. Shall I pay for the bill out of petty cash, or would you rather I charge it to the company?"

When should you not attend meetings?

When you know they are a waste of time.

When they are held for insignificant reasons and will not add to your visibility.

When they are called by a rival who wants to dominate what you are doing.

Rivalry is everywhere, especially in large bureaucratic corporations such as government agencies, where power and turf are the name of the game. Lorna, a city commissioner in charge of transportation, skipped meetings purposely when she found herself in a territorial power play with the commissioner of communications:

This job is the first one I've had in the public sector, and at first I didn't know about the internal politics of politics. I learned it in a hurry. The most time-consuming activities here are fielding curves, creating an image of dominance for yourself, and attending meetings. Usually, the three are a package, as they were in my battle with Daphne. Before I came in and took charge, Daphne controlled my department. Needless to say, she did not bow out willingly. She did everything in her power to look bigger than I: no mean ambition considering the fact that I am five ten and weigh in at 180, before lunch. But she has gall. She'd issue memos directing my staff to submit reports to her, an activity I promptly snuffed by telling my people they were not to respond. When that didn't work, she inaugurated a series of report meetings for all department heads in her private office. She figured by playing gracious hostess and concerned executive to the other commissioners, she could get them to acknowledge that she was top dog. They loved being invited and walked dutifully into her web every week. Not me. I knew what her motive was, and I intended to keep my activities under my own thumb. Getting credit is very important in this business.

When I got Daphne's first meeting memo, I lobbed it into the wastebasket and went onto something else. Daphne is not accustomed to being ignored and had a fit. Ten minutes after her meeting, her secretary called and said Daphne wondered where I'd been. I wasn't about to make excuses. I just said, "Please tell her I'm sure it was a constructive meeting." The next week Daphne called herself, before the meeting. "Lorna dear," she oozed, "we are all so pleased with the wonderful job you are doing. The mayor himself told me he's happy he hired you." She was implying that she had His Potency's ear and if I knew what was good for me, I'd better be good to her. She went on: "I want to be sure you are at my next meeting so we can all hear the marvelous plans you have for transportation. We want to work with you to make them as effective as possible." Condescending bitch. OK, I thought, I'll play the game. But watch out because you are not going to win. What I did was send my notoriously loyal assistant to the meeting, a four-fold message Daphne caught on to immediately. One, I was putting her down by sending a subordinate. Two, the subordinate was a spy. Three, my assistant would only say what I told her to say, and could not be probed. Four, if Daphne argued with my assistant, she would only put herself at an assistant's level. The old girl never tried to put a lasso around my territory again.

You have just seen two very strong, career-oriented women in a classic battle of wits. Lorna may not like her rival, but Daphne is an intelligent woman. She recognized Lorna's signals as soon as the assistant showed up at the meeting. She realized that she could not win over a strong rival. She backed off before she weakened herself. Daphne was disarmed, and there was nobody she could complain to.

Should I take the minutes at a meeting?

Yes, if you are the official recording secretary. Yes, but not too often, if you just happen to be the only woman at the meetings. There is nothing terrible about taking notes once in a while. But if you agree to do it too often, the men will naturally assume that the secretarial duty is your strong suit. You will be typecast as the perennial stenographer.

The same thing holds true when you are in meetings with other women. You cannot sit there taking notes at every meeting if you want to be a leader. For one thing, it's impossible to perform both functions simultaneously. For another, it's a signal that you are willing to give up the leadership to somebody else.

In meetings with men or with women, the smart thing to do when they say, "Who will take notes?" is to look expectantly at somebody else. If nobody volunteers, say, "Frank, how about you?" Or, you can set it up so you take notes only at a few of the meetings: "I was happy to take the notes last month. Why don't we take turns, and let a different person do it at each meeting?"

How do you take the notes as recording secretary in a formal meeting?

Formal meetings may follow parliamentary procedure, and the recording secretary will write notes accordingly. The style is brief and factual, as follows:

Type of meeting and/or purpose	**STAFF MEETING**
Date	February 3, 1980
Place	Held in Conference Room B
Time meeting was called to order; name of presiding officer.	The meeting was called to order by the department manager, Ms. Constance Brown, at 3:30 P.M.

Attending	Present: Diane Black, Constance Brown, Edward Green, Stephen Grey, Ellen Jones, Tom White
Absent	Absent: Michael Squires
Statement that minutes of last meeting were read and approved, approved without reading, or not read.	The minutes of the staff meeting of January 27, 1980, were approved without reading.

Report of Special Committee

The report of the committee on arrangements for the spring sales meeting was read by Edward Green, chairman. It was moved by Ms. Jones to accept the report. The motion was carried.

Statement of reports read; and whether accepted as read, amended, or referred for further study.

Unfinished Business

It was moved by Mr. White that the administrative manager take the necessary steps to acquire additional temporary help for the department. The motion was carried.

Main motions, and whether carried or not, referred to committee, or postponed. Use exact wording of the person who made the motion.

New Business

It was moved by Ms. Black "that our usual budget for department representatives attending the spring sales meeting be increased this year by $900." The motion was seconded by Mr. Green.

Subsidiary motions, if the main motion is passed.

It was moved by Mr. Grey "to amend the motion by inserting the words, 'to cover the increased cost of travel' after the figure $900."

State number of affirmative and negative votes. If no action taken, state

Mr. Grey's amendment was passed, and Ms. Black's original motion, as amended, was carried unanimously.

that fact and mention that there was a discussion of the matter.	Ms. Brown moved "to adjourn." The motion was carried unanimously.
Exact time of adjournment.	The meeting was adjourned at 4:15 P.M.
Your signature.	Jane Miller, Secretary

How can I get so I can talk up in meetings and not blush or stammer?

Some people are so afraid their ideas will be rejected or made fun of, they become spastic when they're called on to speak. You have to begin by believing in your ideas. And you have to practice speaking up so other people will believe in your ideas, too.

Nadine, a New York wit who has long since advanced to the position of head writer for a well-known TV comedy series, recalls her early days as a timid young trainee in the advertising department of a discount department store:

> It was my first job and I was so scared I would blow it, I used to take my wastebasket home nights so nobody would see the mountains of crumpled paper and dumb mistakes I made during the day. It was also the first time in my life anybody had ever called on me to come up with ideas that might actually see the light of day, a responsibility I took very seriously.
>
> Oh my, I was serious. And nervous. I will never forget the first time I was asked to attend a meeting. They said to bring along copy for a big spring sale they were planning. Remember, this was my first job and I had never been at any kind of a meeting before in my life. I had no idea what to expect, except that it sounded official. Do you curtsy and kiss somebody's ring? Should you dress formal? My concept of the mysterious Meeting was as daffy as that. Anyway, I wrote out two full pages of spring sale stuff and showed up in the conference room on the dot. The meeting started with the ad chief telling the president of the company that his advertising department was going to make this the most profitable, bell-ringing sale of the decade, and that *Nadine* would now read the copy. Oh God.
>
> I wobbled to my feet, which immediately turned to Jello, and began to mumble, so nobody could hear the dumb things I was saying. The president requested, very courteously, that I speak louder please,

as he and the rest of the room would like to hear what I was saying. I started over again and this time it came out a bellow. My voice cracked, like a thirteen-year-old boy's. And then I got a coughing fit that would have made Camille sound healthy. Thank heaven for my boss. She understood, having been in the same position herself not too long ago. She handed me a glass of water and suggested that I try it again.

I did. Here's how I sounded. "Big B Stores presents Crazy Days? You'll think we've gone . . . tee hee . . . berserk? Our prices are so low we're. Ourpricesaresolow we're making April Fools of ourselves?" And on like that. I was so self-conscious, thinking I was on trial and not the copy, and so sure that everybody in the room would judge me negatively, I presented every line as a query. Two or three minutes of this and my wonderful boss said quietly, "Nadine, just read the copy, straight." That was all it took. Her quiet, uncritical guidance leveled me off. The good copy lines came across. The president, the buyers, and the ad chief laughed and applauded in all the right places, and Nadine's Crazy Days theme was accepted. For a whole day I was the house hero, and I even got a personal thank-you note from the president of the company. But I'll tell you, as bright as my ideas and copy were, they'd never have got into print if my boss hadn't shown me how to sell them at that meeting. It was a lesson I have never forgotten.

Do many people have trouble talking at a meeting where there are strangers?

Yes. Most people have a shyness quotient that makes them uncomfortable in strange situations. They do self-defeating things like walk into a conference room and instantly disappear, instead of introducing themselves right away so they'll be included in conversations. It's hard to start introducing yourself after everyone else is already on a first-name footing.

Or they can't think of anything to say so they stay mute. They might as well be the wallpaper or piped music, for all anybody is aware of their presence.

What to Do.

Practice. Get used to striking up conversations.

Who to Practice On.

Strangers. Force yourself. It's a good way to get used to rummaging around in the small-talk bin, because strangers aren't apt to reject you. And if they do, so what? They're not rejecting *you*, they're just having the same trouble you are.

Where to Practice.

In line at the supermarket. Seated in a waiting room. At the ball game, theater, or any relaxed, informal place.

What to Say.

Introduce yourself to your neighbor. "Hello, my name is Carole."
Compliment them: "What a beautiful scarf." Add a question they can respond to: "Did you get it in this country?" Or, "I see you're reading an Agatha Christie mystery. Is it a good one?"
Lean on a common experience: "Gosh, this is a long line. I hope the movie is worth the wait. Have you heard anything about it?"
Use the old standby, weather: "This has been the most gorgeous July I can remember. Do you think it will hold up for August?"
What you'll find, when you've broken the conversational ice with a few people is (1) it's easy, and (2) you'll have a repertoire of usable chatter you can riff through whenever the going seems stalled.

What do I say in meetings when they ask my opinions and I have none?

There are several ways to handle that situation. You have to assess the group and your standing in it to select the technique that works best.

Answer last.

Maneuver so that you hear what other people are thinking before you have to voice your opinion. You can then latch onto one of their ideas, or if it is politically right, you can second the leader's opinion. One way to get yourself in a position so you answer last is to reply to the questioner, "Would you go around the room and come back to me? I think better if I jot down notes first."

Stall.

"I'd like to get back to you on that. There's a report on my desk that I think would shed fresh light on the subject. I want to study it so we'll have complete information before we lock ourselves into a decision."

Be honest.

"I haven't formulated any opinion as yet. I'd like to hear some further discussion." Or, if the discussion has already gone on and on and this is the moment of truth: "I can see the merits in Stephanie's solution, and I also agree with Bea's. I'm afraid I can't cast a strong vote one way or the other at this point. I'll pass, this time." By adding "this time" you have let them know that you usually do have valuable opinions and they should continue to call on you. You have also put yourself in a position where the opposing factions will seek you out after the meeting, to try to convince you to see things their way. Or they may leave you alone, since the decision has been made anyway. At least you haven't lost points by babbling some harebrained opinion. Babble for the sake of babble almost always works against you.

Be an active listener, so you can formulate valid opinions.

What is active listening?

Really hearing what people say. Participating in the meeting even when you are silent.

You've watched people who sit there obviously not focused on what's going on. They doodle on their note pads or make lists of things to do after the meeting. You can tell by their eyes and lack of responsiveness that their thoughts are continents away. They miss the point of what is taking place and never contribute an opinion or fact. If you ask for one, they ask to have the question rephrased. They are inert listeners.

Active listeners get visibility. They make themselves part of the discussion verbally and nonverbally. They nod, smile, indicate agreement or comprehension. When they miss a point they ask for clarification. If they don't understand a buzzword that is used repeatedly, they ask what it means. They involve themselves in the discussion, and they learn what they need to know by listening carefully.

Active listeners are seductive to a speaker. Be careful of them when you are holding the floor.

How do good listeners seduce you?

They are so supportive of everything you say, nodding and smiling at the points you make, you find yourself locked into that one person in the room. You begin to speak just to him or her, and forget that there are others you need to impress. Then the people you are ignoring become inattentive and drift away. You have lost your audience.

The way to recapture an audience is to involve them, the way your fifth-grade teacher used to involve you in class. Remember? You'd be dreaming about who you'd play with after school or what you would wear to Jamie's birthday party, and *whammo*—you'd hear your name. The teacher was asking you a question. You had to snap out of your fog and return to the here and now. It's an ancient technique and it works as well on grown-ups as it does on fifth-graders. Try it and see. Next time you lose your audience at a meeting or the dinner table, speak his or her name and then ask a question. You will bring him back into the fold in a hurry.

How do I overcome my fear of addressing large groups?

Study, prepare, and practice.

Take a course in public speaking. Look for one that has a television monitor on hand. Study yourself in replay. Watch how your gestures come across. See if you waggle your eyebrows, scowl, twitch your head like a bird. Listen to how you sound. Is your voice resonant, inflected, believable? Get help in class and then practice correcting your faults in front of your mirror at home. The more time you spend practicing in private, the more comfortable you will be in public.

One of the best ways to hone your public-speaking skills, and at the same time gain valuable exposure, is to address small groups at trade association meetings. Prepare as thoroughly as you would for any speaking engagement. Know what you are going to say. Rehearse it endlessly. Type your speech on five-by-eight-inch cards, or letter it jumbo-size so you won't have to squint. Number the cards in case they get shuffled. Plan every detail: what you will wear, what you will do with your hands, when you will allow for laughter or applause, your nods and smiles, and how you will stand. Finally, learn how to give yourself last-minute self-confidence. Just before you go on, tell yourself, "This is going to be a wonderful speech and the audience is going to love it."

Once you get past the basics of platform speaking, you can relax and move out into the audience with a portable microphone. This works well with groups up to about three hundred, where you can walk up and down the aisles and make frequent eye contact. In larger rooms, you are apt to become invisible—isolated from too many of your listeners.

Why do I freeze when they ask questions from the floor?

Because you don't like unexpected demands. You can remove the surprise element and field questions more comfortably if you realize that there are only six basic types of questions they will throw at you:

1. Questions that pertain to your subject, to which you already know the answers. You can prepare yourself for pertinent questions two ways:

a. Before the meeting, role-play probable questions with a friend. Have them frame the questions different ways, so you can practice different responses.

b. At the meeting, buy time while you plan your answer. Use a compliment: "That's a very good question. I'm glad you asked it. Many other people have asked me the same thing." Or stall openly: "That's an excellent question, and I have never heard it before. Let me think about it for just a moment."

2. Irrelevant questions. Do not let them lure you away from your point. Answer, "That is an interesting question, but it is not our topic today. I plan to take it up at another meeting." That gets rid of the questioner without putting them down. Or switch the comment back to your point. Answer, "The last time I heard that question was from somebody who also wanted to know about . . ." And then career right on into the subject you want to discuss.

3. Angry questions. Take the steam out. "I understand that this is an important question for you, and I am disturbed by it, too. I would like you to know that we are doing something about it." Then you thank the irate questioner for being concerned, and get on with your show. Notice that you have not only placated them, but made them right.

4. Declarative questions. These are not questions, they are orations. The person wants to use your time to make a lengthy statement. Try to force a realistic question by saying, "I didn't understand the question. Could you restate it briefly in question form?" If their statement goes on too long, don't hesitate to interrupt and check the flow. This is your time to speak, and the audience is entitled to hear what you have to say.

5. Foggy questions. Some people cannot express questions clearly. Try to define what is on their mind. "What I think you are saying is. . . . Is that correct? Would you like to add anything?" If the person is totally inarticulate, don't hold up the meeting in a vain struggle for clarity. Say, "I can see that you have something important in mind, and I'd like to discuss it with you after the meeting."

6. Dirty talk. When they ask, "Do you sleep in the nude?" or "Do you ever (blip)?" answer, "That is inappropriate," and move on to the next questioner.

What if there are too many questions to handle?

When you are going into a large meeting and you know there will be many questions, supply the audience with three-by-five-inch cards on which to write their questions. Have helpers collect the cards before the question-and-answer period, skim through them, and select the questions you want to answer.

How do you get people to participate?

Keep an open climate. The trick is to leave people free to express their opinions without fear of negative criticism. Let them know you are interested in whatever they have to say. Encourage them to share their thoughts with the rest of the group. Do not cut them off with killer phrases like, "That's a stupid idea and it's out of the question. Let's just forget you ever said anything and move this meeting along."

Killer phrases not only impede meetings, but make enemies of the people you aim them at. Open, neutral, nonjudgmental statements make friends: for you and for the ideas you are trying to sell.

Incidentally, effective bosses use the open-climate technique all the time, not just in meetings. It is one of the ways to get the agreement and cooperation you need on your path to the top.

What are some open-climate phrases?

- That's an interesting idea. Tell me more about it.
- What are the pros and cons of your idea?
- Do you feel the advantages outweigh the disadvantages?
- That's a fascinating subject, but it doesn't fit into our agenda today. Please remind me of it later, and we'll put it into another meeting.
- I'm not clear about what you are saying. Could you rephrase your statement please?

Will people argue with me in a meeting?

They may. Some people are born disruptive and will make mayhem of your meetings if you let them. There are shouters who make scenes and throw tantrums. Comics who interrupt your thought flow with gag lines. Mental lightweights whose remarks are beside the point. Constant warriors who will argue a fact just for the sake of arguing.

How do I deal with arguers?

Positively. It is no good to try to outshout a shouter, tell a nitwit he or she is stupid, or argue back with a battler. What you have to do is concentrate on deflating the attack, not the attackers. There are several ways to take control:

- Stay on your own agenda. Say, "Thank you for your contribution. You have a lot of good things to say, but our time is running short and we must get on to the next point. I'll be glad to discuss your suggestion with you when the meeting is over."
- Quickly summarize what they have said and make them an offer: "Is there anything you would like to add to that, in the forty or fifty seconds we have left?"

226

• Put things in terms of your feelings: "When somebody blocks the meeting, it makes me uncomfortable and I get off track. Let's get back to the subject. We were saying . . ."

• List their problem and the possible solutions on your blackboard or chart. State only the facts and ignore emotions:

PROBLEM	SOLUTIONS
This project will take too much time.	A. Divide project among three task forces.
	B. Do part of the project now and part later.
	C. Assign project to another committee.

• Draw realistic answers out of your audience. "You say the problem is the project will take too much time. How long would it take you—five hours, seven days? Give me a period of time that's too much. Is five hours too much time? Can you do the work over a period of two weeks? Or would you prefer to do it on overtime and get extra pay?"

• Direct their desire for leadership. Delegate a task that will give them something positive to do.

Do not be upset or frightened when somebody disagrees with you. Arguments in meetings are healthy. They prove that people are interested in what is going on, and add vitality to the group process.

How can I control somebody who wants to take over?

Betty, the director of women at an eastern college, got a takeover artist out of her way by giving him something else to do. Betty is twenty-six: small, brunet, introspective. She smokes too much and worries a lot, mostly about the fact that she must constantly work to gain respect among university people who are years her senior. She says that although she is by nature a conciliatory person, she has learned to stick up for her rights when she has to:

I had an idea for a project that could put our small college on the map. All it needed was funding, so with the board of directors' blessing

227

and a lot of professional advice, I wrote up a grant proposal. It was accepted and the board put me in charge of implementing the project. Then along came Lloyd, a psychologist they'd hired to head up student counseling. He is one of those loud, opinionated types who assumes that he is always right. He's ambitious, too, as I realized at a staff meeting we attended. He was bent on refuting whatever I said, and he did it in tones of such Olympian authority he began to weaken my credibility. I didn't like the way he operated and I was afraid that he'd monopolize all my meetings and take over my grant project. So I invented a plot to short-circuit him.

A week before the first project meeting was to take place, I sent all the board members a memo. It went:

> In preparation for our meeting on May 10, I have contacted all department heads to discuss the details of the project in advance. At this point, I should like to recommend that we appoint Lloyd to head up a special task force, so that we can take advantage of his area of expertise. I plan to devote the last ten minutes of our May meeting to his presentation.

Then I outlined an agenda that had me in charge of presenting the program to the board. Having been given his due as an authority, Lloyd would be busy making points with his task force and wouldn't need to jump all over me. Besides, I was the one who gave him his due; he could hardly afford to argue and make me wrong after that. My strategy worked and it was because I concentrated on his needs instead of putting him down. He'd only have resented and fought me for that.

Give me a checklist for large meetings.

The larger your meeting, the more details that can be overlooked. If you want your meeting to run smoothly, you have to check and double-check every element, to make sure nothing goes wrong. A standing checklist in your meetings file will help remind you of the primary rule for running a meeting: Assume nothing; check everything:

Function room reservation
Seating arrangements for audience
Seating arrangements for head table
Public-address system

Lighting and controls
Heat, air conditioning
Slides, projector, screen
Electric outlets
Flip chart, markers
Refreshments
Invitations
Invitations to reporters
Photographer
Press contact
Press kits
Name tags
Note pads, pencils
Hospitality committee: receptionists, name tags, seating, refreshments, phone messages
Arrangements for speaker: airport escort, hotel reservation, thank-you gift/letter

What are some of the things that can make a well-planned meeting go wrong?

A blizzard. Power outage. Speaker who doesn't appear. Gremlins, like the ones that got Margaret-Ann:

> I was doing publicity for a fabric house, and the project was to introduce a revolutionary new material to the trade. It looked like wool and it felt like wool, but it wasn't wool: You could wash it. It was a sensational fabric and deserved to be presented with a big splash. I named it TumbleWeave, dreamed up a three-ring presentation, and invited the company's most important customers to a demonstration. I personally saw to it that every fashion and new-products editor would attend. I hired a brass band, klieg lights, disco dancers—the whole bit. The centerpiece of the show was a dramatic live demonstration of our wonderful new washable wool. I had two washing machines hooked up on stage and made sure they were in working order. I had spectacular twin models to parade matching dresses: one made of TumbleWeave and the other of wool. The bit was, the models were to sashay around, then duck behind a screen, shuck the dresses, and toss them out to the president of the company. His job was to plop the wool dress into one washing machine and the Tumbleweave into the other. While the band played on, the dresses would whirl

through their wash cycles, the lights would die, and a brilliant spot-light would showcase the president as he removed the two dresses: one shrunk to toddler size and ours still gorgeous. We got the show started and everything went off perfectly. We didn't miss a beat. Right up to the very end, the moment of magic when the spotlight show-cased the president as he opened the lids of the machines, reached in, and held up *two* tiny, shrunken, toddler-size dresses.

I invented some abstruse chemical explanation, invited the guests to another demonstration, and promised them the earth, sun, and a fortune in profits the minute they ordered glorious unshrinkable TumbleWeave. It didn't work!

THE IMPORTANCE OF VISIBILITY

How will publicity help me succeed?

It will make you visible. Bring you credit for what you do. Make people see that you are a valuable asset.

You have to let people know it when you do something good. Otherwise you will sit alone in the background, while somebody else takes the credit. People who work hard rarely get praised for their deeds unless they make the effort to publicize them. You have to toot your own horn if you want others to hear you.

There was once a myth that said good girls are silent and demure. It led us nowhere. Goodness, as Mae West pointed out, has little to do with getting ahead. Look around at the people who get to the top. They are not necessarily the hardest-working grinds in their company. They get ahead because they know how to promote themselves. They announce their achievements, let you know they're important, deliberately keep a spotlight on their performance. They understand the value of keeping their name out front.

Why should I learn about publicity while I'm an assistant?

It's something you may have to do for the person you work for. And it's a skill you will need when you move ahead in your career. Publicity is a tool successful career people use to capitalize on their accomplishments. The more tools you have, the better you will understand how to get what you want.

What is a publicity or news release?

The standard form you send to editors about events you want to publicize.

An effective release contains newsworthy information and follows a format that is easy for busy editors to process quickly. The guidelines are:

- Use eight-and-a-half-by-eleven-inch paper.
- Type everything double-spaced.
- Type one side of the paper only.

- Leave wide margins on the top, bottom, and sides so the editor can make notes.
- State the following in the heading: your company's name, address and phone number; the name of the person to be contacted for further information; and the release date, or "For Immediate Release."
- Include in the body of the release the basic information readers will need: full name and address of company, prices, advantages of the product or service, and so on.
- Exclude superlatives, tricky phrases, obscure references.
- Stick to a single subject.
- Be as brief as possible.

Show me a sample news release format.

GRAND SERVICES INC.
11 Main Street, Wyman, Ohio 45000
(513) 555-1777

NEWS RELEASE

(Name and title of addressee, if the release is personalized)	TO: J. J. Jones, Editor WYMAN DAILY SUN	CONTACT: Susan Smith, New Products Manager
(Subject matter) (Or, Hold for a certain release date) (If a glossy is enclosed)	RE: New Product FOR IMMEDIATE RELEASE Photo and caption enclosed	
(Lead tells who, what, where, when, why)	_____ _____ _____.	
(Include a quote if possible, or attribute a statement)	_____ _____ _____ _____.	

(Expendable infor-
mation goes last)

_____

_____

_____

_____

(use a symbol:
"-0-", "###" or
"END" to indicate
end of release)

How do you write the body of a release?

Follow these two basic rules:

1. Construct a release in the shape of an upside-down triangle so that all the basic, vital facts are at the top: who, what, where, when, how. Place the next-most important facts in paragraph two. Continue with your facts in decreasing order of importance. Place expendable information last, at the bottom of the triangle. The reason for this is that editors chop from the bottom up when their space is limited and they have to eliminate copy.

2. Write in simple, short, declarative sentences. All they want is the facts, not artsy frills and adjectives. Remember that you are writing plain, basic news, not a feature story, and leave the hyperbole, evocative symbolism, and tricky suspense-building to professional feature writers.

Show me the body of a publishable release.

Jane Doe has been appointed director of Life Sciences for the University of Wicker, it was announced today by the office of Chancellor Frederick Smith.

Who, what, where, when, how. Chancellor's name adds authentication.

A native of Wicker, Ms. Doe has been professor of Biochemistry and Doar Scholar at the university since 1971. In addition, she is a contributing editor of *Life Sciences Monthly.*

Important credentials.

As director of the Life Sciences department, Ms. Doe plans to expand the current program to include oceano-

Subject reminder. Repeat subject's name once or twice.

graphic and geological studies. Monthly field trips will be a curriculum feature. Says Chancellor Smith, "Ms. Doe brings to the department a special expertise. She has explored many little-known aspects of the life sciences, and her work can have enormous impact on our search for new energy sources. I feel that her background, intense interest, and ability to communicate knowledge are a great asset to the university."

Immediate activities.

Quote attributed to authority. Quotes personalize a release and add believability.

Ms. Doe is married to James Doe, vice-president in charge of sales for the Grand Tire Company. They have two children, ages five and twelve.

Extra information that can be chopped.

Now work your way backward through the sample release, as if you were an editor. First eliminate the last paragraph. No loss: the story is still intact. Do the same with the next to last paragraph, starting with the quote, "Says Chancellor Smith. . . ." The story still stands. Get rid of all of that paragraph and you still have the vital facts. If all that remains is paragraph one, your important message will appear in full.

At what point in my career might I need to do a release?
• When you are working for someone who wants visibility.
• When you accept a new job, get an award, or want to publicize some other milestone.
• When you are in business for yourself as a shop owner, free-lancer, or company head.
• When you are between jobs and want people to know what you could do for them.

Will I have to write all my own releases?
No. You can use your company's public relations department or outside agency. If you work for a company that has PR help, be sure to check with them first. Ask them to write the release for you. They are professionals and probably have better press contacts than you do.

They may even advise you to withhold your news; it could conflict with other company plans.

Cultivate writers and editors you meet. Keep in touch so you can phone or take them to lunch when you have news to announce. If they are interested in the details, they will tell you whether their own people will write up the story or if you should supply a release.

What events do editors consider newsworthy?

New job or appointment	Publication of book or article
Award	Business anniversary
New business address	Committee chairmanship
Degree	New business concept
New client	Civic activity
Speaking engagement	New sales record
Teaching appointment	Famous visitor
Store opening	New trade or company name
New product	Unusual sale
Open house	Convention news
Business expansion	Price change

What are the usual publicity outlets?

Local newspapers	Radio news
National newspapers	Television news
Wire services	Company newsletters
Consumer magazines	Professional association news-
Trade magazines	letters

When should you not try to get publicity?

When you do not have a legitimately newsworthy, interesting announcement. If you barrage people with inconsequential information, they will learn to put you on their "Who's She?" lists. If you keep interrupting their schedules with trivia, you will only put your story in disfavor.

The first thing to ask when you call reporters or editors is, "Is this a good time to speak with you?" Put yourself in their shoes: They don't want to hear about your inventing the New World when they are crashing to deadline, trying to finish up the old. Ask them what deadline they are working on: Your material may be too late to be usable. And be sure your material fits their needs. A financial editor won't care that you've been promoted to first violinist in the local orchestra—unless there is a financial peg to your story: "The Harmony Orchestra, funded entirely by local business, is an example of the trend toward corporate financing of the arts."

Editors are not interested in nonnews, either. Angela, a free-lance publicist, has a client whose news judgment is questionable. She says she earns her fee just by keeping him away from editors. Steve is a real estate developer given to chasing every goal on the horizon, a tunnel-vision type who is apt to call Angela in the middle of the night, in a panic and screaming for help:

> Remember the release you sent out for me about breaking ground next spring for the new luxury tower? I just heard that the financing's been held up and we can't break ground until fall. I want you to send them another release right away, before every editor in town gets on my neck, wanting to know what happened!

Angela explained to the frantic developer that his chances of receiving a single inquiry were practically nil. The delay was nothing to write about, any more than if you did *not* get a job, or failed to win an award. You publicize the positive events, not empty holes in the ground.

Now, if the developer's delay were due to financial shenanigans, that would be a story. People love a good scandal. Then Angela's job would be to squelch the bad news, to avoid adverse publicity.

How do you keep bad news out of the papers?

There is no pat answer. It depends on the size and quality of your scandal, the relationships of the people involved, and a variety of other factors. Some of the techniques are:

- The "No comment" routine.
- The underground method. "She is out of town and cannot be reached at this time." "The accused has been hospitalized, doctors say for exhaustion."

- The indignant nonresponse.

Allegation

The developer has diverted corporate funds for his private use, including travel and a limousine used for private pleasures.

Response

"What am I, a freak? I'm the chairman of the corporation!"

- The outraged denial.

Allegation

The chairman of the board purchased an expensive limousine out of corporate funds and proceeded to use it for matters that did not pertain to company business.

Response

1. Distort the statement: "Your columnist has accused me of using a limousine for unseemly purposes, such as private transportation for my secretary and other sins."
2. Then deny the distortion: "My secretary does not require transportation, nor has anything unseemly ever occurred in my limousine."
3. Next, assert that you have denied the original statement: "The accusation proves to be no more than an unwarranted and vicious personal attack."
4. Finally, write, "the fact is" and launch into your own true but unrelated statement: "The fact is, the two banks that had agreed to underwrite the construction portion of this building failed to negotiate in good faith. . . ."

- The altered point of view. I asked Angela to explain what she would have done if the developer's hypothetical scandal had been real:

I'd have provided the press with information that would reshape their thinking. I'd have told my client, "Your best bet is not to avoid the reporters when they call, but to give them information that will alter their focus and diminish the importance of their charges. For instance, when they ask you, "Is it true that there was an overexpenditure?" tell them, "Yes, but that is not as important as the fact that the money was spent on superior construction. The public has had far too much foisted on it in the way of shoddy housing. In my opinion, we have made an important stride in reversing that costly and unfair trend."

How can I be sure they will run my news accurately?

You can't. They may misspell your name, garble the facts, and omit vital data. It happens all the time. Don't be upset. And don't give up. You need reporters, even though all of them are not perfect and they don't always have time to dig into all the facts.

What should I do with press clippings?

Keep them in a publicity scrapbook so you will have a documentary record of your accomplishments. And before you paste an item into your scrapbook, get all the mileage you can from it when it appears. Reproduce it in quantity and mail a copy, along with a personal note, to people who can influence your career. Do your mailing quickly, when your news is hot off the press. There is nothing more dead than last week's news.

Take advantage of other people's publicity, too. Phone or write them a congratulatory note whenever they make the news. It's a way of making them aware of you as an active, alert, friendly contact.

And don't forget to say thank you to the people who write about you. A short note will let them know you appreciate what they did, and will help you maintain good relationships:

Dear Bill,
    That was a wonderful piece in this morning's paper. You captured the gist of my statements perfectly. Thank you for the mention; it will be very helpful to me. I'll try to return the favor by keeping you posted on developments that might be useful to you.
                                                            Best,
                                                            Ann Mills

Everybody likes to be noticed and praised.

Who else should you write to?

People who can help your career. Even strangers will pay attention to a well-written, logical, interesting letter. You don't have to want anything specific from them. Your purpose is to build relationships you can call on in the future. Renée, a political scientist, wrote streams of letters to strangers when her career was young. She says she owes a lot of her success to her mail-order contacts; without them she still might be an unknown.

Renée is in what publicists call an unsexy field: Political science does not have the warmth and immediacy that touches people's emotions. Renée herself is a scholarly type: cerebral, dispassionate, closer to cold facts than hot issues. Although she can talk comfortably on her subject with almost anyone, she used to be terribly ill at ease with people. She says the change is due mostly to the recognition she has acquired as a professional:

> Intellectually, I knew I had to make contacts with the important people in my field, even though I preferred the solitude of my ivory tower. But my constitutional inability to mix with people was hindering my career: You can't function effectively in a vacuum. So I devised an alternate strategy that would put me in touch with the scientists I had to get to know. Whenever I read a paper or magazine that had an interesting statement by a prominent historian or economist, I would compose a letter to him or her.

Here's one letter Renée wrote to a famous economist:

Dear Professor Grant:

As a political scientist, I am profoundly interested in the economic implications of international monetary policies and their effect on the United States voting process. Your comments, quoted by UPI, on the possible alignment of European and Latin American nations to control the flow of U.S. dollars strikes me as an important breakthrough in terms of the Senate's present efforts to contain campaign financing. I should like to add a suggestion that would perhaps augment your efforts to "purify

Introduces herself and makes the connection with his sphere of interest.

Précis of his article shows she has studied it carefully.

Demonstrates keen interest and activity of thought. Quotes the professor.

241

America's elections." If there were a way to police the funds that we now know are habitually diverted by American labor unions through foreign nations so as to remain technically legal, would that not strengthen the democratic aspect of our voting process? I wonder if you have thought about it, and if you believe there is a practical way to implement such a procedure.

> Presents an idea to stimulate further thought.

> Implies that a reply is invited.

I would like to express my admiration of your clarity of thought and presentation of complex ideas. It is my opinion that your talents and expertise have done much to further the progress of societal attitudes in America.

> Adds laudatory comment.

> Very truly,
> Renée Martin

P.S.   I am enclosing a clipping of the UPI article as it appeared in this morning's paper, so you will have an extra copy for your files.

> Knows he probably has a clipping service. The enclosure, marked with her name, is to remind him of her interest.

The professor answered Renée's letter, she wrote back to him, and added another correspondent to the collection of pen pals she's maintained over the years. What happened later on makes the point of Renée's strategy. Two years later when she needed an influential person to introduce a paper she'd written for a national conference, she wrote and asked him if he'd be at the workshop, and if he'd make the introductory remarks. He agreed, and his name attracted overflow attendance. After the workshop, Professor G. complimented Renée on her paper and introduced her to several prominent scientists she might otherwise never have met. Renée says, "That conference and the people I met there went a long way in enabling me to speak comfortably and create an authority with strangers. Linking my name with the professor's helped immeasurably to further my career."

When might I have to be on radio or TV?

When you are the local expert on a certain subject. When you have an unusual shop or service. When you are asked to be spokesperson for a trade association, a women's group, or a community cause. When your company selects you to represent them.

Whether you are representing yourself or the company you work for, a radio or TV appearance is a golden publicity opportunity. It showcases you dramatically. It brings your name and expertise to the attention of thousands of people at a time. At least some of them are bound to remember your credentials and call on you when they need help.

What techniques should I practice for TV?

Speak more slowly than you usually do.

Move your hands, head, and body sparingly. Use slow, broad gestures.

Look at the camera with the red light on, or else at the person you are speaking with on the set.

Look and sound confident.

Smile. A frequent, relaxed, pleasing smile gets people on your side. Even if what you say is not brilliant, or the person interviewing you tries to nail you to the cross, smile and the audience will be with you. Answer tough questions as if you were explaining yourself to a good friend. If the interviewer keeps on acting tough, he or she will come out like a monster attacking a lamb.

How should I dress when I have to appear on TV?

Very carefully. This is a special situation for career women that is becoming more and more common as the spotlight sharpens on women at work. Local stations love to call on designers, boutique owners, women of special ability in various fields. You have to be prepared for the fact that you could wake up one morning and say, "What should I wear on TV?"

Selma, forty-six, bakery owner: They called and asked me to be on an interview show about women enntrepreneurs. My first thought was, "I can't do it; I haven't a thing to wear." My second thought was, "You oaf. This is a fantastic shot at getting your brand name over to thousands and thousands of people who buy cake and bread, and you're worrying about what to wear. Grow up." So I did: I asked my twenty-three-year-old daughter what would look right. She loaned me her gray suit, and we gussied it up with some pearls, found some high-heeled pumps in the closet, and I think I made a good appearance. Not too severe and not frilly or loud—up to date but not faddish. It was my image—the way I'd see myself dressing for work if I didn't wear jeans every day. And the way I'd costume myself if I were being cast in a movie about a successful business owner.

Betsy, twenty-two, writer: I called three friends and they each gave me different advice. One said, "Wear something in a medium tone, not blinding white or a blur of black." The second said, "Look the way you want people to think of you. You're a serious biographer; wear something serious, like your camel-colored suit. It has a full skirt that won't ride up over your knees when you sit down." My third friend pointed out that I'd better do something about my hair. I took all their advice, and they were absolutely right. There was one thing nobody thought to mention to me, however, and I nearly blew the fuse out of three cameras with it. The blouse I chose was in a bold red and green geometric stripe, and when I walked into the studio, the director took one look and had a fit. There was a lot of scurrying around and strangled conversation while I sat there trying to be invisible. Finally the director came over to me and explained what I had done to cause the furor. He said, "The blouse you're wearing is beautiful, but on camera it will have a very dizzying effect. Would you please remove it, and we'll loan you a plain silk scarf instead. Thank you very much." His words were polite, but I'll bet underneath he was furious over having one more problem on his hands.

Give me two techniques for selecting TV clothes.

First, watch the professional newscasters and talk-show hostesses on TV. Really look at them. See what colors they favor, the styles they wear, their jewelry, necklines, hairstyles, everything about them. And bear in mind that each performer has been carefully packaged to give a particular impression to her audience. Comic, homey, intellectual, dynamic—whatever personality she wants to convey is reflected in how she looks.

The other technique is to role-dress. Think of yourself not as Mary Jones, but as the entity you want viewers to see: The Warm-hearted Florist. The Calm Computer Expert. The Well-Traveled Gourmet. Choose what you wear to suit the role.

How can you control a TV interview?

Stay on your agenda, the way Marikka did when they asked her on to talk about female entrepreneurs.

> My corporate party service is something new and different in this city, especially because they're not used to women who start their own businesses here. When the local TV station heard about me, from releases I'd sent them, they asked me to come talk about myself on their morning show. I leaped at the chance: It'd be advertising I couldn't possibly have paid for out of my own pocket. I could see a solid half hour of plugs for Corporate Catering Inc. At show time, however, I almost lost out to competition. It turned out they had another guest besides me, the author of a new book on hairwashing whose subject interested the hostess a lot more than corporate catering. Let me tell you, I worked like a demon to stick to my subject.

Marikka gave me a partial transcript of the interview to show how she accomplished this:

HOSTESS: Good morning everybody! And what a good morning it is. I have with me not one but two celebrities. Allow me to introduce Marikka, a wonderful woman with her very own business. Isn't that right, Marikka?

MARIKKA: It is indeed. My business is called Corporate Catering, and I plan and run parties for local business people. My organization is ——

HOSTESS: Lovely. My other guest is Ilsa-Sue, who has just written a fantastic book called *Creative Hairwashing*. Tell us all about it, Ilsa-Sue. Exactly what is creative hairwashing?

ILSA-SUE: Well . . . (Went on for four full minutes plugging her book, which had already been mentioned twice by the rapt interviewer. Marikka was totally ignored. The instant there was a pause for breath, she broke in.)

MARIKKA: Your book sounds fascinating. I'd love to have done the publicity party for it. You'd have had a menu they'd never forget, the same one I did for the Post Corporation. We had . . .

Marikka related her strategy.

And then I launched into a mouth-watering menu and told how effective my corporate party-of-the-year had been. The rest of the half hour was pretty much a replay of that opening. They'd get into the book, I'd interrupt and swing the talk to catering. It was hard work, but I must say, I think I carried it off very well. I got in my half-hour's worth of plugs for Corporate Caterers and still came across as a nice, agreeable person you'd like to do business with.

How do you talk about yourself without sounding like a braggart?

Subtly. In ways that offer other people something they need. With ideas that let them know you are a valuable contact they should cultivate. By seeming to be casual even though you have a clear purpose in mind.

Read the hidden messages in the following statements, and compare the probable effect of subtlety with out-and-out bragging.

SUBTLE	*BRAGGING*
I'm having a party December sixth for Edward Bigwig. You probably saw in the papers that he'll be in town. Would you like to meet him? *(Links your name with an important person; tells people you can be useful to them)*	Do you know that I went to school with Edward Bigwig? I'm one of the few people he'll see when he's in town next month. *(Gives people nothing to respond to.)*
I saw Jim yesterday, over at Prime Manufacturing, and he said he'd love to have one of your salespeople call on him. *(Lets them know you are active in business, have good contacts, and can do them a favor.)*	I called on the head of Prime Manufacturing yesterday. The president's door is always open to me. *(A dead-end brag that may impress some people, and make others jealous or bored.)*

You can sell people on how valuable you are if you think from their point of view. You have to remember that they are less interested in your accomplishments than they are in what your accomplishments can do for them. Speak up and let them know you are an influential person, but tell them in a way that will benefit them. The purpose of promoting yourself is to make people want more of you. You can do it if you give them something they can use.

How can I publicize myself in the office if my work is just routine?

Dramatize your work: Make it look like more than it is. Use memos to document what you do, and make people think of you as an important, active cog in their wheel.

You can use memos to get visibility from the most ordinary tasks. When you come back from a routine trip, the first thing to do is shower everybody in the office with reports of the people you saw and the things you did. When you're involved in a project or serving on a committee, send memos at every stage of your work to the person you work for, and to his or her boss as well. You can even use memos as a vehicle to get a promotion. The vice-president of a Missouri sales organization told me that's how a young woman he'd hired as a receptionist got his favorable attention:

Martha was straight out of secretarial school, with no work experience. In the job interview, I judged her as intelligent, willing, and a person who asks good questions. I hired her for the front office because she was ornamental, and because I thought she'd be competent and could learn her job fast. She was there a month and a half when my IN box began to be flooded with memos signed Martha. Every day there was another sheet filled with her comments and criticisms about every conceivable aspect of our business: the number of people covering certain territories, the efficiency of their sales reports, why we should use a computer to keep track of inventory, the merits of installing two extra coffee machines, whether we should buy an automatic envelope sealer. Some of Martha's memos were plain silly and some were to the point. I mentioned them one day to another of our vice-presidents and he said, "I know. I've been getting them, too. So has everyone else in the organization. My God, when does she find the time?" I didn't think much more about Martha until a third colleague brought up the subject of her memos. He said, "Look, I don't know if this kid Martha is good, bad or indifferent, but she certainly is putting in a lot of effort analyzing our company policies. Why don't we give her a promotion?" His instinct was right. I gave her a promotion and she really proved herself. She's one of our crackerjack research assistants. I sometimes think what a good bet I'd have missed if she hadn't got our attention with those memos. If she'd been content just to sit at the receptionist's desk, answering phones and sorting the mail.

Show me how to write memos so I can get credit for my ideas.
Here's a sample heading for a memo:

Date: March 6, 1980

From: Shirley Smith

To: J. Brown. Copies to W. Black, G. Gray, D. Smith, R. Green, B. White, S. Brown — Copies to your boss and other concerned management, as well as the people working on your project.

Re: Sales Training Course: Research

Following are three memos Shirley wrote about her project:

(1.) March 6 memo
To implement the sales training idea I discussed with you last week, I have formed a five-person task force and will meet with them 3/10 in my office to outline my workshop plan and ask for additional suggestions.

Emphasize that it's your idea.
Show you are doing something about it.

(2.) March 11 memo
To keep you informed: I met with my task force last night from 5:00 to 7:00, and we agreed on the following:

Let them know when you work overtime.

1. I will be responsible for workshop attendance.

Keep yourself actively involved in your project.

2. Dennis and Roz will report to me 3/17 on the costs of a workshop series.

Show you know how to delegate.

3. Brian and Sonia have agreed to investigate appropriate function rooms.

Show you know how to get people's cooperation.

(3.) March 18 memo

Attached are copies of the reports prepared for last night's meeting of my task force: attendance, projected costs, recommended function room. I have added a working checklist for the actual sessions: flip charts, projectors, and so on. I think you will agree that my research indicates that the sales training course I suggested is a feasible undertaking. I will be happy to continue to work with you on the project until it is successfully completed.

Deliver what you have promised.

Make the point that they can rely on you to follow up on details.

Offer to fill their additional needs. Keep your name attached to your project throughout.

What other ways can I make a name for myself around the office?

Take on committee work that people will have to notice. Head up refreshments, program-planning, anything that will get your name around as a person who makes things happen.

Use the company newsletter to announce the projects you're active in. Speak to the editor in person, send in releases, keep feeding them information they can use.

Pin *signed* notices on the company bulletin board that will bring you to people's attention: services you can offer, new procedures you have installed, information about interesting meetings.

Develop contacts with people who can help you, people who are in the inner circle. Find reasons to talk with them. Invite them to lunch. Offer ideas. Cultivate their respect and trust. Incidentally, this is an excellent way to break into all-male cliques where women aren't welcome as a body. If you cultivate one member as an ally and make him your friend, you will probably find that soon he will invite one after another of colleagues to join you at lunch or for chats in the office

Will they call me the office flirt if I cultivate male friendships?

They may gossip about you, but you have to remember why. Chances are, they envy your ability to get ahead. People who are afraid to succeed have trouble understanding others who do things to improve their position. They think you should be just like they are and stay in the background, taking orders and not moving ahead. Or they have a chip on their shoulder, like Meredith:

> I've watched this woman get promoted over and over again, and it's only because she swings her hips. Oh, she does her job competently, but in my book she is just plain devious. The only people she fools are the men she flatters and swishes her behind at. She's getting their egos, and it's disgusting that she gets rewarded for that. Rewards should be for intelligence and merit. The day she got her last promotion I got so upset I was shaking. Sat at my desk and snapped a pencil in two. My boss caught me, and do you know what he said? "I think it's good when a woman uses her feminism and is charming. It's a mature and productive way of getting along with people." I had a fit.

Meredith also had a lesson if she'd been willing to listen. She could have learned to soften her personality, relax, and be charming. She needn't have adopted the other woman's style, but she could have developed her own and made it work for her. If you don't want to stay isolated, stuck where you are, you have to be the kind of person other people really want to know.

Is it true that outside activities can help you in the office?

Absolutely. The visibility and recognition you get through outside organizations comes back to you where you work. When you are active in trade associations, women's and civic groups, your name becomes known by other active people. The higher-ups in your company begin to realize that you are someone to watch, somebody who speaks for their company, an achiever they would do well to recognize and push up in the organization.

Remember that outside organizations have newsletters, too: Keep your name in print wherever you are. Help chair committees. Speak before groups. Be an asset, the same as you are in the office. And make sure that people who count know they can count on you.

Will people be jealous when I get publicity?

Some people are always jealous when others succeed: friends, relatives, rivals in business. It helps to be able to poke a bit of fun at your own fame. Smile and say, "Oh sure. Next thing I'll be the centerfold in *Bigshot* magazine." A little self-deprecation takes the weight off the fact that you are overshadowing somebody else. Notice that I say, "a *little* self-deprecation." You don't have to give up what you have worked hard to earn just because somebody else is jealous.

Judy says that when she began to attract national attention for her work in pediatrics, she wasn't bothered by the fact that her colleagues felt threatened. She could handle them. It was her home life that suffered:

> When my new diagnostic procedure was announced, the press picked it up and almost overnight I was a celebrity. They interviewed, photographed, tape recorded, and televised me to a fare-thee-well. People recognized me in the street. The phone rang night and day. I certainly had the limelight—and I never felt so alone. I was losing my husband. Jack and I had almost no time together anymore, except at breakfast. It was as if he'd become the Prince Consort. One night as I was dressing to dash off to another speaking engagement, I overheard him say on the phone, "Judy is very busy playing Superwoman these days. All this publicity is so ridiculous. You'd think she was really a somebody."
>
> I cried all the way to the rostrum. But next day, I did some heavy thinking and realized that Jack's reaction was perfectly human. I'd ignored him in the heat of what was happening to me, and he was left outside. I'd abandoned him, really. Hadn't even troubled to thank him for making it possible for me to succeed. I made amends and Jack, who is after all a big man, forgave me. But I was lucky. I wish I could tell everybody that it's fine to get applause when you've earned it—but you have to remember to give credit to the people who helped you to earn it.

LEAVING A JOB:

Rights, Privileges, Options

Is it normal to be afraid I'll be fired?

Yes, especially if you are new in your job. Most new people who care about their performance are scared to death they won't handle their responsibilities properly. They worry that somebody will find out they are inadequate. They panic every payday, thinking, "Here comes the pink slip." Sometimes they are right. More often, their terror helps them succeed. It keeps them on their toes, forces them to learn to do their job right. I've heard more than one top executive say that sheer paranoid fear was their key to success.

Lois is on her way to the top. She's a twenty-seven-year-old first-time manager who came up the corporate ranks from secretary. Suddenly she is in charge of a twenty-person office and doesn't know the first thing about managing people. Lois knows her performance will be formally evaluated, and she is terrified. She feels tense, pressured, anxious, and that's her creative stimulus. It makes her learn fast, stretch her abilities, work extra hard to succeed. Lois is mature enough to know how to survive the tension. She'll get away from it all from time to time: step back and assess herself, gain perspective on the situation. And she'll confine her worries to things she is able to control.

What do you do about things you can't control?

Lois used to worry a lot about conflicts she thought she couldn't manage. She was afraid she'd be fired because of her need to devote time to her four-year-old son:

> I was so afraid of being late to work in the morning and at the same time I had such guilt about leaving Josh. He cried terribly every day when I left the house. Really sobbed. I couldn't stand it. My sister-in-law was the one who told me what to do about it. She said, "Josh is only behaving that way because he knows how to get you. Try an experiment. Tomorrow morning when you leave and Josh screams, tell him good bye and then stand just outside the door for a few minutes. I'll bet you a ten-dollar lunch he'll stop, once he thinks you're not there to emote for." She was right. I played the scene every

day for a week, to convince myself, and like clockwork he stopped crying within two minutes and went back to his play. I can't tell you what a release that was for me. It freed me of guilt, once I had the facts, and it proved that I wasn't stuck with a problem. I still have anxieties that they'll replace me with somebody who doesn't have to dash from the office on the tick of five, to take over from the baby-sitter. And what if Josh gets sick, as kids do? Too much of that and I could be deported on account of parenthood.

Most of the people you work for will make allowances for the fact that you have young children, as long as your obligations don't interfere with their business in any major way. And as long as you've told them what to expect. Let them know up front that you may have to take time off if your child is ill. Get their prior agreement if you plan to travel with your husband. Tell them in advance if you know you'll be away from work for more than a day. Employers don't like to hire somebody and then find they're not getting what they paid for. They think they are being taken advantage of, and you can't blame them. Long, unexpected absences mean you are not living up to your job requirements. They have a right to dismiss you for that.

What are six signs that I might lose my job?

1. Business is bad. If it keeps on being bad, your company will have to cut back and eliminate nonessential jobs. You are on the expendable list if you work in one of the following departments: publicity, community relations, newsletter, dining room. They may do away with the entire department if things are really tight, or they may keep a few people on. The rule of thumb is, the last people hired are the first people fired.

2. Your industry is waning. All things change; the hot fields of a decade or two ago can be stone cold tomorrow. Plastics and teaching used to be job bandwagons people clamored to get on. Today they've shrunk, and the active fields are electronics, computing, and government. You have to keep up on industry news to know what's hot and what's not. When you see signs of industry slippage, it's time to consider the fact that your company could fold and you might be out of a job. Start looking around at other fields you can adapt your skills to.

3. New management brings in their own style. Style and function

go hand in hand, especially in the creative end of business. If you are strongly aligned with your creative group, the new team may move you out in favor of their own people who understand their techniques. Size up the situation. If you suspect they will think you don't fit in, start looking elsewhere. It is always better to look for a job while you still have a paycheck than to wait until you are fired and desperate.

4. New management is bottom-line oriented. New teams often concentrate on making their numbers look good: Their prime goal is to see a profit from their investment. This means heads will roll, and support people in frill jobs will be lopped. A company take-over is handwriting on the wall: a warning signal that you could be on your way out.

5. You don't get along with your boss or a colleague. There are only three ways to resolve a personality conflict: It's smoothed over, they go, or you go. If you are involved in a personality war and the rumbles disrupt your office, take warning. It's a sign that you may be dismissed.

6. You hate your job and it shows. You are inviting a discharge if distaste makes you careless, disrespectful, openly bored, negative, or a goof-off. Nobody wants an unpleasant, unwilling person around. If you really hate your job, the best thing to do is to find another position that suits you better. In the meantime, work at hiding your feelings. You never know when you will need references or meet the people you work with again.

Is new management apt to fire me?

Yes, if they see that you are not a cooperative member and an asset to the company. If your new boss is a good manager, he or she will wait for a while and give you a chance to adjust to their style. Good managers know that some people react badly to change: They're afraid of the unknown so they act hostile or sulk. It can take time to build trust and respect.

There are reasons a new boss will hang onto an inadequate worker. They want to use the person to find out where bodies are buried. The worker may be well connected with the company's owner or an important customer. But when their usefulness has ended, they can expect to get the ax.

Ellen waited nearly a year to clean house when she took over—
it was a difficult decision to make:

I'd never worked a day in my life until I suddenly found myself at
the age of thirty-four in the president's chair of a commercial printing
company. My father, whose company it was, died in 1975 and my
husband, who had been his vice-president in charge of sales, moved
up to the presidency. Two years later, we ended our marriage and the
divorce settlement gave me all rights to the company. My ex-husband
was out. That was fine, but now there was nobody to run the place.
I had to step in. It was a crash course for me in business administration, trying to become an instant expert. But I have always believed
that you can do anything you have to do, so I did it. Step by cautious
step, with the help of people who'd been with the company for years,
I learned the business. One of the people was Matthew, who'd been
my dad's accountant for thirty-five years. He was a rather creaky
gentleman and I knew he was skeptical of my taking over. I'm not
sure if it was because he didn't like me as a person, if it was because
I was a woman, or because he thought nobody could ever live up to
my father's standards. Matthew gave me a hard time. He was always
making disparaging remarks to me. The nicest thing he could bring
himself to say was, "You're not managing too badly, Ellen. I didn't
think you could do it at all. I only hope that in another year we'll
still have our heads above water." I felt so unsure, and Matthew knew
how much I needed his instruction and support. Yet he'd do things
like come in and hand me a balance sheet, without a word of explanation. Balance sheet! The only thing I'd ever balanced was my own
checkbook—sometimes. I had no idea what his entries and abbrevia-
tions meant, or what I should be looking for. When I asked, he acted
irritated and impatient. Or I'd ask, "Matthew, where would you suggest that I invest my capital so it will earn good interest?" His answer
was archetypically sexist; I get upset all over again just remembering.
"You can't make decisions about stocks, and you don't know anything
about when to buy and sell. Your father always kept his funds in a
savings bank and so should you." It was all I could do not to swat him.

I stewed for about eight months. On the one hand, Matthew was
all wrong for me. On the other, my father had trusted him completely.
I finally faced reality and said, "Matthew, I would like to invest my
money and get a better return on it. You tell me that investing is not
your area of interest and that it should not be mine. I need somebody
who can advise me on personal matters as well as on corporate affairs.

You can't, so I am going to have to replace you with somebody who will cover all the bases for me." He took it like a wounded buffalo. You never saw anybody so angry. I tried to smooth his ruffled feathers or whatever buffalo have, and move the interview to a civilized conclusion. "I'm sure, Matthew, that you are so efficient and keep your records in such good condition, it will be a simple matter for you to effect an orderly transfer."

The end of the Matthew era freed me. I realized that what worked for my father didn't necessarily work for me, and that it was OK to do things my way. For a while I toyed with the idea of taking a financial accounting course, so I'd be completely independent. Then I said, "No, that's foolish. You don't have to know everything. There are plenty of experts out there you can hire." I looked around until I found somebody who had the capabilities I needed and a mind-set I could connect with. Now, when I have questions or problems, I simply define what I need, get his answers, and then make my decision.

What are some other ways new managers evaluate the people they inherit?

Linda, a thirty-two-year-old store manager, uses a number of excellent techniques:

A week before I went to work, I went to a store meeting where the crew and I could size each other up. They got to see whether I come on like a machine gun or a reasonable human being. And I got a chance to learn something about them. I told them the experience I'd be bringing to the job and my philosophy of working with people: how I like to identify problems, analyze what's needed to solve them, and assign people to carry out projects. To get clues about them, I asked them each to hand in a written job description and to write down their ideas on how the store's operation could be improved. When I came to work a week later, I found that some of the people hadn't bothered to turn in their write-ups. To be fair, I asked again. Some responded and some did not. The write-ups that were turned in were revealing in terms of attitude as well as content. Some were incomplete, and some made it evident that they hadn't taken my request seriously. Now I knew which people might have to go.

I didn't fire them all. Some of them got rid of themselves. One woman who had given me a careless half-answer came to my office after a couple of weeks and said she was nervous about her status. How did I think she would fit in? I repeated my management philosophy and added, "I like to delegate responsibility and then let people fulfill it their own way. I never hover, even when people don't do their jobs. I just replace them with somebody else." That confirmed her fears. She came in the next day and said, "I've been offered another job, Linda. I like it here but I'm wondering if I shouldn't take the opportunity. What do you think?" I advised her to take it.

Another staff member, Dave, was one of those people who, whatever you ask for, have forty-nine reasons why it can't be done. "It would cause too many difficulties. We've never done it that way before. It's not my responsibility. Edith and I don't get along, so your suggestion about teaming up wouldn't work." I thought, this is probably one of those types who can't get from here to there. It's better to call this type of person in and say, "Look, Dave, this just isn't going to work out. I think you'd better find another position elsewhere."

Tell me how it feels to be fired..

I asked several executives to tell me their personal experiences. Here is how four different people reacted:

Frances, stockbroker: It was completely unexpected and my first reaction was physical shock. I couldn't breathe. My blood pressure plunged to zero. I thought I was going to black out. It was a really awful sensation for about three minutes, then the juices began to flow again and I could speak. I like to think it was because I was unprepared that I spat out all the wrong things. "This is outrageous!" I shouted. "You can't just up and fire someone. I'm very good at what I do. I hope the next person who comes along is rotten so you'll see how good I was. But don't call me back. I wouldn't work for an outfit like this, now that I know how you treat people."

I have to tell you that I was twenty-four years old at the time and have learned a lot since. Looking back, I can see that I deserved to be fired. I was a snippy kid who knew it all, wouldn't cooperate, never gave them a drop of myself in extra time or effort. And I didn't understand that firing somebody is a miserable task. I should have been more considerate of the woman who had to give me the ax. I could have taken her off the hook if I'd said, graciously, "I'm very sorry that things haven't worked out." After all, this was a business situation, not her personal revenge. I could have added, "I hope we'll stay in touch. I've learned so much from you and the organization." That would have left her with good feelings about me, so when we ran into each other again she would be my friend, not my enemy. The longer you're in business the truer the old saying becomes: There are only five hundred people in the world and wherever you go you meet them again.

Bobbie, magazine manager: Getting fired was my own idea. I was a fact-checker at one of those serious magazines with limited circulation. In fact the circulation was getting more and more limited and so was the advertising revenue. All the signs were there: The publication was going down the tubes. So I started to look for another job while I was still on their payroll. I had pangs of disloyalty, using their phones and their time. But I knew I'd be on the pavement soon, so I had to start looking. I told everybody what I was doing so I wouldn't feel sneaky. And because the more people knew I was available, the better my chances of finding another job.

I found a job, and I got fired anyway. I rigged it so I would. The new job was with a magazine that had to wait six months to put me on the payroll. Since I was certain my old company wouldn't last that long, I went to my boss and told him my plan. I said I'd like to stay on one more month, then take a semester to learn more about magazine management before I resume my career. I said, "I could give you notice and quit. But then I'd be completely on my own for tuition, rent, and living expenses. If you'd fire me instead, or agree on a 'mutual disagreement,' I can pick up unemployment insurance and put that toward my tuition." He thought that was a splendid idea, wished me luck, and confided that he'd have done the same in my shoes.

Midge, financial administrator: Getting fired is an awful experience. I went through it four years ago when the company I worked for was bought out and the new owners brought in their own key people. I did not get along with the manager they put in over me. She thought my systems were all wrong because they weren't her systems. She couldn't give me a job to do and then let me go ahead and do it. She hovered and snarled. I had the feeling that she did not respect my work and that once she'd been there a few months, she'd replace me with one of her former cronies. It was all very dispiriting and I thought I should quit. Then I thought again and realized that if I quit I'd be jobless. I'd be less desirable. And I might panic and rush into the wrong thing. So I stayed on and used their phones and desk space as my base for a job search. I also started to goof off so my boss would have a reason to fire me, and I could collect unemployment. Oh, the guilt—goofing off is not my style. I used to slink around the corridors with my chin on my chest, trying to avoid people. Stayed away from the usual lunch-hour haunts. They fired me all right, and it was a hateful experience. But it gave me enough money so I could take my time looking around for a job that was right for me.

Mary Beth, publicity, city-planning department: I was fired with a bang and he had every right to do it. After all, I'd been trying to undermine him for months. I was a do-gooder trying to cripple his housing program and save the citizens' tax money. He did not appreciate my efforts. When he sent word that he'd like to see me at three o'clock on Friday, I knew what was coming. An hour ahead of time, I closeted myself in my office and plunged deep into TM. I did such a good job on myself that by the time three o'clock rolled around, I was about twenty-four inches off the floor and certifiably calm. I rapped on his door, went in, sunk into a chair, and smiled the smile of a saint about to be pastured to heaven. He missed the first beat, he was so steamed up about what I'd done to wreck his program. He sailed in: "You are cashiered. Canned. Eliminated from this office. Do you understand?" I smiled serenely and murmured, with compassion, "I understand. You are letting me go and it is not easy for you to speak." The nerve of me. I even added, "I know this is hurting you worse than it is me." My saintliness suddenly caught up with him and the wind flapped out of his sails. I'd made him feel like such an ogre that he stammered, "I'm not an animal, you know. What can I do to help you get another job?"

I say, if you're going to get fired, do it with dignity. Anything less would be unseemly.

What do they mean when they say "You've been surplussed?"

They mean you've been fired. "Surplussed" is one of the euphemisms people use for an act they detest so much that they try to talk around it. Some of the more ludicrous euphemisms are:

Surplussed (They made too many of you)
Terminated (They've pulled the plug)
Displaced (As in wartime refugee)
Phased out (Like the last of the Studebakers)
Dismissed (Just in time for recess)
Declared redundant (You were one wrinkle too many)
Leveled off (Here comes the bulldozer)
Excised (Like a sick appendix)
Dehired (Do you believe this?)

Then there's:

> Canned
> Laid off
> Discharged
> Cashiered
> Bounced
> Given the boot, gate, or walking papers
> Sent to the showers
> Shown the door

And I almost forgot:

> Dejobbed.

This is all very funny, except to two people: the person who's fired and the person who does the firing. Of the two, I think the latter often has a harder time of it.

Why is it hard to fire people?

It's no fun to behead people unless you're Attila the Hun. It's especially hard for women with a strong need for approval and affection. They let their emotions intrude on the decision-making process. And it's hard for women who are new to management and still equate "control" with "masculinity." They still see their role as stereotypically feminine: the sympathizer and socializer, rather than the leader and authority.

Not that firing somebody is any easier for men. It's just that they have had more role models, so it's easier for them to place efficiency above personal consideration. Male or female, experienced or not, people still feel uneasy about firing: Is this the humane thing to do? Are they going to hate me? There is one saving fact: Bosses have been firing employees for so long, they can rely on certain proved guidelines.

What are some guidelines for firing?

• Give the employee a chance. Call them in, close the door, and talk out the problem. Point out what's wrong, what needs to be changed. Give them a time limit to shape up, so the picture will be perfectly clear for you both. If their performance does not improve after that, you will have no choice but to fire them.

- Get the firing over with rapidly. The surgeon with the swiftest stroke makes the kindest cut of all. Dragged-out preambles, defensive apologies, or conversational goulash like "How nice you look today" only heighten the discomfort.

You have to remember that anticipation is always worse than the real thing—whether it's a trip to the dentist, revving up for a blind date, firing someone, or being fired. Be conclusive: Drop the guillotine quickly:

> John, as you know I've been disappointed by your performance. We talked three months ago about how you could improve, and I think it's clear to us both that it just hasn't worked out. We will be giving you two weeks' pay, and I'd like you to clean out your desk at the end of the day.

- Say something positive about the person if you possibly can. There's no use making them feel more rotten than you have to. Be kind, and let them know they're not all bad. Recognize the good things they've done:

> You have many talents, John, particularly your ability to think analytically. Unfortunately, our company doesn't permit the liberty of extended deadlines. We need someone who can work at a faster pace. I think it would be best for you to find a position where you have the time to go into things more deeply.

- Be clear about the details. Make sure that you both understand exactly what the game rules are: when they are to leave, what the severance pay is to be, and what if anything your company will do to help in the relocation process—if you will offer the services of a company-paid executive search agency, your personal contacts, or letters of recommendation:

> John, it's always difficult when there hasn't been a good match. You've tried very hard, but we have to let you go. I'd like to offer some suggestions, if it would help. You're welcome to stay at your desk

another two weeks, and feel free to use our phones, stationery, and secretaries to send out your résumé. I can recommend a personnel agency if you like. And don't hesitate to call on me for references. If it would be more comfortable for you, we'll give you your two weeks' pay now and you can leave at the end of the day.

Here are the bench marks to test yourself against when you have to fire somebody. You should be able to answer Yes to these five questions when the interview has ended:

1. Do you think you were fair?
2. Were you supportive?
3. Did you stick to facts rather than emotions?
4. If you have to deal with them again and they are in the driver's seat, will they think well of you?
5. Will you sleep well tonight?

Can they fire me for something that's not my fault?

Are you sure that what's happened is not your fault? Or that you can't correct the situation? Consider the plight of Anita, the ultimate whiner for whom everything seems to go wrong, and it is never her fault. Or is it?

I miss a lot of work because I get every virus that's going around and a cold every time somebody sneezes. I can't help these things, and God knows I try to put in my time. It's not as if I stay out on purpose. For instance, last week my youngster had a fever but I was going to go to the office anyway. Wouldn't you know? The sitter canceled out on me. And what are you supposed to do when there's a funeral in the family—not go? I'm late to work a lot, too, but I certainly can't help it if the traffic jams in this city are incredible.

Why doesn't Anita leave the house a half hour earlier so she doesn't get caught in rush hour? Why doesn't she have a backup sitter? What makes her take to bed with every twinge and sniffle? It sounds as if she may have a psychological problem and needs professional help. Maybe she's used to being babied and doesn't want to grow up and be responsible. I'll tell you what's going to happen to Anita: If her work is really valuable, her boss will call her in and tell her that she must resolve her problems and give him the full time he's paying her for, or else leave. And he'll be right. Even though Anita's difficulties are valid, they are not going to stop interfering with her work until *she* puts a stop to them. You can be sure that her co-workers and certainly her boss have lives that are at least as complicated. They are rarely absent from the job: effective people almost never are.

Why do I always get blamed for whatever goes wrong in the office?

The first thing you have to do is sit down and analyze why you are always being blamed. Consider the possibility that you have let yourself be placed in a scapegoat position. Women are apt to do this out of the cultural conditioning that taught them "females are supposed to be subservient." They are so eager to please they act as if they were born guilty. Whatever happens, they automatically offer themselves up as the ones who did wrong. Naturally, everybody automatically takes advantage of them.

You have to stop and pinpoint who is really responsible for what went wrong. You will never win respect or succeed in your career if you let yourself be the company poodle.

You also have to realize that it is entirely possible that the things that go wrong really are your fault. Face the facts about yourself:

- Do you make mistakes in figures?
- Are you clear when you tell people what you want?
- Do you listen carefully to what people tell you, or do you leap to conclusions?

It may very well be that you deserve the blame you are getting. If that is the case, you had better take stock of your errors and concentrate on learning to do your job properly.

What if I'm not smart enough to do everything the job requires?

Maybe you are in over your head. Or maybe you are trying to play the game of "I'm just a flighty female." That's not a game for career people. You have to make it your job to understand the nature of business—how your company works and what its priorities are. You can't just peck away at every task that comes along, or you will bog down in minutiae. You have to learn to tend to the big picture first and not chew up your time concentrating on trivia. Otherwise things will always go wrong.

Give me a trick to keep blame off my back.

One technique that gives you control is to document what you do. Cover your moves in writing. Record phone calls and meetings as soon as they take place. Keep dated memos outlining prices, schedules, assignments, whatever you discuss. And send copies to everyone involved, plus one for your files. That way you will have concrete evidence of the facts if there's a misunderstanding or argument. They can't say it's your fault things went wrong if you can prove that you did just what they said.

Suppose nobody reads my memos?

It doesn't matter. The object is to get on record and have your defense ready in case anyone blames you. If you find you're the target of frequent accusations, you go a step further and borrow the techniques of lawyers and reporters. Make it a precautionary habit to record the date and gist of each conversation in a logbook. Use a tape recorder for conference and phone calls. If your taping makes people uneasy, explain why you want to preserve the conversation: "We have had several misunderstandings in the past. I'm sure you understand that taping this talk is to help us both."

Can they dismiss me if I become pregnant?

No, it's illegal. A recent amendment to Title VII of the Civil Rights Act states that pregnancy must be treated the same as any type of disability. This means you cannot be discriminated against or fired because you are pregnant. Further, they must give you equal treatment under their health, disability and sick-leave plans. You may take a leave of absence if you wish, but they cannot require you to do so as long as you are able and willing to work. When you return, they must reinstate all of your rights, including credit for previous work, accrued retirement benefits, and seniority.

What if I need an abortion?

If you need an abortion, federal law says you get the same health, disability and sick leave benefits as you do for pregnancy, *providing* the abortion is to save your life. You are also protected if medical complications result from the abortion. Incidentally, it's a good idea to check your company's health insurance plan to see if it provides abortion coverage.

Can they fire me if they find out I'm a homosexual?

Some cities have a law against firing you for homosexuality. But few employers anywhere will fire you for that reason; they're afraid you might make a case of it. They'll fire you for another reason instead: "We're lopping our budget. We're eliminating your department." Or else they'll make it uncomfortable for you so you'll quit of your own accord. Being fired for homosexuality is not the point; it hardly ever happens. The point is, will you make them fire you because of the way you handle yourself? Do you make an effort to fit in where you work? If your company is conventional, are you extra-careful to be discreet? If you are in a relaxed community where it's all right to be out of the closet, are you relaxed, too? Or do you make an issue of your sexual preference? Your private life is never something to flaunt around the office. People accept or reject what they see. The passage of time, however, can change their tolerance thresholds, as Michelle discovered. She was held back for years by her personal life, but is finally ready to acknowledge it in public:

> I have been an assistant manager with the same company for twelve years. I have always done a good job, been praised—and passed over. For twelve years running, I have *not* been promoted to manager, and I know perfectly well it's because I'm a lesbian. This is your typical conservative midwestern town, however, and if I'd made an issue of the fact I'd have destroyed myself professionally. Nobody else would hire me. So I've just gone along with the tide, doing my best and enjoying it as much as I could. Things are loosening up, though. A friend got me to join the Gay Coalition, a national activist support group, and they lined up a job for me in Chicago. I'm not really eager to move, but the fact that I could gives me courage. I feel now that I can go in to management and put it on the line. I wouldn't be afraid to say, "We both know that I've done a good job and deserve to be manager, but my sexual orientation has got in the way. It's not your fault and it's not mine, but I have my future to consider. It's time to

review once and for all the question of whether or not I will get my promotion. Can I count on it this year?"

If they don't go along with my proposal, I will hand in my resignation and head for Chicago. Either way, it's going to be a great relief.

What does it mean, to kick someone upstairs?

Karen, the senior vice-president of a large research and development firm, tells how she squeezed a nettlesome staff member out of her department:

Michael was a bright young man, well mannered and probably very able. I couldn't tell when I took over the department because he chose to look busy rather than to work. Michael was forever in meetings, chatting in somebody's office, or nattering away on the phone.

As administrative manager, he should have given me the department's records, documents, and procedural policies to study. Instead, he postponed me and double-talked. "I'll have those answers for you as soon as I get back from my meeting," he'd chirp. Pressed, he would postpone, double-talk, and trot off to more meetings. Obviously, I'd have to find out for myself how the office was run. It was a nuisance, but I did it. What I found out was, the office hadn't been run at all. There were no records and no filing system. Procedures were non-existent. Michael was responsible for chaos and I couldn't fire him: He'd been given the job by the company's chief executive officer, who happens to be his uncle. I had to figure out how to get him off my payroll some other way. What I did was foist him onto Marcy.

Her department was so big the troops stumbled all over each other, and there was nobody to untangle the strands. Marcy was going bonkers. She kept hiring more and more people, in hopes she'd find one who could take charge. "Ah ha," I calculated. "Here is my pigeon. I will help Marcy out." I asked her to lunch and we spent two hours talking about the company. Every time Marcy complained about her staff, I raved about mine. Naturally, she asked about my alleged aide-de-camp, Michael. I didn't actually lie because lies can boomerang on you. I merely gave her the impression that my department was a very tight ship and all hands were to be congratulated. She put two and two together and came up with Michael as the person responsible for keeping everything on a straight course.

I wasn't surprised when the chief executive officer called the next day and told me he was going to transfer Michael from my department to Marcy's. He said she'd expressed a particular interest in him, and could give him a bigger salary than I. I answered that I was crushed, but Michael certainly deserved the promotion. I let Michael break the news himself that he was abandoning my department and going on to help Marcy. If I ever needed help, just call him. I expressed profound regret, wished him well, and I hope to heaven Marcy never figures out how she became the recipient of Marvelous Michael.

When should you quit a job?

• When you need more money, they keep saying No to a raise, and you have other good prospects.

• When you need a job with a better future. When you've gone as far as you can in the organization and there's no room to go further. When you feel you could make better use of your abilities.

• When you want to push your career ahead faster. Studies show that career people who change jobs a few times earn more money than their peers who stay with one company. A marketing person starting at $14,000 could reach a $22,000 salary level in six years if he/she stays with their company. The same person could jump to $30,000 if they make the right three job changes.

• When they repeatedly break promises to you. They promise a raise or promotion and then renege. They give you authority to carry out a project and then step in and take over. They say Yes, you can take a three-week vacation and call you back after ten days.

• When you are bored with what you do or hate it. The zest is gone. There's no challenge or satisfaction. You don't get up each morning eager to knock 'em dead. You are tired or depressed and need a change of pace.

How much notice should you give?

Two to four weeks is usual, and longer notice is acceptable. The purpose of giving notice is so your boss will have time to find a replacement for you. You should use the time to make sure you leave good records behind, to simplify the maze for the new person and shorten the time your boss has to spend training them. Include a work-in-progress report, so everybody will be clear on the details you've been carrying around in your head.

You don't have to abandon everything when you quit. Leave confidential material behind; that belongs to the company. But take a copy of important phone numbers, your contact lists, and special work files with you. The hard work you've put in and connections you've made belong to you. Hang on to them. You are sure to need them as you move on.

Why is it so hard for me to write a letter of resignation?

You may feel a mistaken sense of loyalty. "These people taught me everything I know. I would be wrong to repay them by leaving them in the lurch." The reality is, they won't be in the lurch. There is always somebody else who can do what you do as well and maybe beter than you.

You may be in a rut and afraid to move out of it. You think you might leap from the frying pan into the fire. Take the risk. The reality is, leaving your rut can open doors. It's your opportunity to choose the job that will further your career.

You think they will hate you. For what? The fact is, they are primarily concerned about their own future. And they realize that their world will go on without you. If they are your good friends, they may express concern over your decision to leave. But hate you? It doesn't make sense.

What do you say in a letter of resignation?

In a large, structured organization, it is good form simply to send a brief, formal note:

This is to inform you of my resignation effective March 6.

In a more personal letter, you might add:

I have thoroughly enjoyed my tenure with your organization and have the greatest respect for you, your staff, and the work that you are doing. It is my hope that sometime in the future I will be in a position to serve you again.

I am not in favor of the considered dig, but I can't resist telling you about the barbed letter of resignation Rusty once wrote. It was her first. She has since had a multitude of careers—advertising, television, sales—anything that's fast-moving attracts her. Rusty fairly crackles with energy and zest for whatever she's doing, and is always ready to do something more. That was true even in her very first job, twenty-two years ago:

> I was hired by a laundry company to do I don't know what. Some kind of publicity work. There were only two people in the office, me and a sort of factotum. Yet this office generated hundreds and thousands of dollars from a business that we never saw anything of. After a few months, by piecing together the names of the people who called in and who went to meetings, I realized who really owned the "laundry": the Mafia. I knew it for sure the day they stopped by to check up on their business. The door opened and in stepped a cartoon: four pin-stripe suits, four white silk ties on black silk shirts, four wretched-smelling cigars, and four shiny holsters. That's where my paychecks were coming from? No thanks. I didn't care for it at all. I immediately handed in a superbly wrought letter of resignation:

>> Dear Sirs:
>> At this time I would like to tender my resignation. I am distinctly uncomfortable in your employ for reasons best left undiscussed, and I believe that I can make an honest living elsewhere.

> I was young, and I got my troubles off my chest. I don't think I'd do that today, especially with gangsters. I'd just resign without going into the reasons. I'm lucky they didn't take it into their heads to use me for rifle practice, or wrap my feet in cement.

What do you say when you resign in person?

Something courteous. Always leave a job on an up-note, so there is no bad taste in anyone's mouth. You want to leave people with good feelings about you, even if you think they're savages. Take your leave with all the respect and goodwill you can muster. Otherwise you will give them a reason to dislike you and to say bad things about you to people you will need in the future.

Sometimes it is hard to swallow your righteous indignation when you think you've been treated badly. You want to lash back, give vent to your contempt. You want to let them know that they are the culprit: They were unfair, uncooperative. Don't do it. You will only give them reason to say you were a disloyal, disruptive, undesirable employee. When you make somebody else look bad, it is usually plague on both your houses, in the end.

272

There are many ways to tell somebody you're resigning; it depends on your relationship. When you're on an informal footing, you can approach your boss as a friend. Like the resignation talk I overheard at a research firm in Texas:

SUSAN: Good morning, Kim. I asked to come see you because I have good news for you, and I have bad news. Which would you like to hear first?

KIM: Give me the good news, Sue, quick. Business has been so slow this quarter, I need all the goodies I can collect.

SUSAN: OK. The good news is, I'm going to get you more business.

KIM: That's wonderful How are you going to do it?

SUSAN: Well, that's the bad part. I'm going to do it by leaving you.

KIM: Oh no! Susan!

SUSAN: Yes, Kim. I must move on. I have an opportunity to make a lot more money, and to get into product development. That's something I can't do here, since you have no product-development division. That's my good news. Now I'll get back to the part that's good for you. The job I'm taking is with one of our clients, Lord and Noble. As you probably know, they have a lot of plans that are going to be thrown on somebody's drawing board. I really believe in your company, Kim, and what you are doing. I have the greatest respect for your research and integrity, and I know I'll be able to bring in a lot of L and N's business.

KIM: I appreciate that, Sue. And I'm happy for you. But I hate you for doing this to me! Why, you learned how business works here. And now that you've learned it, you're leaving me high and dry.

SUSAN: I wouldn't do that to you, Kim. I've thought it all through. I'll be here for another month and during that time I plan to keep a daily log of exactly what I do, plus a procedural handbook, so whoever replaces me can just pick up the pieces and nothing will slip through the cracks. May I make a suggestion? How about calling Carla, the research analyst I replaced. Remember, she left because she had a baby to take care of? I spoke with her yesterday and she is feeling antsy and is ready to come back on a part-time basis. She'd be perfect.

KIM: Yes, she would. And I could combine her part time with Maria's, who's in the same position. They could job-share and take up the slack you'll be leaving. With your log and handbook, we can bring them both up to date and work out the logistics.

SUSAN: Still hate me?

KIM: I never did and you know it. It's just that nobody likes to lose a good member of the team. Sue, promise me you'll keep in touch, and if it doesn't work out for you we can always make a place for you here.

WORKING
FOR YOURSELF

What are my chances of making it in my own business?

The Small Business Administration, which keeps track of entrepreneurial successes and failures, says you have a 50 percent chance of surviving the first two years in your own business. After that the odds drop with a thump: Only 20 percent of the people who go into business for themselves make it past the first five years.

What are the most common reasons entrepreneurs fail?

In order of frequency, the five major reasons are:

1. Undercapitalization
2. Inexperience
3. Inadequate research
4. Overexpansion
5. Lack of self-discipline.

Explain the five reasons to me: How much capital do you need?

Enough to get you through the first two years at least. It takes that long for most businesses to get onto their feet, so you need enough start-up money to cover operating costs until you begin to see appreciable profits. Otherwise you will wind up with your initial investment down the drain, and nothing to show for your efforts but debt.

One of the first things you must do before you launch a new business is to project your cash flow. It's important to be pessimistic. Look for trouble. Under *Outgo,* add in every item you can think of: supplies, advertising, travel and entertainment, repairs, bad debts, taxes, a contingency fund. Project a minimum *Income,* and a maximum *Outgo.* Then take steps to ensure that you can weather the worst and still have money to spare. If necessary, get a bank or a personal loan. Or take on a financial partner. Even if you do have to share your profits with someone, at least with sufficient capital you'll have profits to share.

Capitalization is an ongoing thing. You have to be prepared to keep on spending money on your business if you want to succeed.

277

Many women fail in business or stay small because they are afraid to invest in themselves. They worry so much about laying out cash, they are blind to the long-range benefits reinvesting can bring. If you want to grow, you have to have the courage to think big and dare to take realistic financial risks.

Explain the number-two reason for failure: Inexperience.

People crash when they fly blind. You have to be willing to take the time to put in an apprenticeship, so you will know what you are doing when you fly solo. You don't succeed just because you have a feeling for clothes, a love of art, or a good head for figures. You have to take the time to learn what that particular business is all about. Even a course in entrepreneurship won't prepare you well enough; that's just one plank in your platform. What you need is at least two years' practical, everyday experience working for somebody else. That way you can refine your skills, learn the structure and problems of business, get to understand what it is people need, develop contacts, find out which suppliers are which, and build up a good professional reputation.

Inexperienced people set themselves up as patsies. They make every mistake in the book. Often the disasters are more than they can overcome.

What about the third reason for failure: Inadequate research?

The best ideas in the world turn into nightmares when people fail to do their homework, to make sure they can make a living from what they do. They let enthusiasm override good sense. Creative people are especially apt to skip market research. They get into trouble because they won't sit down with a sharp pencil and figure out if they can really make a profit from their beautiful creations. They don't ask the right questions: Will my products be in competition with lower-priced, mass-produced articles? How much will my materials cost? How many hours will I have to spend to produce a limited number of masterpieces? What will my bottom line actually be? Talent is wonderful, but it isn't enough. You have to find out if your talent can pay off.

People fail in business when they don't research their motivations as well as their market. They look at friends who are in business for themselves and think, "Everybody's doing it; why not me?" The fact is, what's right for "everybody" may be all wrong for you. You have to analyze your own position and not ape others for the sake of being on a bandwagon. It's just as important to search your soul honestly as it is to research your market in depth.

Number four: Overexpansion. What does that mean?

Growing too big, too fast. Businesses topple when they can't support their own overhead. You have to look at all the facts before you decide when to grow, how much to grow, or whether you should grow at all. Your figures may show that you can double your volume if you take on two more salespeople. Stop. Figure it out. Add up what the expansion will cost you. Will the salespeople require support? A secretary, a bookkeeper? Will you need to rent larger space? Will you have to buy or lease more equipment? Doubling your volume could mean quadrupling your outlay for salaries, Social Security, and Unemployment taxes, a bigger rent bill, typewriters, a car. That's called overexpansion, and it can put you into the red and out of business.

Explain why undisciplined people fail.

They can't be their own bosses. You have to be honest about yourself. If you can't get up and get dressed in the morning unless you have somebody to report to, you probably won't do it for yourself. If you habitually fritter time, you'll have difficulty learning to treat time as a commodity. If you are relaxed about deadlines, put personal pleasures ahead of business demands, can't organize a schedule by priorities or stick to your commitments, you're going to have a hard time succeeding as head of your own business.

There are ways to overcome your handicap. Here are the tricks some people use:

1. Keep a project schedule in full sight at all times, so you can see where you have to speed up to meet deadlines.
2. Assign an hourly dollar value to your time and keep a daily time sheet, so you can see how much you earn on each project. Or how much you lose.
3. Set a specific schedule for nonwork items such as laundry, shopping, haircuts, reading.

4. Keep an orderly, organized work space so supplies, files, everything you work with is quickly and easily accessible.

5. Set priorities to make the best use of your time. Use this checklist to help find the techniques that work best for you:

PRIORITIES CHECKLIST

- Keep a written or diagrammed timetable for each goal.
- List a daily plan of action. Write it down first thing each morning or the last thing the night before.
- List things to do in order of their importance, starting with the most important. Adhere to it, but be flexible enough to shift your plan when something urgent comes up.
- Recognize the difference between "urgent," "important," and "desirable."
- Stick to your agenda. Control interruptions, distractions, digressions.
- Do nothing that you can delegate to somebody else.

Why do people go into business for themselves?

They're the type whose personality dictates self-employment. If you want to work for yourself, you probably share these traits: You have a strong need to be independent. You tend to be something of a loner—a person who prefers not to play on somebody else's team. You cannot bear to have anybody looking over your shoulder. You need freedom and flexibility. You have to feel you can come and go at will, choose your own tasks, set your own hours. You are strong on *self:* self-discipline, self-expression, self-motivation. You are an initiator rather than a follower, able to feed on your own ideas and resources. You are a visionary, a risk-taker, and an optimist; and you are totally committed to your own success.

There are other reasons. You may be forced to take over somebody else's business. Self-employment may be the only way you can earn a living and stay at home, too. Perhaps you don't fit into any corporate niche. You're overqualified for the going pay scale. Or you can't find a company that will let you reach your full height as a female. See if you relate to any of these stories:

I HAD TO STAY AT HOME WITH YOUNG CHILDREN

Evelyn, thirty, book illustrator: I'd worked at a publishing house since before I was married, and quit when my first child was born. Two years after the second child, I was divorced and had to generate an income again. I also had to stay home with the children, so I went into business for myself as a free-lance illustrator. To get started, I contacted everybody I'd ever known in publishing, and I also let all my friends know what I was doing. You never know who will tell whom. Next, I got up a mailing piece for myself that I could also use as a leave-behind when I went on sales calls. The minute I knew that I had some kind of rolling start, I turned the guest room into my studio. I had shelves built for my supplies, bought a drawing table, installed a good fluorescent light, and plastered every inch of wall with those cork squares you get in hardware stores, to give myself a wraparound bulletin board for sketches, job orders, schedules, and other inspirational pinups. That was about it. I was in business with very little financial investment and had everything at my fingertips— including the children.

I OUTGREW MY CORPORATE NICHE

Betty Ann, thirty-six, commercial realtor: The one thing I could kick myself for is hanging around in institutional life two years longer than I should have. I'd been an associate professor of economics at a university, and thought of myself as a financial person. Yet I knew that I had strength in a number of other disciplines: marketing, analysis, and even negotiation, thanks to some real estate transactions I'd done extracurricular consulting on. There came a point when I began to feel that teaching was no longer a challenge for me. I was bored; it was too easy. I missed the feeling of elation and accomplishment I'd had at first. But I didn't have the nerve to do anything about it, so I puttered along, increasingly discontented. After two years, I knew this was wrong. I took the bit in my teeth, quit the university, and set myself up as a full-time specialist in commercial real estate. It's been fantastic. Everything came together just right. I knew the business and had a network of good contacts from my consultancies. And I had an edge over other realtors because of my M.B.A. in finance. The one thing I was most afraid of, that going into real estate would be a comedown and I'd lose people's respect, turned out to be an empty fear. In fact, it's been just the reverse. My friends, my family, the people I do business with are impressed with the way I handle complicated transactions, and with the money I'm making. I might add, so am I.

I WAS STYMIED BECAUSE OF MY SEX

Jane, forty-four, research company president: I started out in TV, where I worked my way up to producing children's shows. But my ambition outgrew that after a while: What I really wanted was to produce a network news show. Tough luck. In televisionland, the news was man's domain. Women got to produce shows about children, decorating, food, fashion, religion. I thought I was stuck with the system—until it dawned on me that I didn't have to be. I could take my abilities elsewhere and put them to work for myself. That's when I got out and became my own organization.

I gave a lot of thought to deciding what I'd do, and I made a lot of lists in the process. The first one was:

Things I like to do and do well

Produce television shows
Generate ideas
Manage people
Administer and control
Then I had to think about my market:

Local businesses that could buy my services

Three TV stations
Two production houses
It looked as if there was no opportunity to market my abilities, until I thought further and wrote a list titled *Business needs that nobody else is filling*. Three ideas came to mind almost immediately, and none of them had anything to do with television production. The one I liked best was, of all things, opinion surveys. Here's what went through my mind:

Q: People are forever going into new businesses and failing. Why?

A: They don't do enough advance research.

Q: How could they find out whether there actually is a potential for success or not?

A: They could poll people to learn what they do and don't need, and whether they'd be willing to spend money for what they want.

Q: How could they poll people?

A: Hire a professional market researcher who could also analyze the results and give them feasibility reports.

Q: How could I fill that need?

A: I have all the skills, and my TV experience has given me a good marketing sense. I don't know the technical end of the business, but I do know researchers and analysts I could hire.

Q: What's the competition? How many market researchers are there who know this part of the country intimately?

A: Only a couple.

Q: What would I have to do to get started?

A: Get capital. Hire a professional researcher to do what I can't do. Write up some proposals. Sell my idea to product manufacturers, political candidates, whoever needs professional business forecasts.

That was eight years ago. Today I have two partners, a staff of thirty, and an annual billing of a million and a half. And I love what I do. What I'm trying to say is, if nobody will hire you for what you want to do, hire yourself. But look before you leap. Figure out what it is you like to do, what it is you are able to do, and whether there is a market for it. Then go ahead, work like a demon, and the likelihood is that you'll be OK.

What kind of business should I go into?

If you have a marked talent, your work is cut out for you. Writers must write, painters have to paint, musicians and other gifted people have a clear-cut path they must tread. Trust your talent, and let it lead you. Your big question is whether to free-lance or work together with a group. The answer will come from two sources: your personality—whether you are strictly a loner or need the stimulation of other artists—and supply and demand. If your area is flooded with people as good or better than you, you may be able to make a better

283

living if you work collectively rather than as a free lance. Weigh the choices thoughtfully, but don't get so overwrought about making a decision that you stall and do nothing. Remember, you can always switch over to solo or group if your first choice doesn't work out. Recognizing your options is one of the keys to success as an entrepreneur.

If talent is not your long suit, a strong affinity can direct you to a certain field—providing you search out a hole in the marketplace. A good way to start is to think in terms of specialization, which is what business in the eighties is all about. Analyze the successful retailers around you. You'll see that most of them have a special point of view: tennis shops, jeans stores, boutiques for heart-shaped articles, Victorian glassware, gadgets for left-handed people. These retail specialists have made themselves known as the source for one certain thing. They've identified their stores as the place anyone interested in tennis, jeans, or heart-shaped accessories must shop. Successful specialists also know this: You have to be able to adapt to change. When the fashion swings away from tennis, jeans, or your particular specialty, you must be ready to swing with the times. Otherwise your business will die with the fad.

Sometimes an affinity grows on you unexpectedly. Terry is one of those people who fits no corporate niche and has no particular leaning except that she likes to shop. She'd been out of work for months, and whenever she wasn't job-hunting she haunted flea markets and auctions. She found herself especially attracted to old clocks and watches, and picked some up for very little money. Soon Terry began to think, "I'm developing a unique collection here. These timepieces really are fascinating and I've learned a lot about them. I'll bet this could be valuable on the marketplace." She went to a few of the antique dealers in her area and offered to let them take her timepieces on consignment: What they didn't sell, they wouldn't have to pay for. In fact, most of the pieces did sell, and Terry kept adding to her flea-market collection. After a while she began to sell her pieces outright to department stores. By then she had become the expert in her field, to the point of being the person in town who set the prices. Over the course of just two years her business grew to where she now employs a full-time bookkeeper and salesperson, and is interviewing for another salesperson. The shopping she reserves for herself—that's the part she has always loved best.

Another woman, Abby, combined talent, affinity, and good contacts to go into business for herself. Abby worked for a Houston decorating firm, and after a few years she became aware that the corporate clients she served were billing $75,000 to $100,000 a year. She realized that the decorating firm was taking a large markup on merchandise and workmanship, but it was she who gave the clients advice and did all the legwork. Essentially, the clients were buying her expertise, not the company's. So Abby went to two of the clients and suggested that she could serve them equally well as an independent, and at the same time save them from paying the decorating firm's high overhead costs. She said, "Your offices will still have the look of fine quality you're after but instead of paying one hundred thousand dollars a year for it, you will only have to spend sixty thousand dollars. That will give me enough profit as an individual to keep on doing a good job for you." They agreed with her reasoning, and Abby's initial clientele has expanded from two to eight, thanks to word-of-mouth recommendations. Abby has had to add administrative help: a part-time bookkeeper/secretary, but she has put a cap on her growth. She says if she handles more than eight clients at a time, she'll have to charge more to cover her overhead and will no longer have a competitive advantage over the fully staffed firms in town.

What can you do if you're middle aged?
Anything anybody else can do. Women in midlife sometimes think their age makes them a drag on the market. The fact is, they often have more experience and affinities to draw on than younger people. Like Norma, a forty-four-year-old with a teen-ager to support and no business skills whatsoever. However, she had been very good at being a wife: knew how to get home repairs done, liked to shop for household items, had a knack for selecting the right gifts for people, and actually enjoyed running errands. Norma kept hearing her working-women friends groan that they needed a wife: "All those errands, the house—I can't cope." She tuned into the situation and said, "There is a need I can cash in on. I will become the working woman's wife."

And that is exactly what her successful business is all about. If you live in Norma's town and find life is a hassle, all you have to do is call her up and hire her to do the things that are too much for you. She'll shop the sales, balance your checkbook, get your blinds cleaned —do all the things she's always been good at, and is now getting paid to do.

You can translate an affinity for running parties into professional party-planning. You could take your knowledge of museums or music and conduct special-interest travel groups. Have you a green thumb? Consider the possibilities in opening a plant store, or becoming a horticultural adviser. The opportunities are limitless, if you

1. Use your imagination
2. Research your market
3. Figure out your profit potential.

Does it matter what I wear if I work alone at home?

It does. You have to leave the house sometime—to get the mail or groceries, keep a lunch date, or just walk. Somebody will see you, and you want them to see you looking crisp. Dressing well is a lift for your own morale, besides. There is nothing less conducive to efficient, productive behavior than sitting around all day in a tatty chenille robe.

What you do not have to do is spend your time and energy worrying about your appearance. Take care of the basics and move on from there.

How can I overcome my fear of not having a regular paycheck?

Examine your fear to see if it's based on reality or if it's just mental habit that is holding you back. It may help you to analyze your attitude, and decide what you are willing to change. The four areas to look at are:

First, you have to prefer the freedom of independence to the assurance of a regular income.

Second, you must have faith in your ability to make a living on your own.

Third, you have to be willing to risk investing in your own future.

Fourth, you have to be able to discipline yourself about spending during fat times as well as in lean.

Betty Ann, the realtor, says:

Earning my own money and being free to spend it as I choose is very important to me. If you were to offer me a thirty-five-thousand-dollar-a-year job, I'd tell you to get lost. I want my freedom. Even if I never exercise the choice, I want to know that I can go to the Virgin Islands for the next two weeks if I feel like it. Now, if you were to offer me seventy-five thousand dollars, that would be another story. I might give it a go. But I would keep this real estate business alive just the same. I'd hire somebody to work at it so if I tired of the corporate thing, I'd have a business to come back into. And if I fell in love with the corporate job, I'd still keep the business going so I'd always have my own private revenue.

Jane, the research company owner, talks about a friend who asked her advice about whether to take a corporate job at $20,000 or open a stationery boutique of her own:

This woman was very concerned about nitty details. She wanted to know how and when she'd get back her investment in store fixtures. She worried about investing in fifty-dollar catalogs. She had a choice of two locations and said of course she'd take the one that was cheaper. And she thought she'd keep the limited hours so she wouldn't have to pay for help. She was unable to grasp the large picture. The fact that prime locations cost more because they're where the foot traffic is escaped her. It was more important to her to save money on help than to cash in on serving customers at their convenience. Her whole outlook was fastened on the petty details: She thought in nickels and dimes, not dollars. I told her, "I really think you should take the paying job. You'd be better off working for somebody else where you don't have these kinds of concerns."

Her attitude was against her. You have to be able to take other people's needs and ideas into consideration, and not be so opinionated you can't sell to them. You need to have a certain intelligence, a pleasing manner, and know how to deal with people. And you have to be where your market is. This woman may have been tasteful, brainy, and a brilliant salesperson. But she still would have died if she'd gone into business for herself.

Abby, the free-lance decorator who left a company job, says:

Money is a very big factor for me. I have always needed to know that
I'll have a certain amount coming in. Not to be wealthy, but so I won't
have to scrimp. When I started out, it took me a full year to learn to
compensate for my new feast-or-famine status. One month I'd make a
bundle, and the next month not one check would come in. I had to
learn to budget for this, and use the peaks on my chart realistically.
I think of myself as a corporation now, and reassess my position every
three months. But I remember when I began and got paid for three
jobs all at once. All I could see was the gravy. I raced right out and
bought myself a wonderful car, and by the fifteenth of the month I
couldn't even drive it around because I had no money to support it.
That was my first hard lesson. It made me sit down and work out my
needs. I figured out how much I had to have month to month for the
essentials: rent, food, things that are musts. I added a list of fancies:
dinners out, new clothes, the things you can live without but it's more
fun with. And then I set aside a slush fund: money for doctor's bills,
business screw-ups, a cushion in case I should change my mind and
want to start over somewhere else. I will never be without my slush
fund. It's what keeps me from panicking in months when business
goes sour. And it's the security blanket that lets me thumb my nose
at job offers and the world at large.

Why do people incorporate?
Mainly so they won't be personally liable for their company's
debts.

The trade-offs are that you have to pay high corporate taxes, and
you have to do a lot of paperwork to keep proper records.

How can I avoid corporate taxes?
By filing with the Internal Revenue Service under Subchapter S,
which means that you are taxed on your personal income, rather than
at corporate income tax rates. In this way, you may be able to take
advantage of business losses by claiming them on your personal return. Your accountant is the best judge of whether you stand to gain
or lose under Subchapter S.

What if I don't incorporate?
Then you are an individual proprietor. You have complete con-

trol of your business, but you are also personally liable for your business debts.

What does DBA stand for?

"Doing Business As." You take out a DBA certificate when you are in business as a sole proprietor and want to protect your family against liability for your business debts.

When should I consider taking a partner?

When you lack capital and need a working or silent co-owner. When you need somebody to handle the creative, managerial, or administrative tasks you're no good at. When you need somebody to account to, to stimulate your performance.

In many respects, a working business partner is the same as a marriage partner. You must be able to live very closely together on a daily basis. You need similar or at least complementary goals. You have to learn how to get along when you disagree: to give in here, persuade there, see compromise as a good solution. Although your partner's irritating personal habits are literally not your business, you have to keep them from affecting your relationship, just as you would in a marriage. Jealously, rivalry, all the love/hate emotions can crop up. And dissolution, if it comes, can be just as embittering as any divorce. You have to be very careful when you enter into a partnership, and cover all the bases ahead of time.

How do you prevent partner trouble?

Know everything you can about each other before you merge. Business background: successes, failures, weaknesses, and strengths. Check it out as thoroughly as if you were getting references on a key employee. Maybe more thoroughly. You can fire an employee if you've made a mistake; it's a grueling procedure to dissolve a partnership. Talk at great length with your prospective business mate before either of you makes a final decision. Are your philosophies, ethics, and standards compatible? If your partner is financial, will there be a problem about continuing support, about sharing or reinvesting the profits? With a working partner, list the specific ways he or she balances your capabilities. If you need somebody good at administration, is the other person really strong on those skills, and how have they been proved? Is administration what they really want to handle, or might they get bored with it and leave you in the lurch?

Once you are satisfied that yours will be a partnership made in heaven, get your understandings in writing. This is very important, otherwise you risk future disagreement with no recourse or guidelines. Your agreement should be drawn by an attorney and should cover the following points plus any others that pertain to your particular situation:

1. The purpose of your business.
2. Your marketing point of view.
3. The division of responsibilities, spelled out in detail.
4. Business arrangements if either partner should die or become disabled.
5. Your board of directors: people with business acumen who can also act as mediators in disputes.

As clear and specific as your agreement may be, it is only as good as your and your partner's willingness to follow through. Like a marriage contract, it's only enforceable in cast of a rift.

Where do you find a partner?

Through business colleagues or contacts. Through your business or professional association. Through your attorney or accountant. Through advertising in consumer or trade publications.

Betty Ann, a real estate dealer, says that at one point she was looking for a partner to come in with her on another business idea she had. She put an ad in an industry newsletter and in the financial pages of her local newspaper that read as follows:

Seeking active partner in Southwest Missouri for adjunct to established successful real estate firm. High profit potential. Creative sales ability required, plus strong marketing background and knowledge of local real estate market. Reply Box 200.

Betty Ann says she had several dozen responses, of which four looked very interesting. She made appointments with each of the four to discuss the project, to review their business history and get a feeling for what they were like. They were all good people, but something was just a little off-target in each case. One had business commitments that would demand too much of his time. Another represented a group of investors, and Betty Ann felt that she didn't want to have to report to more than one person. The other two simply lacked that dynamic spark she was looking for.

One of them, however, suggested somebody else who he thought would mesh well with Betty Ann's needs and style. He was right. Betty Ann and David were on track in all respects. They met eight times to discuss her idea, and in each meeting they explored and expanded her concept until they reached an agreement.

How many partners should you take?

There is no formula to answer that question. It depends on how you work and what your needs are. I know people in the creative field, where you might think that the more personalities there are to deal with the more chances there are for conflict, who work very well together. I'm thinking in particular of a writer, illustrator, and editor-salesperson who joined forces and have been very successful and happy with the results. Another woman I know, a composer, has put together a trio consisting of herself, a lyricist, and a marketer. By augmenting one another on a business as well as creative basis, each of them now has the sales strength of three. Their arrangement stipulates that they work jointly on joint projects, and that each can also work independently on free-lance assignments.

What do you do when there's conflict in a trio?

Conflicts can be difficult to resolve when three people are involved. Two can gang up on the third, and the result is that nobody comes out really satisfied. In threesomes particularly, it's useful to set policy guidelines at the outset, with the contractual agreement that if even one of you feels strongly about something that departs from policy, the idea will be abandoned without further question. This way you can't get into a two-against-one disagreement.

If you can't resolve a dissent yourselves and you are dissatisfied with the advice of your third-party mediator, the best thing to do is to be very open with one another. Confront the issue straightforwardly. If that doesn't work, be ingenious: Find a way to compensate for whatever it is that's going wrong. Rosa is an entrepreneur who says she's had to do this a few times. She has two separate partnerships, a gift boutique and a needlework shop, and while both are successful, there have been a few distressing clashes along the way:

My needlework partner and I saw a great opportunity to develop a newsletter that would give needlework fans information they couldn't get from the monthly magazines. Since we were already partners and this was to be a spin-off of our basic business, we didn't bother to put anything further in writing. That was a mistake. Before we had got our first newsletter into motion, I learned that she had gone to somebody else in town, somebody with more capital and connections than I had, and was working with him on a fancier newsletter than we had projected. What she did really hurt me; I felt it was disloyal. In a way, though, her action freed me. Now I feel that I can do the same: run wherever I want to with any of my needlework-related ideas without consulting her.

Shortly after that painful episode, my friend Nan told me she'd like to get into a business with me. She said she was eager to open a gift boutique—she loved the buying part and had a lot of experience and contacts in that area. She could see from my needlework shop that there were a lot of gift items the customers would want. What did I think about renting space in a suburban shopping mall and opening a giftware gallery? I must say I did not spark to the idea right away. This was something I wouldn't have done on my own; I'm too cautious. But Nan is a risk-taker by nature, and she persuaded me that her buying ability combined with my retailing experience was an ideal balance. Hmmm, maybe. I called my accountant to get his opinions; I think I was hoping he'd shoot the idea down so I'd have a valid excuse to back out and not have to take chances. But he thought the timing, the location, and the potential were terrific. He checked into my would-be partner's credentials and was thoroughly satisfied. "Rosa," he said, "there's no guarantee that any business will succeed. But this one looks like a winner to me. The worst that can happen is you'll have a tax write-off. Even though that wouldn't mean much in your bracket, I think the odds are with you and you ought to go ahead." Between them, they had me; I succumbed.

Nan's and my giftware gallery has been one of the best ventures I've ever got into, and our relationship has gone swimmingly—touch wood. We've only had one tussle, and we resolved it by departing from our own rules. Nan is a person who hates details. She'll put off paperwork forever if you let her, while I'm a stickler for prompt attention to everything that comes along. She says I'm a born nit-picker, and my answer to that is, patience and nit-picking is what keeps a business running clean and smooth. The problem came up because we got into each other's turf. She was supposed to take care of the paperwork connected with buying, and I was to keep the records connected with sales. When I saw that she was consistently late with her reports, I was fit to be tied. I felt like shaking her and yelling, "Nan, we cannot operate this way. This isn't a game. It's a business, and business is more than flitting around the countryside digging up lovely little items we can sell to suburbanites. It's a lot of follow-up and you'd damn well better buckle down and pull your weight when you're supposed to." That would have made me feel pretty good, getting my gripes off my chest. But I restrained the impulse. What would it have solved? The thing to do was come up with a way to straighten out our difficulty without creating resentment between us. So I sat down with Nan and asked what I could do to help her out. She had the answer: "Let's change our arrangement. You're good at administration, and you like it. It's not my bag at all. I think we should each do what we're good at. If you handle all the paperwork, you can feel safe about leaving the buying activities to me. And I won't be in your hair, overlapping into your territory." That made sense. I'd been so stuck on following our contract as if it were graven in stone, it hadn't occurred to me that there might be another, better way to do things. Sometimes you have to live together awhile before you can tell what works best. That's something else about working for yourself: You have the flexibility to change the system if the system doesn't function well for you.

What is bankruptcy?

A legal judgment that you cannot pay your debts, and that whatever property you or your corporation has shall be distributed among your creditors. You can go bankrupt of your own volition, or you can be forced into bankruptcy by your creditors.

The three kinds of bankruptcy you hear about most frequently are:

Chapter XI,

in which the court says you can settle with your creditors by giving them a percentage of the money you owe them, and then reconstruct your business.

Liquidation,

in which all your assets are sold and your creditors collect whatever the sale brings in.

Preferred Liability,

in which Uncle Sam gets first dibs on whatever you have. After your taxes are paid, it's up to your creditors to collect what they can.

Do self-employed people have any financial edge over payroll people?

A big one: tax deductions. Payroll people get a salary that is fully taxed before they see it. Anything left over is theirs to spend. Entrepreneurs pay taxes, too, but only after they deduct all their expenses for meals, postage, transportation, reference books, office furnishings, repairs, travel, entertaining, and everything else that is business-related. If you work at home, you also write off all or part of your rent and utilities. By the time you add up the tax deductions, your do-it-yourself income can be worth two times a traditional payroll salary or more, in actual spendable dollars.

What are the financial disadvantages of self-employment?

As a solo act, you have no company pension plan or retirement fund in your future. However, there are ways to create these things for yourself. Check with your accountant or bank about retirement plans for the self-employed.

You have no group health insurance to ride on. By all means, get your own. Shop around until you find the best coverage for your money, and don't go a day without it. One injury or illness could wipe you out unless you have help paying for it.

You have to buy your own accident liability insurance. The cost is low, and the return could be high. If somebody trips and falls in your office, they can sue you for their medical expenses. But if you are covered by an accident policy, their suit will be against the insurance company, not you.

Whatever you buy or invest in, shop around first. Research everything for value, and get the best you can buy for the money you can spend.

What is business overhead?

The expenses connected with operating your business:

Rent.

One way to keep overhead down when you are a small organization is to sublet space in somebody else's office, preferably an attractive office with a good address. Subletting gives you several advantages. You are not necessarily locked into a lease. You can arrange for the use of a desk, the copying machine, somebody to answer your phone and screen your visitors. Even if you pay a small fee, the purchase costs, salaries, and payroll taxes will be on the person whose space you're subletting.

Utilities.

Telephone, electricity, and possibly heat. If your business necessitates many long-distance calls, ask the phone company about possible savings from alternate systems such as Wide Area Telephone Service (WATS). Or check with a private phone company to see if you can save money by using an independent communications system.

Taxes.

If you employ people, you will have to pay taxes for their Social Security and Unemployment coverage. Check out the tax costs before you add staff. You may find it's as efficient and more economical to hire consultants or free-lance help instead. Overhead also includes your corporation taxes, income taxes, and in some places such as New York City, an occupancy tax.

Interior Decoration.

This is the cost of furnishing your office, and includes aesthetic as well as functional appointments.

Do you tip the cleaning people?

Yes. Every Christmas and sometimes in between. You also should tip the mailman, the elevator starter, the building superintendent, and anybody else you hope to get special attention from. A tip expresses your thanks for extra service and is an incentive for the building help to keep paying attention to you in the months ahead. I sometimes give small gifts during the year as well as at Christmas.

Should I accept Christmas gifts from people with whom I do business?

Surely. It's your suppliers' way of thanking you for giving them business. It's also a subtle encouragement for you to give them more, but that doesn't mean you have to. As boss of your own business, you are free to choose whatever suppliers will do the job best, regardless of whether they shower you with Christmas booty. Besides, it would be awkward for you as an individual to return a gift. What you can do if you are uncomfortable about presents is what larger companies do: Send a letter early in the holiday season to each of your suppliers stating that it is your policy to forward all gifts over fifty dollars in value to worthy charitable organizations, and that you would prefer that any gifts be made directly to charity instead. This is a procedure that is clearly understood by everyone in the business world. It means, "No payola. No bribery. Take me to lunch or send me a calendar if you like. But please don't embarrass me with TV sets or trips to a fancy resort. I do not want to be beholden to anyone."

Do I have to donate to charities?

Most people earmark a certain percentage of their money for charities. Make your choices according to the charities' worthiness and what the donations will do for you.

Charity donations come in various forms: dues, contributions, ads in special publications, raffles, tickets to lunches and other social events. Some organizations that solicit you are valid, some are not. Watch out for fakers. Check out organizations you're not sure of with your Chamber of Commerce or Better Business Bureau. Ask the solicitor for literature about the organization. Find out how much of their fund-raising goes into administrative salaries, how much to charitable works. Investigate before you donate.

You don't have to investigate every fund-raiser who solicits you. Go ahead and give a small amount of money to causes like the policeman's, fireman's, and postal carrier's balls if you think they will respond better to your needs because you are listed as a donor. Buy tickets to your trade association dance if the association is an active one whose members could be important to you. Attending a dinner-dance could be your introduction to new business contacts and a way to establish yourself as a certifiable member of the industry.

Who pays for my office parties?

The occasion dictates the answer.

Office parties come in all kinds of wrappings, including Christmas, farewell, engagement, promotion, welcome, we just hit the million-dollar mark, and Thank God It's Friday. Parties occur in large offices and small, in the conference room or at restaurants, and they are paid for in a number of ways: from petty cash, by taking up collections from the staff, or, when you choose, out of your pocket as owner.

What else is petty cash used for?

Extra postage. Emergency cabs. Messengers. Coffee. Supplies. Little things that you need in a hurry. Most companies have their people fill out petty cash slips and turn in receipts whenever it's possible. It's a good idea to have one person—your receptionist, secretary, or yourself—in charge of petty cash. And not to keep very much on hand. Where there's money, there's temptation. The idea is to keep possible losses small.

What should I do if I find out somebody has been stealing?

If you are absolutely positive you know who the culprit is, fire him or her immediately. If you are less than positive, investigate the situation. Most important, once you know there's been a hand in the till, do something at once to make the till inaccessible.

Pilferage is one of the most common of all business problems. It's unsettling when you find it because you want to be able to trust everyone. The fact of life is, you can't. Claudia found that out after she'd been in business two years. She owns a bakery, the outgrowth of a home kitchen catering service she'd started when her children were small and needed her presence most of the time.

We were exceedingly busy, filling orders for every good restaurant and specialty shop in the county. For all that, profits were down. I'd fine-combed the books—purchasing, production, overhead—and couldn't spot what was wrong. So I had to consider the nasty possibility that my customers were receiving short orders. If that was so, it meant somebody in my own organization was light-fingered. I began watching them very closely. For a week I noted the number of items loaded onto a truck, and then asked the driver for his tallies. They never matched. Where I'd counted eighty-five pies, he told me he'd loaded seventy. Then I had somebody follow the truck to see what happened at the other end. Sixty pies would go to my customers and twenty-five to some stranger who would hand cash to the driver. It was plain what was going on, except that I knew that driver couldn't have maneuvered the deal all by himself. I did some more sleuthing and found out that both my general manager and my kitchen manager were in cahoots with the driver. The three of them were running their own business, and I was their goat. I was particularly upset because I had trusted and befriended them over the years. Then to have them steal from me—I felt defiled. I learned then and there that in business you must always have some system of checks and balances, no matter how much you want to rely on people's integrity. And that you never show mercy to cannibals. I fired the three thieves, hired a checker to oversee and double-check the new driver and manager's inventory, and informed everyone that there would be lie detector tests if I found anything amiss. The entire episode was extremely upleasant, but it taught me never to run a loose ship again.

What basic equipment will I have to buy?

A desk and chair, file drawers, a typewriter or whatever tools you need for your trade. Shop the catalogs, retail and discount stores to find furnishings that are attractive as well as durable. You're going to have to live with this furniture day in and day out for a long time; you owe it to your psyche to give yourself a decoratively pleasing environment.

Letterheads, envelopes, and business cards. Your stationery is your signature. It reflects your professional image and conveys a certain impression of you to the people with whom you do business. Please do not skimp or go the four-dollar-rubber-stamp route. Invest in professional, well-designed graphics and good quality stock. It's a small bill to pay for a long-playing ad.

A telephone answering service or machine, if you don't have a secretary. This is an investment that pays for itself the first time it takes a business call you would otherwise have missed. If you use a machine, keep your outgoing message simple; something like:

> This is Susan Jones. Please leave your name, phone number, and a brief message if you like. I will return your call as soon as I return to the office.

If you use an answering service, instruct them how you want your phone answered: by phone number, company name, or your own name. Be explicit: "Good morning. This is Susan Jones's office. She is out just now. May I take a message for her?"

How do you know how much to charge for your services?

When you deal in service rather than product, you can set realistic rates based on your competition. If you are a consultant, a writer, or provide some other intangible, find out how much other people in your field are charging. The rates will vary depending on whether they are beginners, middle-stagers, or top recognized professionals. Set your own rates according to the category you fit into. To be completely realistic and fair, you also need to judge when to be flexible about your rates and when to be firm. For example, Evelyn's illustrating fee of $100 an hour—high because she is a proved, successful professional—would be absurd if she were to apply it to an ambitious booklet she knows will take thirty hours to complete. In a case like that, she gives the client a package, or project price: $1,500 for the whole booklet, instead of the hog-wild $3,000 it would cost by the hour. She still comes out making a good profit and gives her client good value for his money. On the other hand, if somebody wants her to churn out drawings at a beginner's rate, she tells them exactly how she stands. "If you can only pay twenty dollars an hour, you will have to go to somebody less experienced than I am. If you want somebody you can trust to deliver top-notch work that will achieve your objective and not waste your time with false starts, I'll be happy to do the job for you. My fee is one hundred dollars an hour, and I estimate this as a four-hour job. Let me know if four hundred dollars fits your budget and when you would like delivery."

In addition to service charges, you also have to decide how you will charge for out-of-pocket expenses. Standard practice varies from industry to industry. Sometimes you can get your costs paid in advance, and sometimes you submit an itemized bill after the fact. In other arrangements, depending on your agreement with your client and the business you're in, you can bill for costs plus a markup, or have your suppliers submit their bills directly to the client. Whichever way you handle expenses, there is one key point you must always remember: *Get it in writing.* Find out what the expenses will be in advance if you can, and include them in your estimate of charges. Or you can submit an estimate of your service fee and add a note that out-of-pocket expenses will be billed at cost. If the bills are to be sent directly to the client, indicate that in your letter of agreement, and include the names and addresses of the suppliers as well, if you are sure who it is you will be using. And make sure you get your client's signature on a letter of agreement before you go ahead with the job. One way to do this is to send your letter in duplicate, and ask that they sign and return one copy to you, and keep the other for their files.

People are forever getting stung because they neglect to get things in writing. Most people make sure they never get stung twice:

Dolores, commercial photographer: I was doing some product shots for a direct-sales company, and we were in a meeting discussing a booklet they could use to recruit salespeople. Toward the tail end of the meeting, they told me they had a hundred or so candids lying around that somebody had shot at one of their house parties. I exclaimed, "That's it! Thats the guts of your recruitment booklet. I could edit them down, get them into logical sequence, hire someone to write captions, and you'd have a marvelous, absolutely real visualization of how it feels to sell your products." Oh, they were crazy about the idea. Loved it. Begged me to get the job done for them in time for their spring sales meeting, which was two months away. Sure, I said, no problem. I gave them a price, and that was the only discussion we ever had.

I never checked to find out where the negatives were and it turned out nobody knew, which immediately raised my costs because I had to go to the expense of converting the prints. And I never verified to make sure there were one hundred candids. It turned out out there were six hundred, which meant hours and hours at the light board. I took a bath. It wasn't the client's fault. What I thought they meant and what they thought they meant were two different things, that's all. I should have written a letter of confirmation before I took a single blessed step.

Here's the letter Dolores should have written:

Dear Les:

This is to confirm that I am to edit 100 candid photos from negatives you will supply for a recruitment brochure to be produced and delivered by me no later than March 14. My fee for this service will be $500 plus expenses for type, photostats, and messengers, to be billed at cost.

If you agree with this understanding, please sign and return the enclosed copy of this letter immediately on receipt, so that I can begin work on the project for on-time delivery.

I will phone you tomorrow to ask if there are any changes you would like to incorporate in this working contract.

Very truly,
Dolores Smith

Approved by

Lester Cooper
ABC Company

What if they say I'm too expensive?

Maybe they're right. Maybe you overestimate your worth. Maybe you are still at the proving stage and haven't got the credentials yet to show that your work is better than most of your competitors. You have to charge what you are worth now, not what you think you would like to be worth in the future.

If you are better than the rest of the pack, however, price yourself accordingly. People will get what they pay for, and you will be paid fairly for what you give.

There are always some clients who give you cliché excuses when they hear your rates:

"We're young. Help us grow and you can grow with us."

Baloney. Let them come back to you when they're all grown up. Or, if you do decide to take a chance with a young company, negotiate futures with them. Tell them, "I'd be happy to help you out now. Let's amortize the fee over a three-job package. I'll do the first job for you at twenty dollars an hour, with the provision that the second and third jobs will be guaranteed me within the next year at my regular forty dollars rate." If they demur and are unwilling to risk guaranteeing you three jobs, there is no reason why you should take a risk with them.

"Just get me out of this one jam. You have to!"

No, you don't have to. And you don't have to set low-priced precedents, either. If these people have been good clients in the past, however, you can negotiate with them on the basis of a quantity discount. "I can deliver the job for you at a 30 percent discount providing you give me ten jobs or more at that rate." It's not a bad deal. In addition to ten guaranteed jobs, you'll have got them all with a single sales call.

"You city people are too expensive."

Not for what you can do for them. Maybe they can get cheaper help in their hometown, but they won't get your expertise, your quality, your scope of resources, or your expert direction. All that is worth money. Don't let them try to talk you out of it.

Do I charge for giving advice?

Yes, when you are hired to give advice. No, when you are tossing out crumbs that can come back to benefit you later. A publicist I know, Vivian, says her life is like a doctor's: People are always approaching her at parties or inviting her to lunch so they can get free advice on how to treat their pain. She has developed a technique that is beautiful. Let's say that Lionel Freeloader is having a one-man photo show and wants to find out how to publicize it without hiring a publicist. He corners Vivian:

LIONEL: This is a really exceptional show, Viv. How can I get people to know about it?

VIVIAN: I was with the editor of *Them* yesterday, and he mentioned that he's looking for photography stories. Here's his name. You know, that information would cost twenty-five hundred dollars if you were one of my fee accounts.

With one stroke, Vivian has done three things:

1. She has put a price ticket on her advice, which marks her a valuable, authoritative publicist.
2. She has shown that she knows who's who, and who's looking for what in the inner professional circles.
3. She has led Lionel to the well with free advice, knowing that he won't get the response she would have got, because publicity is more than knowing who—it's knowing the right angle to present and when.

She really hasn't given anything away. But she has made a friend and a fan. Now when somebody who can afford to pay a publicist asks Lionel's advice, he'll recommend Vivian for her savvy and cooperativeness. And if he should hit the big time himself, he'll know that it will cost at least two hundred dollars a month to hire his favorite publicity expert.

Is it tough to collect payments?

Sometimes it is very tough, and this is something you have to be prepared to handle. There are scalawags everywhere, especially when it comes to money. They may ignore your bills. They may claim your work was no good and they won't pay for it. They may actually roast that old chestnut, "The check is in the mail." Or they may say, "So you have a contract with me, so what? Go sue me." You may have to do just that: Hand the matter over to your attorney and let him or her collect for you.

Usually, that is the last step in the collection chain. First, you telephone:

YOU: I'm calling to remind you of the five thousand dollars you still owe on my bill dated March 1. It was due April 1, and this is now April twenty-first. I'd like to know where you stand on it.

THEY: It's in the mail.

Five days later:

YOU: I haven't received your check for five thousand dollars yet. I know business is tight these days for everyone. Why don't you tell me what the problem is?

THEY: You're right about tight money. Our cash flow has been like mud and I've had to defer certain payments. I'll get yours to you in about ten days.

Two weeks later, a collection agency or your attorney writes:

Dear Mr. Slow:
I am writing on behalf of my client, Joanne White, with reference to your indebtedness to her for services rendered in the amount of five thousands dollars ($5,000). According to the terms of your written agreement with Ms. White, your payment was due in full on April 1. Please remit that amount to my office within ten days of the date of this registered letter, or my office will take the necessary further steps.

If that doesn't work, sue the scalawag. Remember this, though. It's expensive to bring suit, so the size of your bill must warrant the cost of recovery. Also, it pays to be lenient with people you have a long-standing relationship with. Everyone has a cash flow problem sometime. If you've had business dealings with these people before and you know they are good for the money eventually, it's not worth your while to bring suit. You will ruin the mutual trust you've developed. You can tell them, instead, "I understand your position right now; unfortunately, it's costing me money. Let's agree that I'll finance this job and put a surcharge on your next bill: 5 percent for payment later than thirty days, and 6 percent if it goes past sixty days. If that's agreeable with you, we can also arrange that in the future, I'll give you a 5 percent discount any time your bills are paid within two weeks."

Another strategy you can use if your client has no money left in the fiscal-year budget but you need the work, is to defer your billing until the start of their next fiscal year with the understanding that you will add an interest charge to your bill in return for financing them meanwhile.

Where do I get financial advice?

Hire an accountant to do your tax planning and reporting, see that you take all the deductions you are entitled to, and help you set up and keep track of the records you will need.

Hire an attorney, especially if you incorporate or go into partnership, to steer you away from possible litigation or problems.

Both your attorney and your accountant should be people who are familiar with your type of business, and who have successful clients in your field. The greatest tax accountant or lawyer in the world may be useless when it comes to understanding and dealing with the mysteries of theater, publishing, or other specialized professions.

Advisers charge for their services, but that's OK. You have to spend money to earn money. The way to find the right manager is through recommendations and personal interviews. Sound them out for their opinions, philosophies, facts. Test everything you hear. If what you hear doesn't work well for you, don't be afraid to switch your business to somebody else. It's your money and your future you're protecting; you need the best advice you can get.

It is also a good idea to have an arrangement with a friend who is in your field or a business that's close to it. That person will know what your costs and general financial picture are. You'll find that often you can just phone your friend, present your problem, and get a fast answer that comes from practical experience. Once you've done that a few times and keep getting the same answer, you'll be able to figure out many solutions by yourself.

What is a line of credit?

Evidence that people believe you will pay for what you order. It's hard to do business without a good credit rating. Suppliers' bills usually come in long before your clients' or customers' checks arrive. And people expect to be paid within thirty days. You have to establish the fact that you can be counted on to honor your bills, and the way to do this is to open a line of credit. This is a kind of short-term loan from suppliers, good up to a certain amount of money, that allows you to extend your repayment time in return for a certain amount of interest. It is wise to establish lines of credit even if you are bankrolled to the hilt. You never know when you will want to expand, when business will be lean, or when your accounts receivable will be extra slow.

What about bank credit?

Get it. Take out a bank loan, even if you don't really need one. Borrowing and repaying promptly is the only way to confirm to the world that you are solvent and responsible, entitled to further credit when you need it. A bank loan will cost you interest, but it is a necessary cost: an investment in your own financial future.

Should I use credit cards?

Definitely. At least one. Two or three months can elapse between the time you charged a purchase and are billed for it. That two or three months is your grace period—either to get the money you need, or to have your money earn interest for you. With a major purchase—equipment, travel, even a large restaurant or hotel bill—credit cards provide a convenient way to collect the receipts you will need for documentation at tax time.

What is a P & L?

A profit and loss statement. This is a balance sheet that shows your income and expenses, or continuing cash flow. It shows clearly whether your business is making a profit, if you are breaking even, or if your business is costing you money.

How many checkbooks should I keep?

One for each of your business activities, to prevent comingling of funds and to provide clear records of your income and outgo. You might want separate checkbooks for:

Separate business divisions
Separate partnerships
Operating expenses
Clients' monies
Investments.

Your personal money should always be in a personal account.

Should I pay for a publicist?

If you need publicity, yes. You won't save money by doing it yourself. You'll only waste your time on amateur efforts and give people a poor impression of you. You should hire a professional to place stories about you or to create your promotional brochures. You don't have to pay retainer fees or hire a large, well-known firm. Shop around to find a free-lance, per-project publicist who is right for you. Ask people in your field to recommend someone. Then check the publicist's samples and effectiveness for yourself.

One thing you can do yourself is write formula releases to announce hard news such as a change of address or a special event. They are not hard to write: See pages 234–235 for instructions.

Promotional brochures with good artwork, typography, and reproduction can be expensive to produce. But you don't have to pay for it all yourself. Sometimes you can piggyback on somebody else's budget if you come up with an idea they can benefit from, too. A Florida art dealer got a Dutch shipping line to sponsor her mailing announcing an exhibit by a Dutch artist. The director of a nonprofit organization that wanted to attract visitors to a historic home in Virginia latched onto an auction house that was promoting artifacts of the region, and used their resources to promote her mansion. An Illinois hotel manager stipulated in her contract with the band she hired for the dining room that the name of her hotel would be featured in all of the band's promotional literature for a year.

How do you get new business?

By making sales calls.

Through visibility: activity in professional and civic groups, publicity, advertising, keeping people aware of what you do.

Through contacts. People you knew where you formerly worked. People they know, who probably know others who can use what you sell. Friends. Your friends' friends. The whole endless grapevine of connections. People with whom you have no connection at all, but who your research tells you have a need that you can fill. You can usually get to them through a mutual contact, or a contact who knows somebody else who can reach them.

Evelyn, the illustrator who works at home, worked up a whole second career through a contact's casual phone call:

When you work at home, your friends somehow don't take it seriously. They think you're just dabbling or sitting around and eating chocolate-covered candies all day. So they feel free to phone you whenever they want to pass the time of day. That's fine; it's a way of staying connected with the world. But it's awkward when they get talkative and interrupt your work for twenty or thirty minutes at a clip. You don't like to be rude and shut them off, but you do have to limit their length.

One day a neighbor called just to chat. As I was about to get rid of her, she commented, "Oh, Evelyn, I envy you so much! You're such a good artist. I wish my husband would use you for his brochures and annual reports. I'm going to have him call you." I thanked her and said goodbye. It was a good idea, but I knew better than to depend on her to do my sales job. The next day I phoned her husband, said that his wife had suggested I call, and made an appointment to go see him. He liked my samples and ideas, and said he'd give me a whack at his next brochure. The job turned out well—he loved what I did—and I've kept him as a steady account for the past four years. Besides which, he referred several business colleagues to me, and I now have a respectable number of what I call bread-and-butter accounts. Better than bread and butter. They've become a whole second business and frankly, they're a lot more reliable and bring in faster money than book illustrating. Brochures and mailing pieces don't take a whole lot of time to research and produce, so I can combine them with my book assignments. Plus there are more local business people who can use me than there are publishers. It may be commercial work, but it's supporting my art.

How do I write a sales letter?

The way you write any other business letter: simply and clearly. Follow these twelve rules and you will have all the letter-writing techniques you will ever need:

1. Before you write, list the main points that you want to communicate, and organize them in a logical sequence.

2. State the reason for your letter immediately. Try to make your first sentence capture the reader's interest, so they will want to read more of what you have to say.

3. Write from the reader's point of view. Give them benefits that will make them want what you have to sell.

4. Write as if you were speaking face-to-face: in conversational language, not legalese.

5. Keep your sentences and paragraphs short.

6. Use action verbs in the active voice: "I will call your office," not "Your office will be called." Limit your adjectives and adverbs: "Our new-product ideas" is more believable than "Our fantastic new-product ideas."

7. Be positive and straightforward.

8. Be specific.

9. Be brief.

10. Stay on the subject.

11. End your letter with a call to action.

12. Be a perfectionist. Leave wide margins all around for a clear, legible appearance. Type your letter as many times as it takes to get out a clean, perfect letter. No smudges, no typos, no strikeouts. Remember, your letter is your ambassador, in appearance as well as in content.

Write me a sample business letter.

September 15, 1980

Ms. Florence Green
Newell Specialty Stores, Inc.
1400 Hale Drive
Newell, Pennsylvania 19000

Dear Florence:

It was a joy to meet you at the new-products seminar in Atlanta last week. Your comments on the absurdity of the new line the vacuum cleaner salesmen were touting entertained me for days. Thank you for the fun.

I also enjoyed speaking with you about our new-product ideas and was delighted by your enthusiasm. You seemed particularly interested in our new line of decorator bathroom tiles for the do-it-yourselfer. I am enclosing a brochure that describes in full how the tiles are mounted, our full range of colors, and a price list. I will call your office next week, when you have had a chance to discuss the possibilities with your sales manager, Sam Jones.

I am looking forward to speaking with you again, and feel certain that this is the beginning of a long and mutually rewarding association.

Cordially,
Mary Smith

Should you chase every new-business lead?

No. You could be chasing rainbows at your own expense, as Laura did when she was a young marketing consultant:

There I was, still in my twenties, with a staff of eight and a headful of ambition. I couldn't wait to get away from my Mom-and-Pop clients and move up into the majors. The minute one of my clients told me he'd recommended me to a babywear manufacturer in Dallas, I saw my chance to get a big national account. I called up the babywear president, who he said he was very enthusiastic about what he'd heard of my work, and would I come to see him in his office. I flew to Texas the next day thinking, "Oh, boy, I've got it made. Nobody asks you to travel five hundred miles unless they're pretty sure they're going to hire you. Here's where Laura breaks into the big time."

We had an excellent meeting. I streaked back home and whipped up a thirty-page proposal in three days. I knew it would knock him dead and seal the deal for me. No sooner did I get the proposal into the hands of an air express carrier than I learned that the manufacturer had hired a consultant in Dallas. My first reaction was, "The nerve! How immature! He simply doesn't know the etiquette of business." Then I realized that I was blaming the wrong party: When there's a fire and you get burned, it's not the fire's fault. I should have done some research on this person and talked in more depth with him on the phone before I blew seven hundred dollars on plane fare and hotel expenses. Plus the office time it cost me to produce a proposal he didn't truly want.

Should I take every job I can get?

Only if you are in a survival situation.

Some women hate to say No to anybody, but this is a trait that can get you into trouble in business. You need to learn to protect yourself and not be afraid to turn down jobs that won't pay off. You have to put a dollar value on your time, and you have to figure that your emotions are worth something, too.

As your own boss, you can pretty much choose who you will and will not do business with. For many entrepreneurs, the No list includes:

- People who try to get something for nothing.
- People who haggle about bills even when the price has already been agreed on.
- Prospects who ask you to invest considerable money in working up a proposal for them with no agreement to reimburse you and no indication that they are earnest about hiring you.
- Clients who refuse to accept a reasonable price increase and want you to keep working for them at rates you can no longer afford.
- People who back down on their promises, such as reneging on an agreement to pay you extra for work that is not included in your retainer contract.

How do you reject a client?

Amicably. Remember that they may have legitimate business friends to whom they may talk about you. You want that talk to be favorable: You never know where your next job will come from, or who will be a valuable contact.

Describe three kinds of people who are hard to deal with.

The Brat.

This is the client who, when you bring him a proposal, rips it up and throws it in your face. (Your rejoinder: "I have a copy of the proposal in my briefcase. Let me know when you're ready to talk about it.") They rip you up one side and down the other just because they don't know better. (You don't react; they get angrier.) They abuse tabletops with their fists (better the table than you), slam telephones down with a whack (while you pray the phone slams on their fingers), carry on like lunatics in a D movie.

You have three courses of action with a brat:

311

1. Decide they're not worth putting up with and get them out of your life.

2. Put up with their shenanigans because they're worth a bundle and you need their business.

3. Bring a third person into the act to keep peace: someone you both respect who has the judgment, seniority, and objectivity to set rules of behavior.

The Make-Out Artist.

There is a switch in some people's mind that flips to ON when they meet a woman in business by herself. It's as if they are out of town and can play around because nobody's looking. They feel free to pursue libidinous notions they'd probably suppress in an organizational setting. It only proves that female entrepreneurs are as attractive as anyone else. However, if the make-out artist comes on with "You play ball with me or I'll take my business elsewhere," and won't take No for an answer, let him or her go. The chances are you won't hang onto their business very long anyway, even if you are an expert at evasion techniques.

The Monuments.

These people aren't people, they're celebrities—institutions. Whether you meet them as customers or stand next to them at public events, their presence is paralyzing. Your brain freezes. You can't think of a thing to say. You discard "How nice you look" as a sappy comment to make to somebody who's encrusted in eight-hundred-watt diamonds. "Isn't the weather lovely?" sounds inane; where will you go from there after they say Yes! "Have you known the guest of honor long?" will make you sound like either bone-ignorant or a busybody. Gulp.

You have to understand that Big Names stand around at parties groping for small talk with people they don't know the same as you and I. They put on their bikinis one leg at a time in the morning, brush their teeth, and wonder what kind of new refrigerator to buy just like other mortals. You also have to remember that Mr. or Ms. Monument may be your prospective client the same as anybody else in the room. Whatever mental stunt it takes to melt the celebrity barrier in your mind, do it. It's the only way you will get on a person-to-person footing with them.

Having given all that excellent advice, I must confess that certain monuments do not melt. They remain awesome and intimidating. The best you can do is try to get through your meetings with them gracefully.

Should you be friends with the people with whom you do business?

Not necessarily. You have to be prepared to deal with all kinds of people, even those you wouldn't choose as personal friends. People don't have to talk like you, dress like you, have the same cultural background you do to make good clients. They can be positively outrageous and still be acceptable business associates.

Do you have any overall advice about women and work?

- You can do whatever you want to do.
- You deserve to win whatever you want to win.
- Take as much success as you are able to handle.

Index